MW01629833

MAGICAL SECRETS ABOUT CHINE COLLÉ

BRIAN SHURE

# Magical Secrets about Chine Collé

## PASTING, PRINTING, MOUNTING, AND LEAFING STEP-BY-STEP

CROWN POINT PRESS   SAN FRANCISCO

Historically, the French term *chine collé* (also called *papier collé* or *chine appliqué*) refers to a printing process in which a thin sheet of paper is printed on and at the same time mounted on a sturdier sheet. In this book, I expand that meaning to include mounting in a press as a separate step in the printing process. In French, the word *chine*, spelled with a small c means paper, and *collé* is the past participle of *collér*, "to stick down." When we say we have colléd one sheet to another, we mean that we have stuck it down.

*Magical Secrets about Chine Collé* is a revision of *Chine Collé: A Printer's Handbook* that I wrote in 2000 and is now out of print. This new book incorporates all the practical material I presented there and expands upon it considerably. In this book, I have dropped the historical section that appeared in the earlier one because I plan to explore the history of chine collé in a future publication.

The series on printmkaing of which this book is a part begins with Kathan Brown's *Magical Secrets about Thinking Creatively*, which introduces various approaches to printmaking and focuses on the creative process. In the second book, Catherine Brooks lays out approaches to line work, and in the third book, Emily York describes the tonal processes. Yet to come is *Magical Secrets about Photogravure* by Dena Schuckit. The focus of the books in the Magical Secrets series so far has been on creating plates and properly inking and printing them, so those books make minimal mention of the role of paper.

My contribution to the series focuses on paper (or occasionally fabric), which as the receptor of the image is an essential part of any printed material. In artists' prints, paper is as elemental as drawing, tonal work, or color. The way ink sits on (or in the case of intaglio printing *in*) the surface of the paper varies with the chosen paper (or fabric), with how it is prepared in terms of sizing, and with the amount of moisture used to soften it for printing. In addition to discussing chine collé and giving detailed instructions for it, in this book I describe and demonstrate the sizing of paper, Asian mounting procedures, and some collage techniques used without a press. There is also a chapter on the technique of gold leafing, a time-honored craft that is dependent on sizing.

When we talk about images, usually we talk about what the artist drew, but in Tom Marioni's 1991 etching *Finger Line* (pl. 1), elements pasted onto the paper are equal to the drawing in importance. The pasted elements were applied using chine collé. Marioni's use of the process is slightly unorthodox.

In Marioni's *Finger Line*, the main image is a silhouette of a violin, its outline broken so that it floats in a pictorial space between vertical lines and a rectangle of wood veneer that suggests the wood used in making a violin. The veneer is pasted diagonally across a yellow background tone, and a yellow matboard rectangle, also pasted, seems to float on top of everything. On the matboard there is a pencil

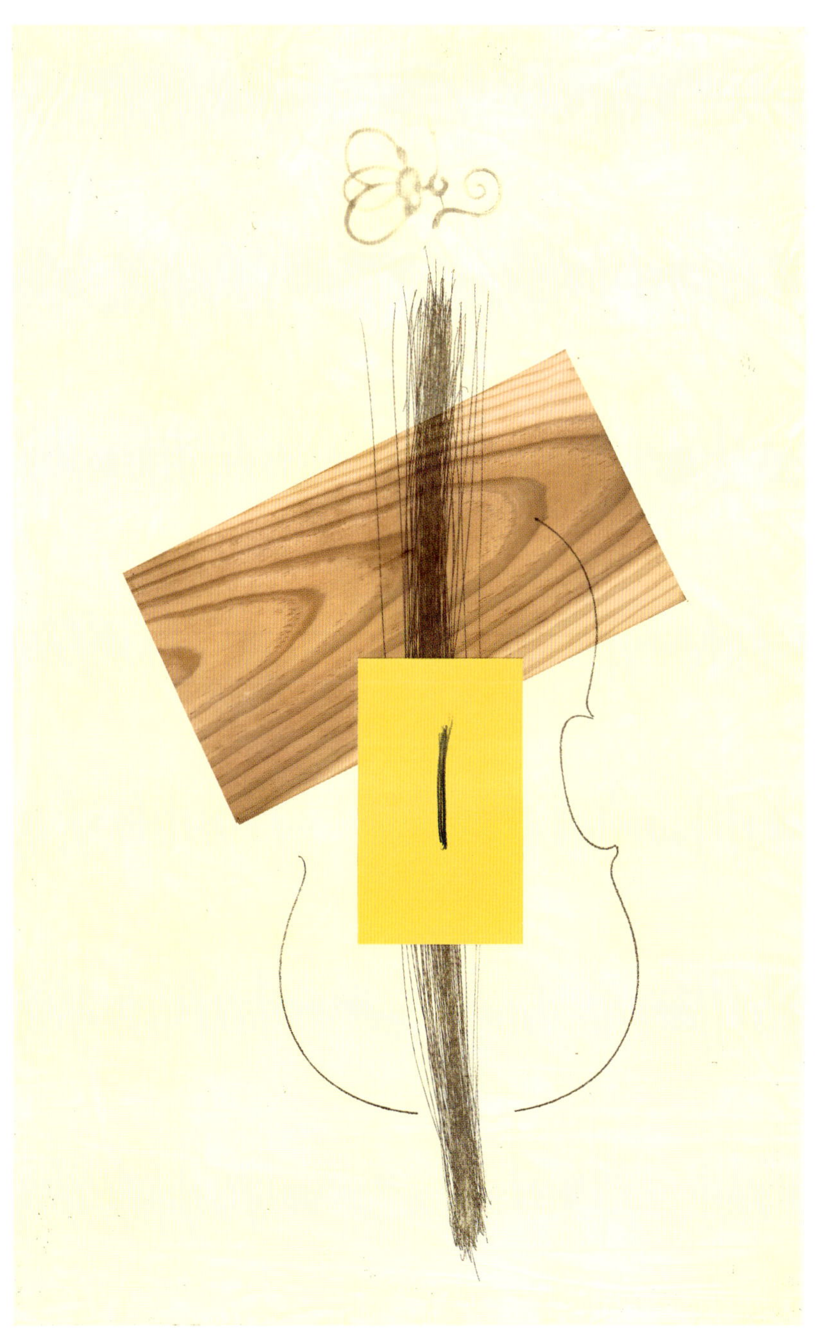

PLATE 1
Tom Marioni, *Finger Line*, 1991.
Color soft ground and hard ground
etching and spit bite aquatint with
wood veneer and a drawing chine collé,
27 × 17 inches.

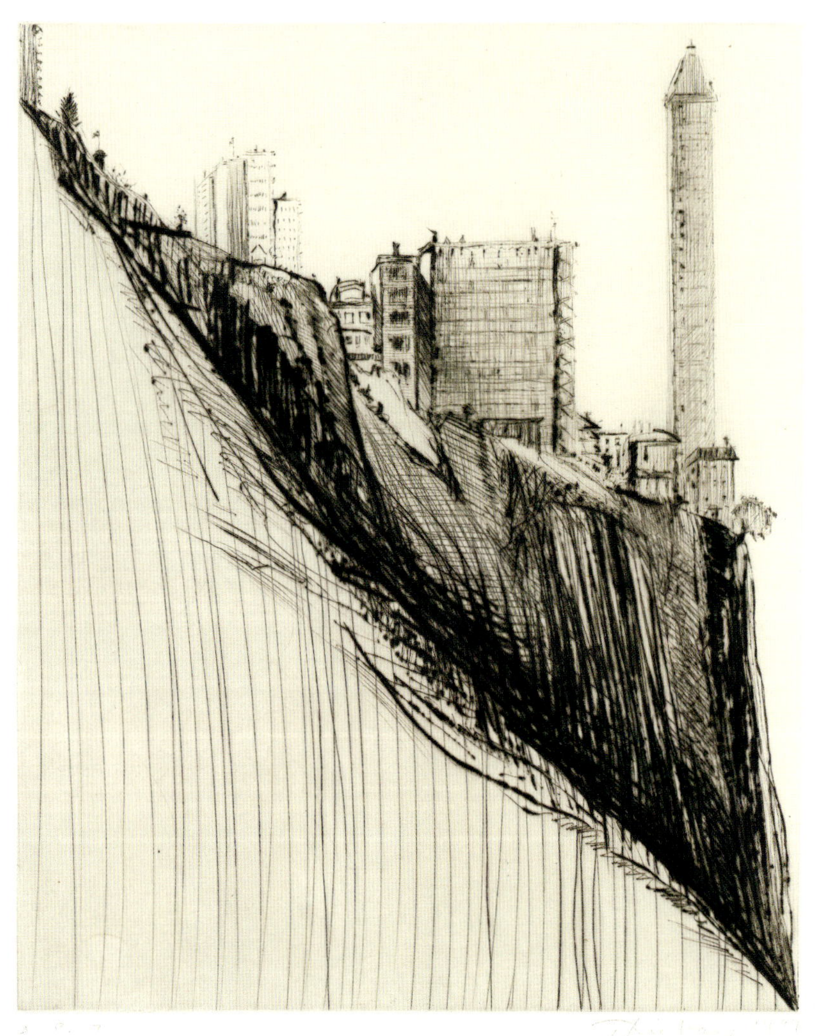

PLATE 2
Wayne Thiebaud, *Marina Ridge*, 1997.
Drypoint printed on gampi paper chine collé, 11 × 9 inches.

drawing of a group of short vertical lines that, like the longer ones behind them, are records of body activity. Marioni drew the short lines by curling and uncurling a finger with a pencil attached to it. He drew the long ones by pivoting from his elbow while holding an etching needle. Both sets of lines appear where the strings of the instrument would be. The short lines are dense like the violin's sound hole. The long lines seem to vibrate as if a bow were being pulled across them.

Floating above the violin is a lyrical spit bite aquatint image (a different kind of line) that recalls the profile of the graceful baroque scroll that holds a violin's tuning pegs. The image is actually a diagram of the cochlea, the part of the ear responsible for our sense of balance.

The pictorial language of this print, its power and delicacy, expands as you look at it. You are drawn into lingering over the beautiful surfaces: the papers, the raised ink lines, the lines drawn with pencil, the veneer with its pronounced grain, and the matboard rectangle saturated with the rich yellow that is Marioni's signature color.

When I asked Tom Marioni about *Finger Line*, he said he had "run Picasso through my noodle machine"—a concise description of the creative process, and especially fitting for this book because Picasso developed the use of collage in painting. *Finger Line* refers

to a century-old style and uses traditional processes in a new way. It demonstrates two points that I will come back to again and again in this book. The first is that all innovation builds upon tradition, and the second is that the chine collé elements are essential and completely integrated with the printed marks.

The same two points are demonstrated in *Marina Ridge* (pl. 2) by Wayne Thiebaud, a more traditional use of chine collé. *Marina Ridge* is a simple drypoint, printed on a Japanese gampi paper so thin that it had to be mounted on a heavier sheet of rag paper during the printing process in order to be stable enough to handle. The two papers integrate with the printed drypoint drawing to form the image in the final print.

Artists are always keenly aware of the support on which their images are printed. However, sometimes a surface that has just the right sheen or color, or is soft enough to pick up the finest details, is too thin or flimsy for printers to work with when registering multiple plates, and too frail to be exhibited properly. The chine collé process not only allows an artist to use more than one kind of paper in a single image, but also makes it possible to have both the best printing surface and a stable backing paper.

I saw my first examples of this kind of print when I was in junior high school. I made

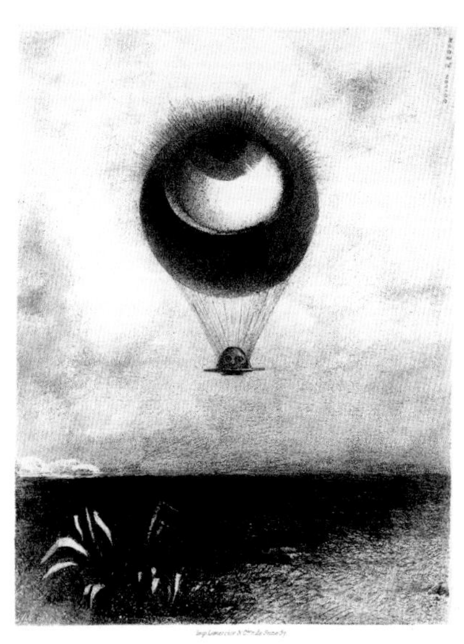

Odilon Redon, *L'Oeil, Comme un Balloon se Dirige Verg L'Infiniti*, 1882. Lithograph printed chine collé, 10½ × 8 inches.

my first prints in the Cleveland Institute of Art's Saturday morning classes. After class I usually went across the street to the Cleveland Museum of Art to look at the prints exhibited in the slanted cases downstairs. I liked best the prints in which the ink was particularly rich and soft. These images were often printed on an unusual paper that seemed incorporated, as if by magic, into the larger sheet.

Down the hall in the museum were more cases filled with exhibits of Chinese ink paintings. Their labels introduced me to the culture that invented printing and papermaking and developed these processes to high art long before they were known in the West. Some of the Chinese paintings were on silk; others were painted on a paper that looked like the unusual sheets I had admired in the cases of Western prints. Henri Fantin-Latour, Odilon Redon, and Redon's teacher Rodolphe Bresdin all used Chinese paper pasted onto heavier sheets of European paper for lithographs printed chine collé, which fascinated me with their rich tones and deep blacks.

Alan Jones, my printmaking professor at Antioch College, responded to my continuing struggle to achieve that kind of richness by arranging an internship with master lithographer Ernest de Soto in San Francisco in 1971. I stretched that apprenticeship into a career, printing with de Soto for six more years after I graduated from college. At the de Soto workshop I sometimes used the chine collé method de Soto had learned at the Tamarind Lithography Workshop when he was one of the fellows in the Tamarind printer training program. Later, I worked for seven years at Editions Press in San Francisco;

there I included chine collé in as many projects as I could in my selfish desire to understand the process.

I often referred to *The Tamarind Book of Lithography*, published in 1971,[2] and to a Tamarind research paper on chine collé [3] published in 1981. These sources give a practical account of the process, but they leave many details unclear. The research paper suggested a method for making wheat starch paste that takes a month and advised the use of only non-yellowing paste yet included in the formula a toxic fungicide that darkens over time. It also suggested using sizing as a bonding agent. Sizing, however, becomes brittle with age when used in sufficient quantity to act as an adhesive.

Like many printers, I was able to get results, often wonderfully delicate impressions that made the troublesome process worthwhile. Yet nothing seemed to work consistently. When I encountered problems, I always assumed that I had not used enough paste or that the paste lacked sufficient strength. Neither of those assumptions was true. As time went on, I realized that I was not the only printer getting mixed results. The fear that an edition will delaminate after it is released to the public has caused many of my colleagues to resort to strong synthetic adhesives developed for the bookbinding trade. These work well and meet certain industry standards, but their permanence is still in question, and their excessive strength is likely to cause buckling or warping over time.

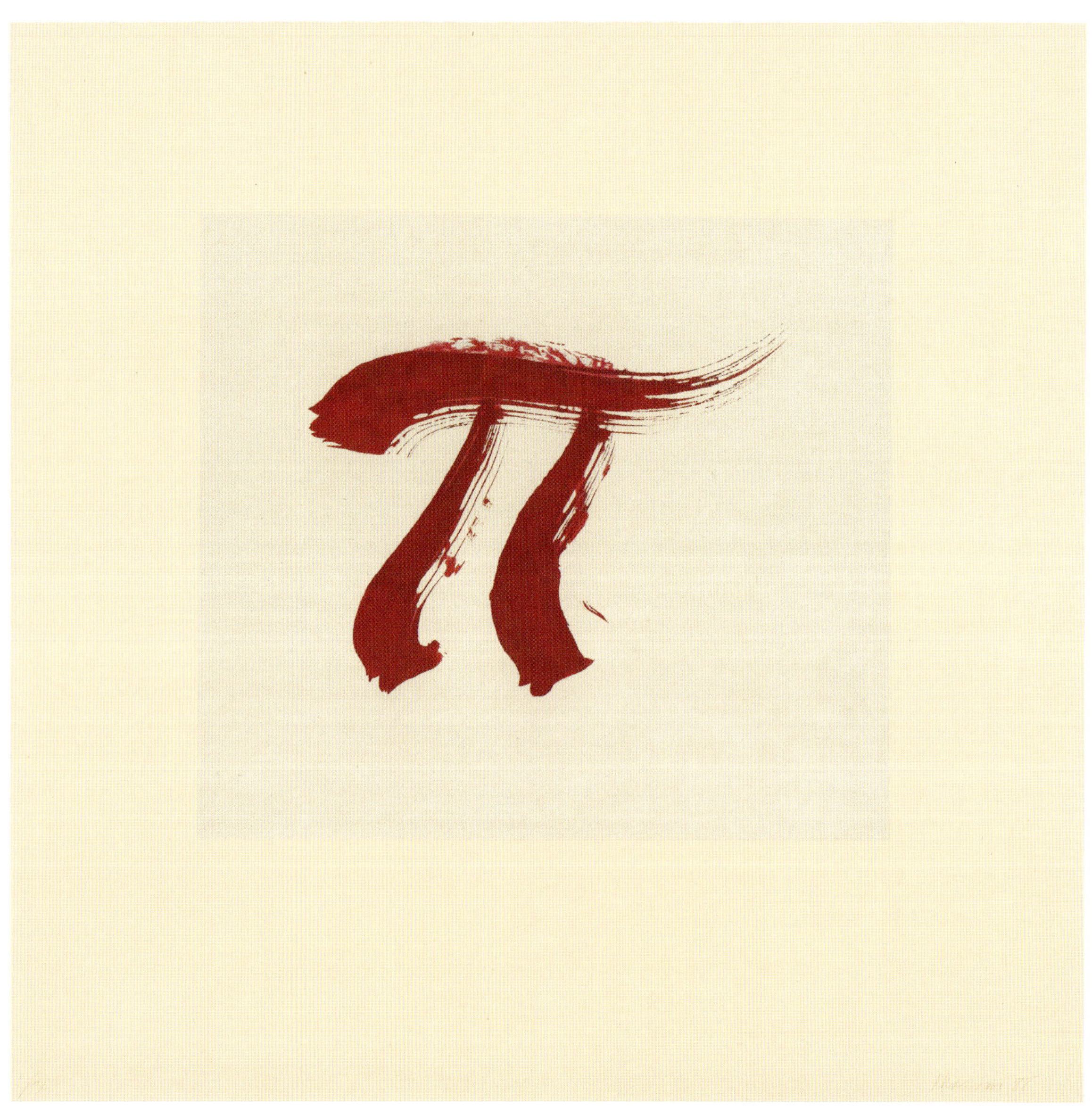

In 1987 I became a printer at Crown Point Press. Kathan Brown was just beginning the China Woodblock Project, which sent Crown Point artists to China to work in traditional woodblock studios. A few months after I started, some proofs of a woodblock print by Tom Marioni arrived from China. *Pi* (pl. 3) was a calligraphic rendering of the symbol π printed on gossamer rectangles of silk that had been simply folded up and stuffed in a crumpled mailing envelope. They arrived wrinkled but undamaged. The wrinkles would come out in the mounting process.

*Pi* isn't an etching, nor is it printed chine collé, but it played a critical role in my understanding of the collé process. Crown Point had done two earlier projects with an established woodblock studio in China, works by Francesco Clemente and Robert Bechtle. But the Marioni print was done by an independent printer whom Kathan Brown had engaged as an experiment. The earlier prints on silk had arrived supported by a paper backing, but this time the printer had printed directly on the fabric without any sizing or backing. I spent several weeks trying to mount the *Pi* prints on a Western backing paper, and eventually, with the help of two skilled paper conservators, I had success with a few pieces. But I had no sense of a workable method, and even more worrisome than that was a nagging feeling that it shouldn't be so hard.

Printers in the Crown Point etching workshop had developed successful Asian-style chine collé techniques in the early 1980s with the help of Shoichi Ida, an artist from Japan whose prints Crown Point Press published. At Crown Point, we worked frequently with paste, adhering different kinds of papers using the chine collé method, but in the case of *Pi* any excess dampening in applying glue or removing wrinkles caused the water-based ink to bleed. I thought that we needed to size the prints before we mounted them, but no method we tried worked consistently. In the same time period, I began mounting Robert Bechtle's woodcuts on Western backing papers.

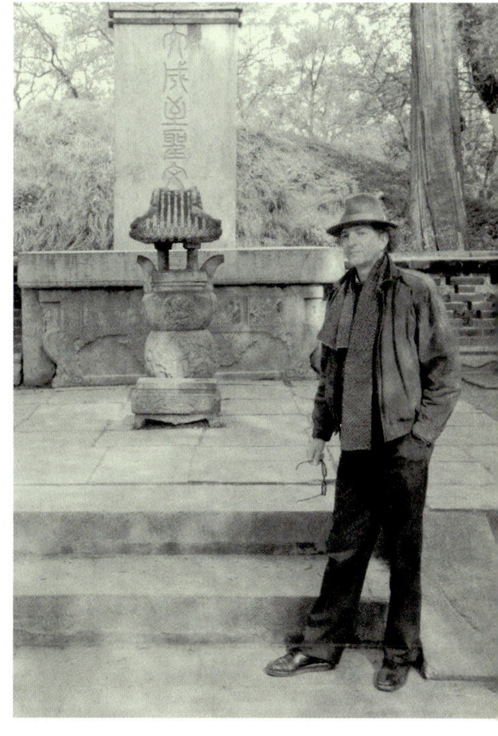

After more than a year of unpredictable results, in the spring
of 1989 Kathan Brown arranged for me to take lessons in
scroll mounting from masters on a visit with her to the print
shops we were working with in China, and then to meet with
a paper conservator and a master scroll mounter in Kyoto,
Japan, where Crown Point had established its Japan Woodblock
Project in 1981.[4] I packed up some of the unmounted
woodblock prints on silk, samples of the papers we use at
Crown Point, and a few of the more interesting failures I
had produced when I tried to combine the two. We headed
to China, completing the arc these materials had traveled,
returning to their source in search of answers. The scroll
mounters there, understanding me to be a craftsperson
like themselves, freely shared their technical expertise and
provided us with new solutions for the mounting of the
Chinese woodblock prints and a clearer understanding of the
chine collé process.

At the Duoyunxuan woodblock studio in Shanghai,
the room used for mounting was filled with enormous red
lacquer tables. I had encountered considerable trouble in
California when I had tried to mount Marioni's and Bechtle's
relatively small woodcuts on silk to backing sheets. Here,
technicians were unrolling onto the tables ink paintings on
silk 4 feet wide and 12 feet in length, getting them ready to
mount onto scrolls.

A mounter began by breaking a lump off a block of paste
that looked like white jelly and was floating in a bucket under

one of the red tables. With the heel of her hand she mashed the paste on the table's edge, then spread it out on the surface and worked water into it with a palm-fiber brush until it was thin and smooth.

She sniffed the paste and touched it to her tongue. (I believe that if she had tasted mold she would not have used it.) She spread the paste thinly on a huge sheet of *xuan* paper. I had used this paper for chine collé and found that it fell to pieces as soon as it was wet. Here, it was used as backing for silk that would be printed on later or for drawings being mounted onto scrolls.

Two waiting mounters grabbed the corners of the pasted paper and lofted it with such vigorous shaking motions that I could not keep myself from laughing out loud. I thought the weak, wet paper should have been hopelessly wrinkled, folded over on itself, and torn to pieces. But the mounters floated it across the room. It billowed in the air currents and gently settled atop a long piece of silk, already damp and spread face down on another table.

As I watched this procedure repeated again and again, I realized that what at first sight appeared to be reckless motion was in truth the extremely skillful, loose movement required for handling the weak paper without damaging it. The mounters never stopped suddenly or moved forcefully. They coaxed the sheet gently, following as much as leading it in one general direction until it ended up just where they wanted it. They checked the moisture content of the paper by its feel

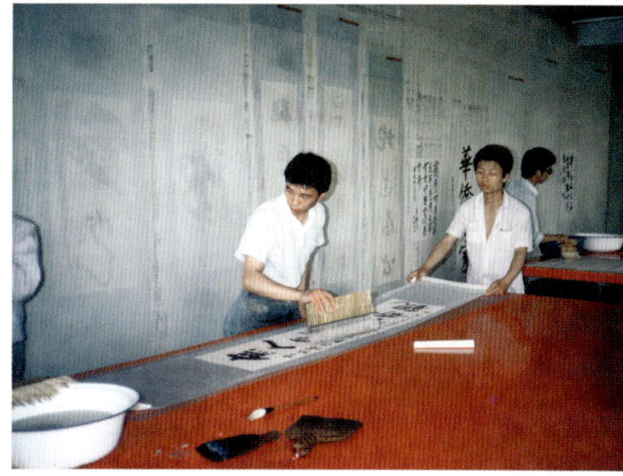

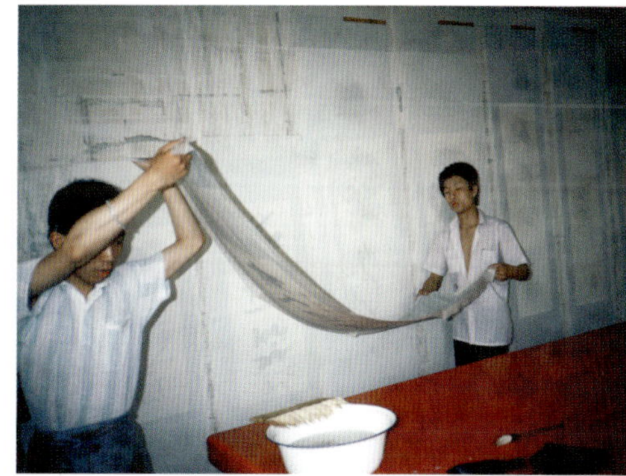

Duoyunxuan Studio, Shanghai

against the cheek as they floated it across the room between them. If the paper was very wet, they moved more slowly; if it was too dry, another mounter misted the part of the room they were moving toward. As they transferred the paper, they equalized the moisture content in both the silk and the paper so that the bond could occur without stress between the different materials. I came to realize that the adjustment in humidity and the thinness of the paste were the keys to making the process work.

After leaving China, Kathan Brown and I flew to Japan, where I met in Kyoto with a paper conservator and a mounter. The paper conservator took a spoonful of aged paste from a jar he kept buried in the garden behind his studio. It was brown and smelled putrid. This fermented wheat starch paste had been aged for a decade; it is the most precious paste, used to conserve very old, fragile, important documents and works of art. It is applied so thinly that the paper seems almost not to be coated at all, but can hold firmly, even for centuries.

The master mounter touched against his tongue Tom Marioni's Chinese woodblock print on silk that I had brought to him. This was to taste the alum and thus determine the amount of sizing present. Next, he thinned his paste to the consistency of watery milk and brushed a tiny amount across the back of the print.

He had already brushed plain water over a sheet of Arches cover paper I had brought with me. He pressed a flexible plastic ruler against one edge of the pasted silk, picked up the silk, and, guiding it with the ruler now stuck to it, flipped it over and positioned it on the Arches. The thin layer of water on the surface of the Arches pulled the print down tight so that the texture of the Arches showed clearly through the silk. He gently pressed out the wrinkles with a flat brush.

Then, to my surprise, the mounter flipped the whole thing over and applied a half-inch band of paste around the edges of the Arches on its reverse side. When he flipped the sheet over again and laid it face up on a drying board, I was surprised to see the silk still in place. I was hardly willing to believe it would stay attached when dry.

When I returned the next morning, the mounter gently lifted the sheet of Arches away from the drying board. It came away without tearing and without the paste on the back sticking or even being visible. The silk remained firmly attached.

In watching these skilled craftspeople, I found the solution to the problems I was having mounting Chinese woodblock prints, and I also learned why I had been unable to get consistent results with chine collé. The keys to success are to use minimal paste and to pay careful attention to the dampness of the papers and the humidity of the environment.

After seven years at Crown Point Press, during which time I became a master printer, I left in 1994 to concentrate on my own work and—as it turned out—to teach printmaking. My approach to my own work and what I have to offer as a teacher are both built around the skills I learned as a printer, so when Kathan Brown proposed to me five years after I had left Crown

Point that I write a book about the chine collé process for
Crown Point to publish, I was very pleased. My earlier book on
chine collé was the result. When I'm teaching chine collé or
pasting down papers or fabrics, I often see in my mind's eye
the professional scroll mounters in China as they apparently
effortlessly worked with large sheets of very thin and relatively
weak backing papers. Watching them for a few hours taught me
more than the months I had spent with the collé process using
only my own experience and descriptions of the experiences of
other printers and conservators.

This book not only expands my original text on chine collé
but also offers video footage. I returned to Beijing and Shanghai
and videotaped a new generation of mounters who continue the
tradition of scroll mounting that dates back well over a thousand
years. I'm very pleased to be able to share these images with you
on the included DVD, along with images of a Japanese master
scroll mounter demonstrating mounting techniques.

When I return to Crown Point Press, as I do often, I always
find the same beautifully appointed studios, clean and sparely
furnished, with room not only for large plates and big sheets
of paper but also for a magical kind of space for ideas to grow.
Having transferred my viewpoint from the professional print
workshop to my studio and the classroom, I know that the
skills of printers through history have been developed in
competitive, commercially viable, and highly professional
atmospheres and that those skills are best preserved and
enhanced today in similar atmospheres. The idea behind the
Magical Secrets series is to pass skills on to you, to present
information too often hidden, at times lost, or, worst of all,
misunderstood, mistranslated, or just innocently distorted.

The rigors of the professional publishing world, with its
historically tenuous economic footing, involve the serious risk

of producing work on speculation for a public often lagging
in understanding the ideas of artists. These rigors refine and
optimize skills out of a necessity that does not exist to the same
extent in printing operations with underwritten support or
in school situations. Shops like Crown Point Press pay careful
attention to providing an optimal working atmosphere for
artists and constantly push for the highest quality produced in
the most efficient manner possible.

Although my career as a printer at Crown Point Press
ended in 1994, this book is informed by my experiences there,
and I still feel very much a part of the Crown Point family.

1  R. H. Gulik, *Chinese Pictorial Art as Viewed by the Connoisseur* (New York: Hacker Art Books, 1981), 58. Reprint of 1958 edition.

2  Garo Antreasian with Clinton Adams, *The Tamarind Book of Lithograhy: Art and Techniques* (New York: Harry N. Abrams, 1971), 417-22.

3  Elizabeth N. Jordan and John Sommers, "The Collé Process," *The Tamarind Papers* IV-2 (summer, 1981: 39-41).

4  For information about the Crown Point programs in Japan and China, see Kathan Brown, *Ink, Paper, Metal, Wood: Painters and Sculptors at Crown Point Press* (San Francisco: Chronicle Books, 1996).

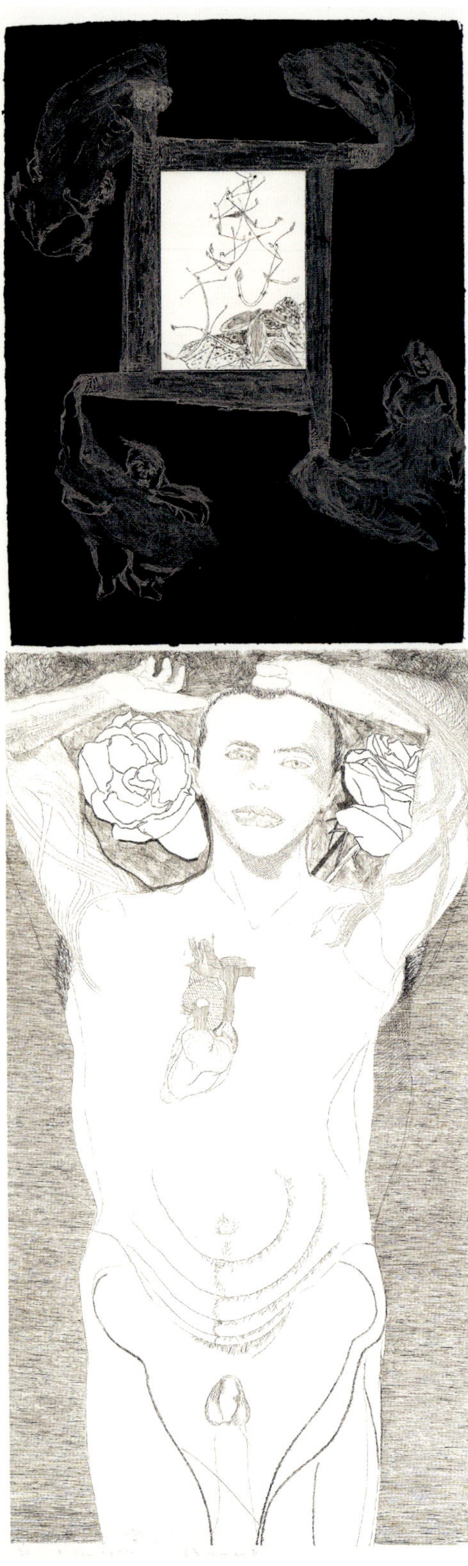

PLATE 4
Francesco Clemente, *Telemone #2*, 1981.
Soft ground etching with aquatint and
drypoint in black and silver on Farnsworth
paper chine collé on Arches 88 with hard
ground etching, 61 × 19 inches.

# Secret #1. THE PASTE

*Less is more.*

Many adhesives can be used to paste one paper to another to make a successful chine collé print. In this book, I focus on wheat starch paste. Traditional mounters in Asia use it, as do paper conservators around the world, and I believe it has the best properties for chine collé. It requires advance preparation and attention to proper storage, but if you have good printing habits, it is easy to use. Precooked starch powders and reversable PVA (polyvinyl acetate) adhesives are now on the market. The precooked powder may work fine, but nothing beats the real thing. The aging characteristics of PVA, a synthetic adhesive, are not as good as those of starch paste. Wheat starch paste is very stable and remains reversible with cold water.

We used a PVA adhesive for chine collé at Crown Point Press until 1984. Francesco Clemente's *Telemone #2* (pl. 4), 1981, is an example. Although it is more than twenty years old, I'm pleased to say that it has not yellowed or become brittle. However, this type of glue is so strong that it changes the basic characteristics of the paper or fabric to which it is applied, and the prints on which we used it, including this one, are noticeably stiff.

Wheat starch paste maintains a print's flexibility, and if you prepare your own paste with no preservatives and apply it correctly, it will not darken or become brittle with

age, a potential problem with commercial preparations, which are appropriate only for temporary work. Neutral pH prepared pastes have added preservatives to keep them from molding or fermenting, and generally the preservatives darken with age.

Paste made from any starch—rice, potato, methyl cellulose, and carboxymethyl-cellulose—remains responsive to changes in humidity even after it has dried, just as paper and fabrics do. Most papers are made of a network of interlocked fibers with small open spaces between them, and fabrics are mostly air. Even vinyl acetate sheets absorb moisture. If you use starch paste, the moisture in the air carried from the impression sheet of a chine collé–printed work to its support sheet can move right through the thin adhesive and not upset the balance in tension set up during the pasting and drying processes. If the adhesive is a thicker layer, impervious to moisture as most synthetic adhesives are, you are placing a barrier between the two sheets and the balance is upset every time the humidity changes. This can lead to curling, buckling, and even delamination.

Wheat starch paste is stronger than other starch pastes, so you can use less of it for better results in the chine collé process. Wheat starch paste is also versatile and can be adapted to solve almost any problem you may encounter in working with chine collé. The normal approach to pasting for chine collé is to apply the paste just before printing, but you can also apply wheat starch paste to paper and dry it in advance of its use. You can store the prepasted paper for years, then reactivate the paste and use the paper to make a chine collé print. This applies, as well, to collage papers— that is, papers pasted together without being run through a press. Prepasted fabric can also be reactivated and used at a later time.

If you wish to detach the backing paper completely from a chine collé print made with wheat starch paste, you can use water to soften the paste and successfully make the separation. If you wish to redampen a print to smooth out minor handling damage but not detach it from its support, you can use less water, and it will not detach.

Wheat starch is wheat flour with the gluten removed. Wheat flour actually makes a stronger paste, but since gluten inevitably attracts insects that will damage the paper, and it darkens as it ages, flour should not be used if the work is meant to be permanent.

In the step-by-step section of this chapter, I describe how to make and store wheat starch paste. You will need to prepare your paste a day in advance to give it time to gel completely. In a few circumstances, which I describe later (pages 115 and 124), you might use this gel with little or no thinning, but normally you will thin it significantly before use. In general,

the thinner the layer you can successfully use, the less likely you will have problems either in the printing process or later with the papers curling after they dry. If you consistently begin any pasting process by trying a small batch of the thinnest possible paste, you will avoid a lot of the problems associated with chine collé. If you find that your papers aren't laminating properly, you can thicken the mixture slightly and continue your trials until the results are optimal. Remember that after you have adhered papers with a thin paste, you must allow time for slow, even evaporation of any excess moisture so that the paste can set up and create a strong bond. My advice overall is to use the least amount of paste and the least amount of moisture possible. Less is more.

To give you an example of how important this is, I'm going to talk in detail about one image in a set of four small aquatints with drypoint by Shoichi Ida printed chine collé at Crown Point Press in 1987. I worked on this project soon after I became a printer at Crown Point; the master printer in charge was Nancy Anello. When Ida first came from Japan to work at Crown Point in 1984, he brought with him chine collé techniques that included the use of wheat starch paste, although in a different formula from the one we use today. "Chine collé," Ida said in a 1989 interview, "reminds me of skin. I can see what's happening on the other side. It's like a screen, a projection screen. I'm always interested in

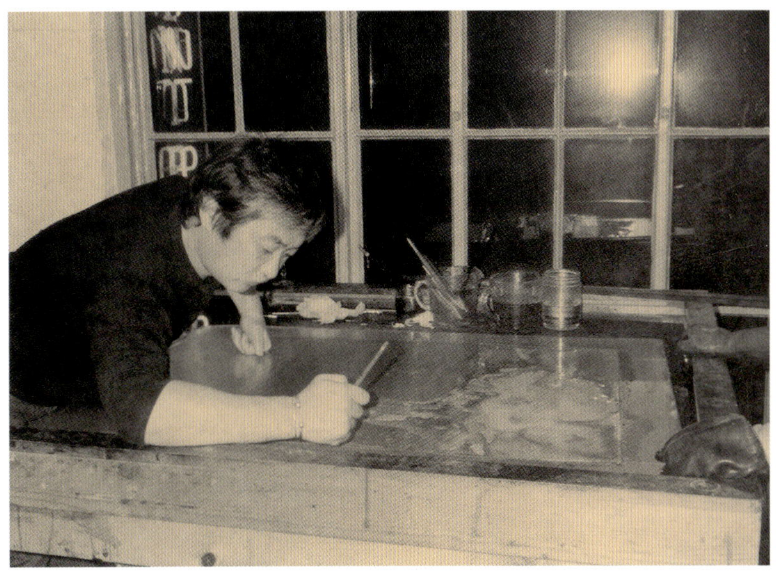

what's happening in the between." Ida died in 2006. His legacy to Crown Point Press includes not only his art but also his mix of innovation and tradition in chine collé.

For the set of etchings titled *Between Vertical and Horizon—Descended Triangle*, Ida explored the descended triangle idea in two horizontal images, designated *A* (pl. 5) and *B* (pl. 6), and two vertical ones, designated *C* and *D* (pl. 7). In each of these prints, thin gampi paper is colléd over an image already printed on the support paper, and another image is printed on top of the gampi. You can see that the circles in *B* and *D* are veiled by the gampi, while in *A* the triangle and square are veiled and the circle, printed on top of the gampi, is clearly exposed. I particularly want to discuss *D*, where one of the veiled circles was heavily inked.

In making this set of prints, Ida asked the printers to pull many proofs of the plates in different combinations, changing the plate sequences and the points at which the gampi was adhered. In intaglio proofing (unlike traditional hand lithography), it is possible to print all the plates in one consecutive press run, so in proofing, the artist can explore the potential of an image exhaustively.

In *Descended Triangle (D)*, we printed the plate with the heavily inked circle on the backing paper first. Then in a second run through the press, we adhered the gampi paper over that image and at the same time printed the line plate on the gampi. Ida created the rich circular spit bite aquatint by cutting a circle out of a scrap of printing paper, soaking it in a very strong nitric acid/gum arabic solution, and then placing it on a plate that was prepared for aquatint. The result was

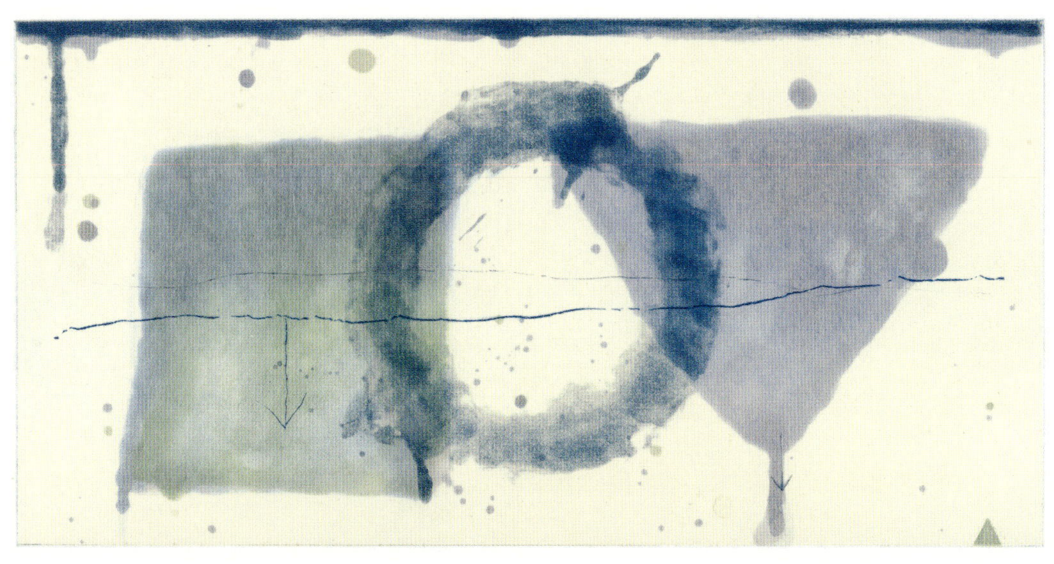

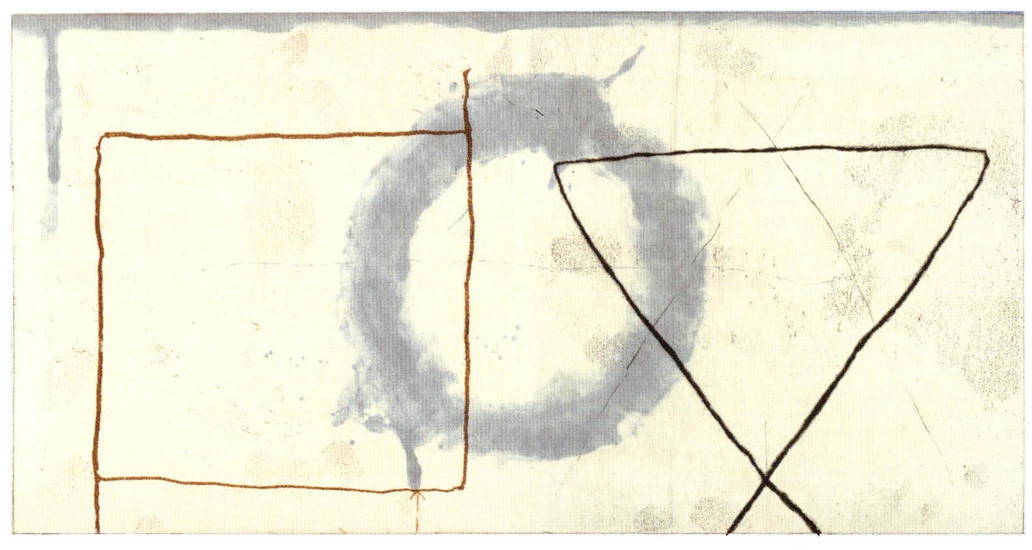

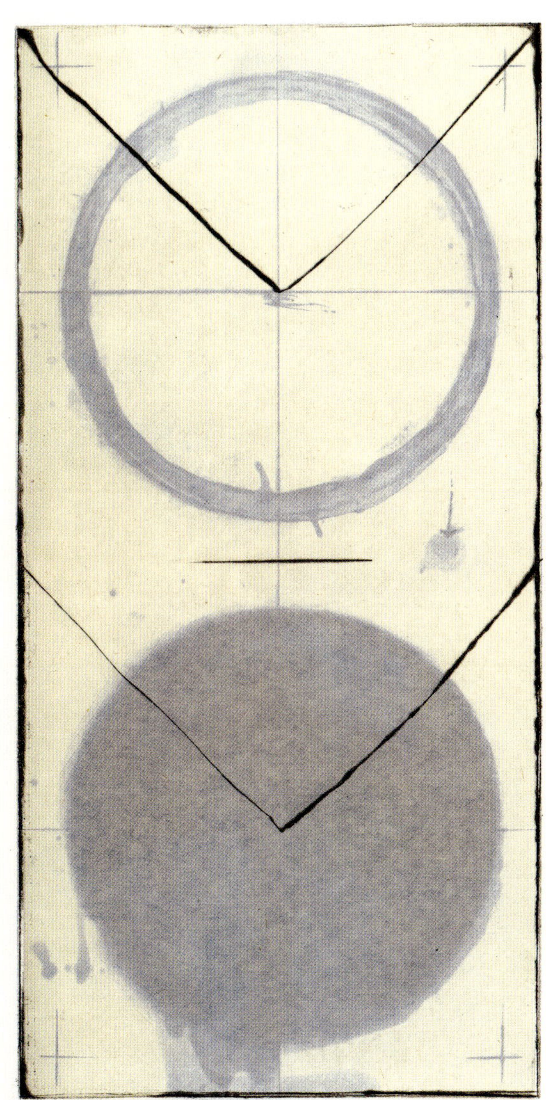

PLATE 5 (OPPOSITE TOP)
Shoichi Ida, *Between Vertical and Horizon—Descended Triangle (A)*, 1987.
Color spit bite aquatint with drypoint printed on gampi paper chine collé, 7 × 14 inches.

PLATE 6 (OPPOSITE BOTTOM)
Shoichi Ida, *Between Vertical and Horizon—Descended Triangle (B)*, 1987.
Color spit bite aquatint with soft ground etching and drypoint printed on gampi paper chine collé, 7 × 14 inches.

PLATE 7 (LEFT)
Shoichi Ida, *Between Vertical and Horizon—Descended Triangle (D)*, 1987.
Color spit bite aquatint with drypoint printed on gampi paper chine collé, 14 × 7 inches.

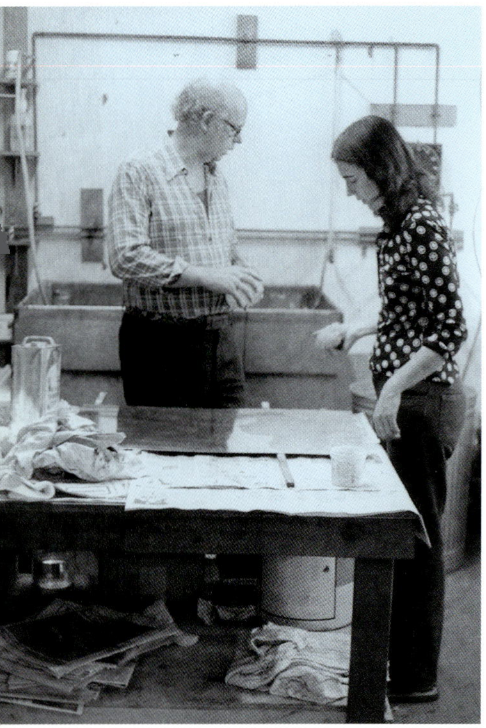

Claes Oldenburg, Kathan Brown



a deep, sturdy matrix that held a lot of ink. This aquatint held so much ink that the gampi would not stick to it.

We tried adding more paste, but it just squeezed out from under the gampi when we ran it through the press, and the gampi still bubbled away from the ink on the backing paper when we lifted the print. The secret was less paste, not more. The amount we finally used was minimal; it had to be because there was nowhere for it to go—it was sticking directly to a thick layer of wet oil-based ink. We also realized that we needed to minimize the moisture level in the gampi to the point that at first the paste would be too dry to stick. The moisture in the backing sheet would be sufficient to activate it when it was run through the press. To accomplish this, we applied the paste to the gampi in advance and let it dry. Then we made a damp pack by lightly moistening several sheets of printing paper and wrapping them in plastic. Before printing on the prepasted sheets, we placed them between the moistened papers until they relaxed but were not wet. You will find instructions for prepasting in chapter 3. The story of *Descended Triangle (D)* is in this beginning chapter to demonstrate a fundamental point: minimal paste and just enough moisture were the magical secrets here, as they are in most cases of successful adhesion.

To conclude these introductory remarks about paste, I'd like to show you two examples of early Crown Point Press chine collé prints: *Sailboat and Hat* by Claes Oldenburg, 1975 (pl. 8), and *Not St. Girolamo* by Francesco Clemente, 1981 (pl. 9). Neither was adhered with wheat starch paste; both could have been if information about its use had been available to the printers at the time. In the 1970s and early 1980s, chine collé was not in the consciousness of many artists or printers.

The Oldenburg etching was the first chine collé print made at Crown Point, which had been founded thirteen years earlier by Kathan Brown. Neither Brown nor Oldenburg's printer, John Slivon, can remember why the image was done chine collé or what glue was used. The project, published by

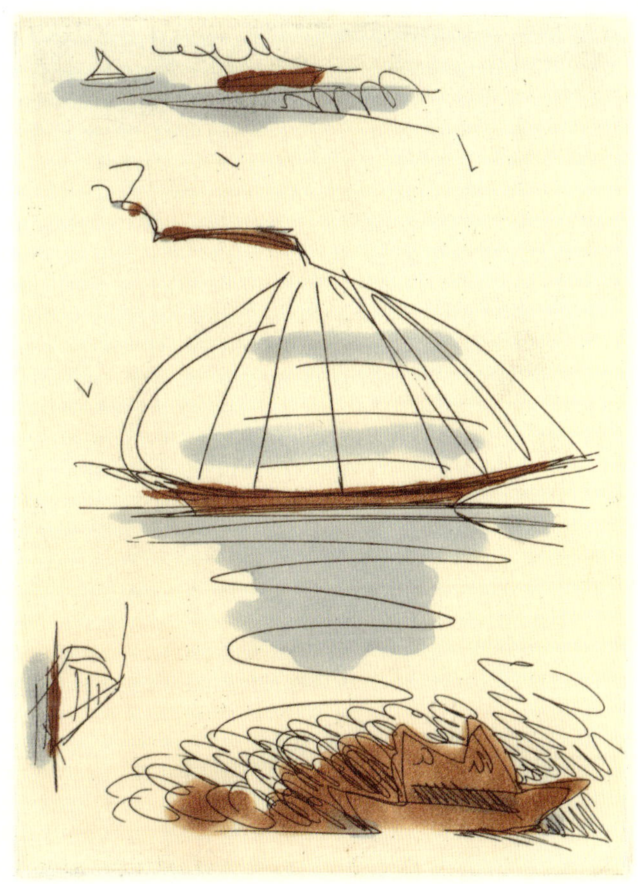

**CLAES OLDENBURG**  *When I come to San Francisco, I always try to get a room overlooking the bay so I can see the behavior of the skies and water.*

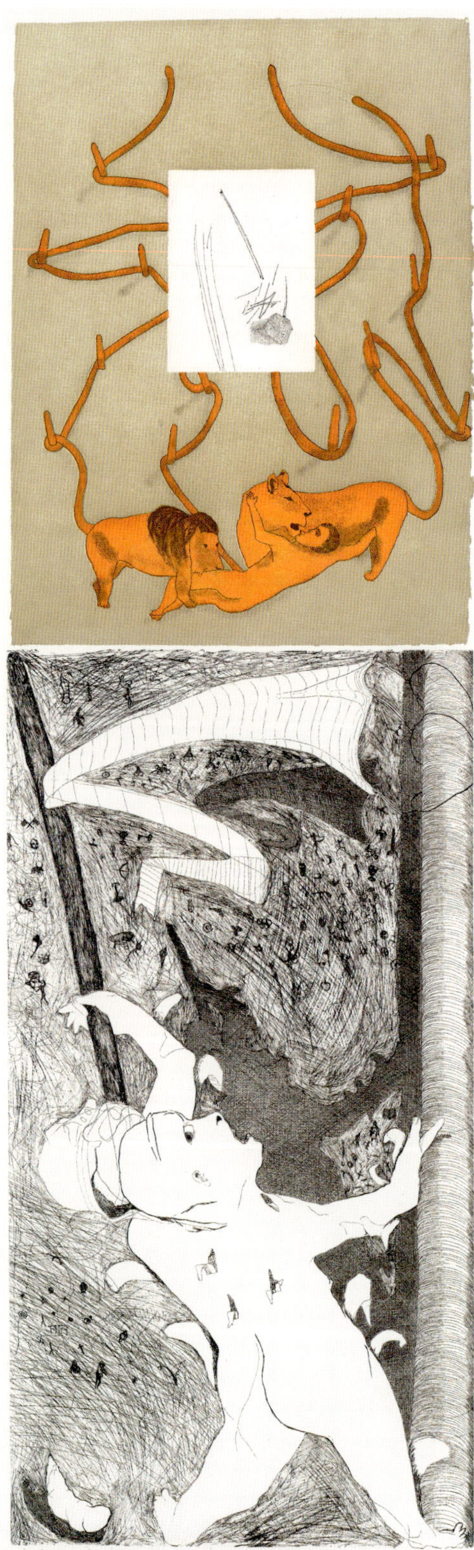


Francesco Clemente, *Not St. Girolamo*, 1981.
Color soft ground etching with aquatint
and drypoint printed on Farnsworth paper
chine collé on Arches 88 with hard ground
etching, 61 × 19 inches.

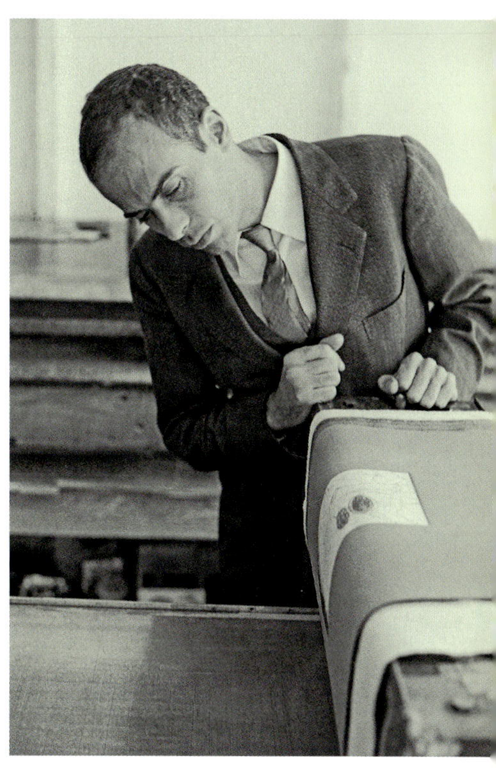

Marion Goodman's New York gallery (then called Multiples), was focused on an ambitious large color aquatint called *Floating Three-Way Plug*. Oldenburg was constantly sketching in a sketchbook he carried, and Brown thinks the chine collé element in the small print was used as a way to give that image the quality of a sketch torn from a notebook.

Clemente's *Not St. Girolamo*, one of a series of three that included *Telemone #2* (pl. 4), also became a chine collé print in response to a particular need of the artist. At the time, Clemente was living in Italy and India, and he came to Crown Point Press from India with a stop in Japan. He stayed in a monastery in Japan and asked Brown to send him some small plates so he could draw on them with drypoint. He brought the completed plates with him to Oakland, California, where the press was located at the time. The printers proofed them and pinned them up for Clemente to study.

Clemente next began work on three rectangular prints on paper handmade by a local papermaker, Don Farnsworth, and he asked the printers if the "monastery" images could be incorporated into those works. To receive the small images, Clemente created windowlike areas in the centers of his rectangular images. Wanting to emphasize the deckles in the Farnsworth paper, he made the plates larger than the paper so that the images would bleed, with no plate mark. He then expanded onto new plates where he drew line etchings of bearers, called *telemone*, to be positioned so the bearers appear to support the rectangular images with their "monastery" insets. Clemente's concept instigated the chine collé project illustrated here.

For each image, the printers first printed the small "monastery" plate in the center of the Farnsworth paper, registering it carefully. Because of the deckles, there was no excess paper to keep under the press roller as is normal for registration purposes; the printers taped extra registration tabs to the paper so they could extend it under the roller for the four runs needed to print the small image plus the three plates in the rectangular image. Finally, this sheet was pasted and laid on the final large plate above the inked *telemone* to be adhered during the final pass through the press.

*Not St. Girolamo* is the third print in the series. *Girolamo* is the Italian word for "Jerome," and the image concerns (or doesn't concern) St. Jerome, who tamed a lion. In Clemente's version of the old story, St. Jerome's world, which includes a peaceful image from a Japanese monastery, is in collapse.

Hidekatsu Takada, the master printer who ran this project, told me that all three prints have the Farnsworth handmade paper pasted down to Arches 88 with white (Elmer's brand) glue, thinned with water and applied with a brush. The white glue was used on the advice of a paper conservator at the Museum of Modern Art in New York, with whom the printers conferred because they were having problems adhering the unsized Farnsworth paper. Sizing that paper first would have solved the problem, as it was absorbing too much moisture. But the white glue worked, and the prints have not degraded over time. Today, we would do something like that with wheat starch paste rather than white glue, and—I believe—would have fewer problems in the execution. These etchings, however, in their beauty and complexity, are here for the ages.

# Preparing Wheat Starch Powder Step-by-Step (Optional)

Wheat starch powder is the material from which wheat starch paste is made. If you do not wish to make your own, you can order high-quality wheat starch powder from a supplier of conservation materials (see www.magical-secrets.com for a source). There is no particular advantage to making your own, but it isn't difficult.

1. **MAKE DOUGH FROM FLOUR**

   Use unbleached wheat flour without the bran. Pastry flour works well. Make it into dough with fresh water, and knead for 5 to 10 minutes, as for making bread. Kneading causes the proteins to link and become gluten.

   TIP *If you cannot find wheat flour without bran, sift it to remove the bran yourself. The bran is coarser than the flour and is visible as dark flecks.*

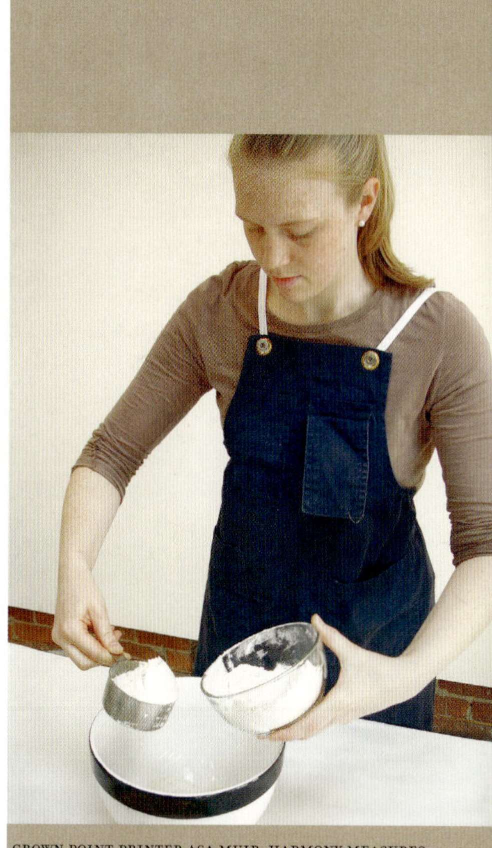

CROWN POINT PRINTER ASA MUIR-HARMONY MEASURES UNBLEACHED WHEAT FLOUR INTO A BOWL.

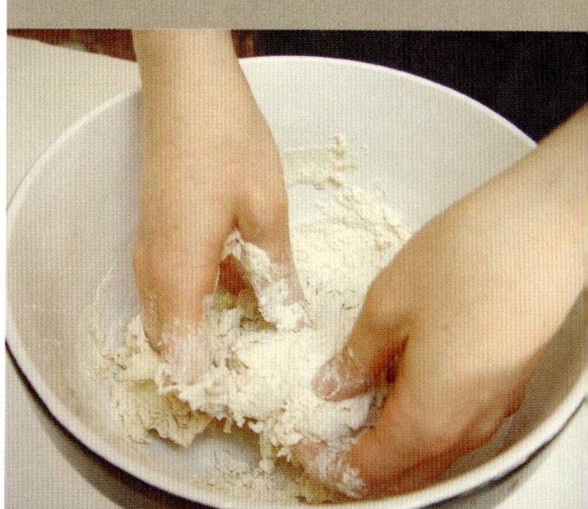

MIX THE FLOUR AND WATER TOGETHER.

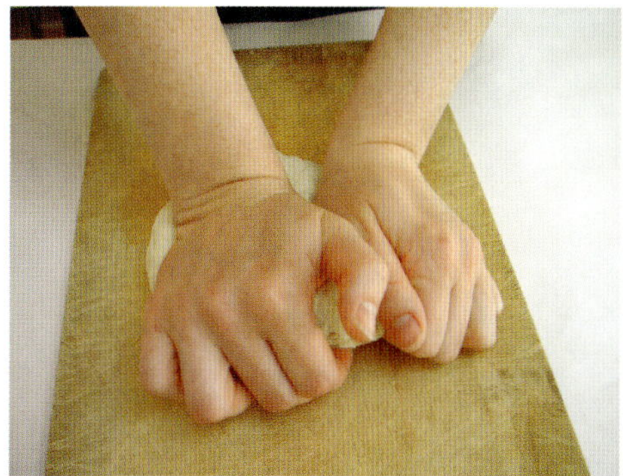

KNEAD THE DOUGH FOR 5 MINUTES.

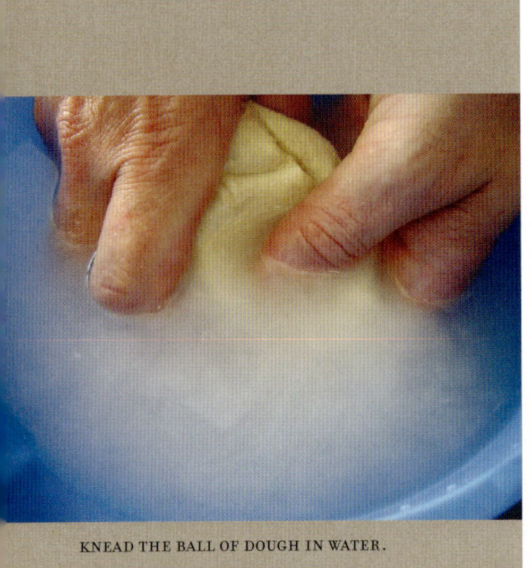

KNEAD THE BALL OF DOUGH IN WATER.

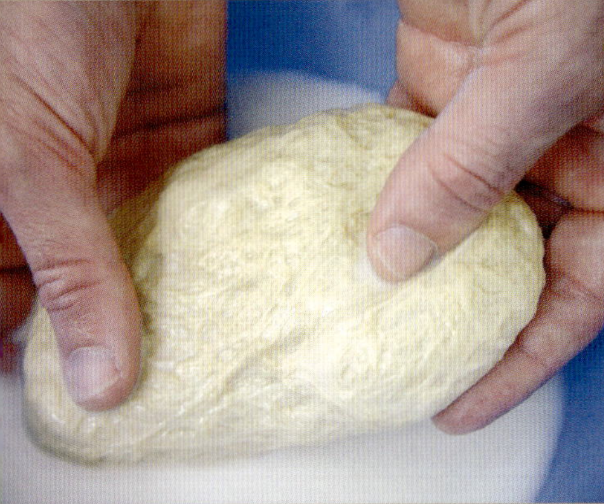

THE POROUS SPONGE OF GLUTEN.

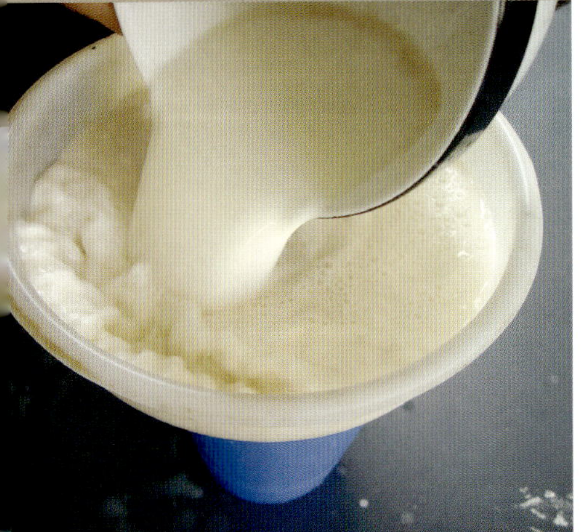

STRAIN THE MILKY WATER AND LET IT SIT
OVERNIGHT.

2.  **CONTINUE KNEADING UNDER WATER**
    Submerge the ball of dough in a big bucket of clear cold water, and gently use your fingers to pull it apart and knead it further. The starch separates out, forming a milky solution and leaving a porous sponge of gluten. In Asia the gluten is eaten—but you can discard it.

3.  **STRAIN AND SAVE THE MILKY WATER**
    Strain the milky water to filter out bits of dough that may have separated from the sponge, and leave the strained water for several hours or overnight, until the starch settles to the bottom.

4.  **POUR OFF THE CLEAR WATER AFTER THE STARCH HAS SETTLED**
    Leave the layer of starch in the bottom of the container until it is dry. This may take 2 or 3 days. Then pound it into a powder, preferably with a mortar and pestle.

    TIP *If you wish to use the starch immediately to make the cooked gel that will eventually become paste, pour off most of the water but leave enough water to approximate the proportion of 1 part starch to 4 parts water. It might take some experience to determine the correct amount of water to leave.*

5.  **STORE THE WHEAT STARCH POWDER IN A COOL, DRY PLACE**
    It will keep indefinitely if stored in an airtight container.

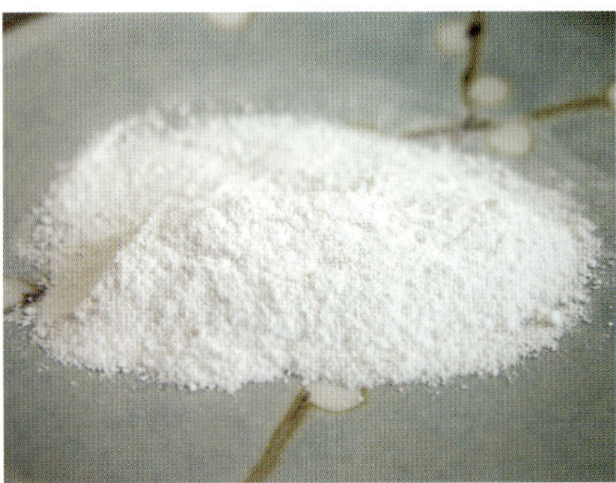

THE FINAL DRIED WHEAT STARCH POWDER.

# Preparing Wheat Starch Paste Step-by-Step

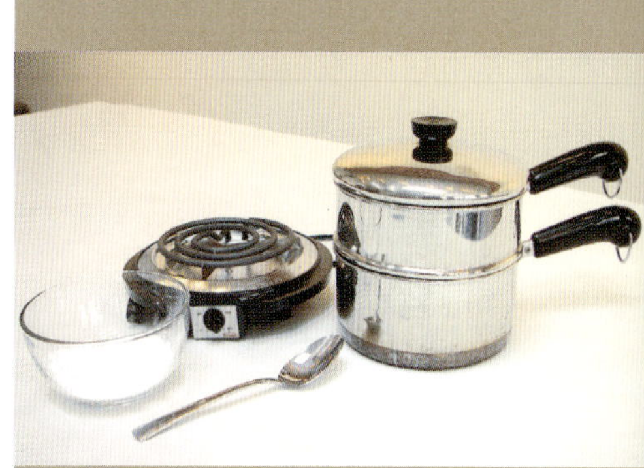

WHEAT STARCH POWER, HOT PLATE, SPOON, AND DOUBLE BOILER.

1. **ASSEMBLE THE MATERIALS**

   Double boiler with a lid

   Adjustable heat source such as a hot plate or stove top

   Cold water (warm water will instantly create a lumpy mixture that is hard to smooth out)

   Spoon for stirring after the mixture is heated

   Wheat starch powder (powder you made yourself following the instructions on pages 31–32 or powder purchased from a supplier)

2. **MIX THE WHEAT STARCH POWDER WITH COLD WATER**

   Use your fingers to mix the powder and water in the top of a double boiler that is not yet on the heat. The basic formula is 1 part wheat starch powder to 4 parts cold water. Different types of wheat, even different crops of the same type of wheat, can require an adjustment in proportions, but start with 1 to 4. Mix until the powder mixture is smooth and thoroughly wet. It will sink to the bottom of the pan.

   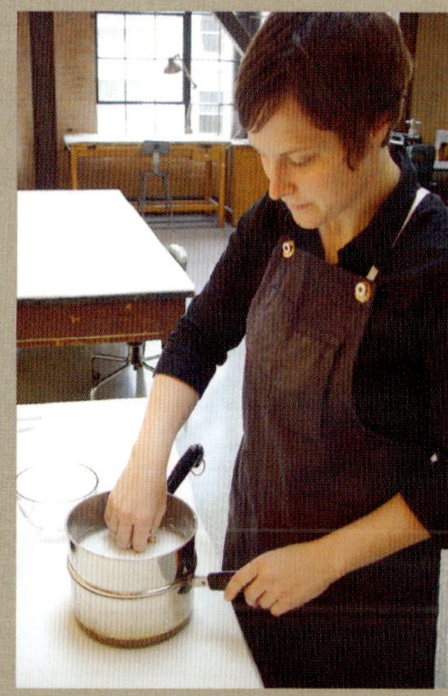

   CROWN POINT PRINTER IANNE KJORLIE MIXES THE WATER AND POWDER WITH HER FINGERS BEFORE HEATING THE MIXTURE.

   TIP *If you are using Zin Shofu, a commercially available starch powder made from Japanese wheat, decrease the water slightly to about 3½ parts to 1 part starch powder. Zin Shofu makes a weaker paste than most wheat starch powders.*

3. **BEGIN THE COOKING PROCESS**

   Fill the lower pan of the double boiler with cold water almost to the level of the upper pan. Bring to a boil. Set the upper pan with the starch mixture on the lower pan. As soon as the mixture begins to thicken, turn the heat down to a simmer and begin stirring. Watch carefully. The starch must never be allowed to boil. Overheating will compromise the strength of the paste. Stir continuously with a spoon as the mixture

   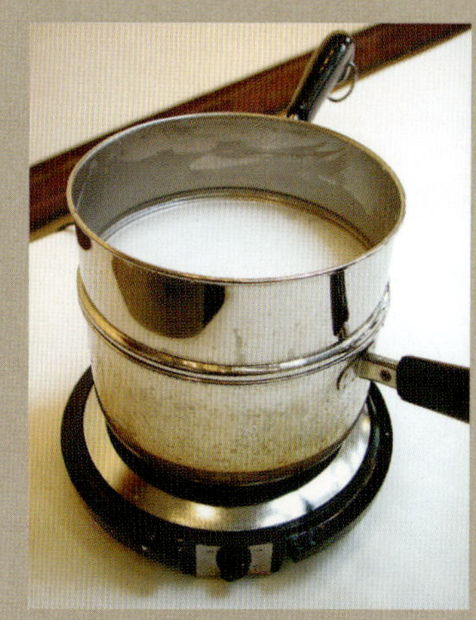

   DO NOT LET THE STARCH BOIL.

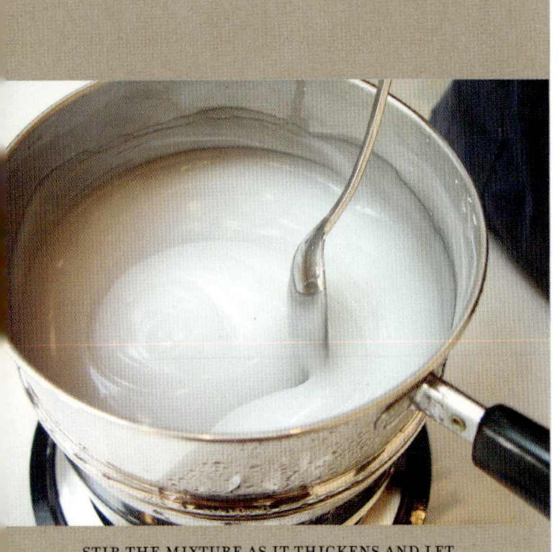



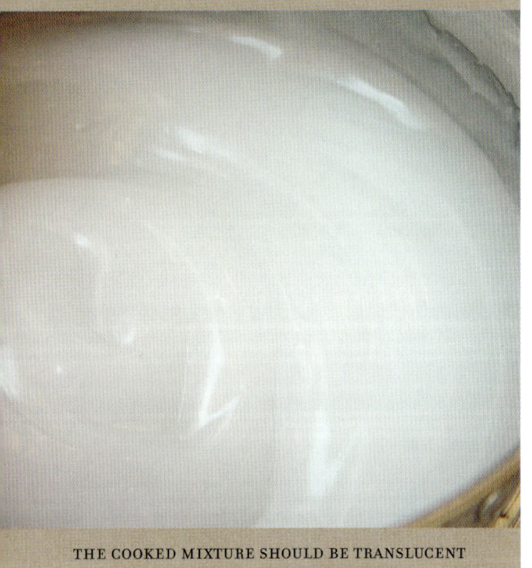



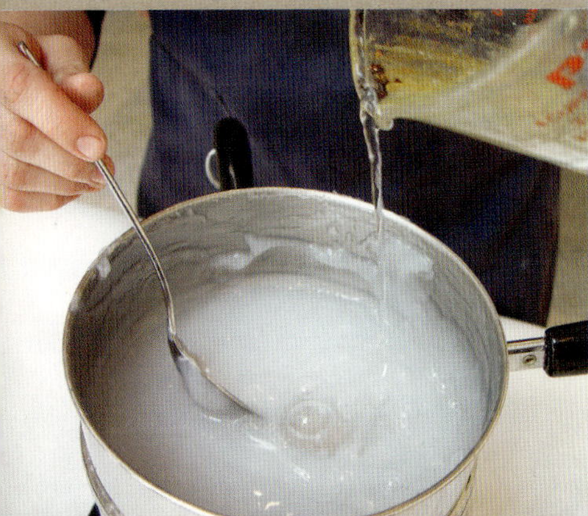



thickens. If it becomes difficult to stir, add a few spoonfuls of water from the bottom pan of the double boiler. Check to be sure the water in the bottom pan is just barely simmering.

4.  COMPLETE THE COOKING PROCESS

Cover the pan and leave the starch to cook over the simmering water for 30 minutes. Give the mixture a quick stir every 5 minutes. After cooking, it should be smooth, translucent, and the consistency of custard.

TIP *The paste can also be prepared in a microwave oven. You must be careful to keep the starch mixture from boiling, which lessens its adhesive strength. To use a microwave oven, dissolve the starch powder in cold water in a glass or plastic container in the proportions given on page 33. Microwave the mixture for 20 to 30 seconds at a time, stirring between each cooking session. Continue this process until the mixture is thick, smooth, and translucent. This method generally takes 3 or 4 minutes of total cooking time.*

5.  THIN THE COOKED STARCH

Turn off the source of heat and add enough hot but not boiling water to double the volume of the starch mixture. Add the water a little at a time, stirring thoroughly to avoid producing lumps.

6.  LET THE THINNED STARCH GEL

When the mixture is completely smooth, cover it again and leave it to gel. You can speed the process along by floating the pan in a sink full of cold water or refrigerating the pan. As the starch mixture cools, it will begin to gel.

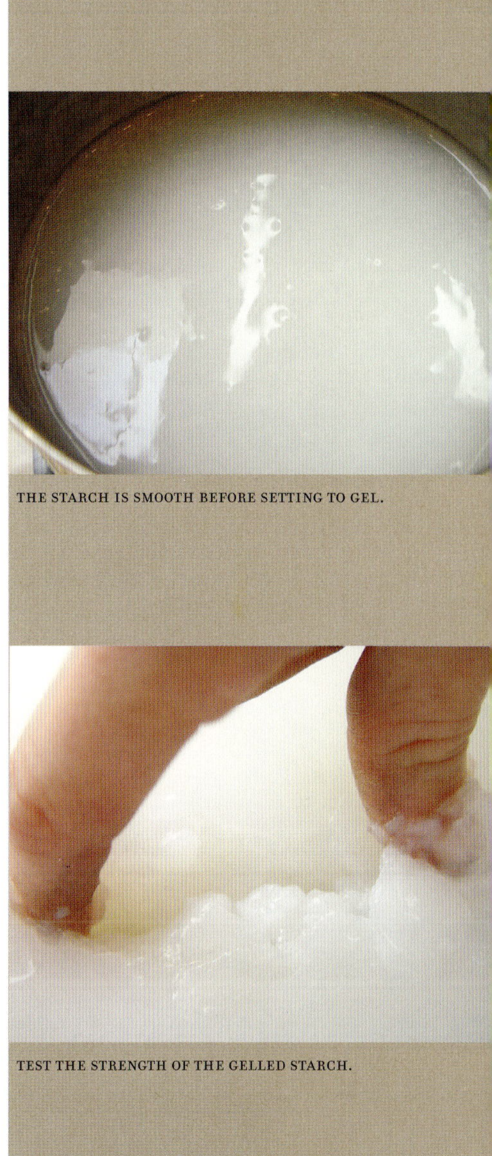

THE STARCH IS SMOOTH BEFORE SETTING TO GEL.

TEST THE STRENGTH OF THE GELLED STARCH.

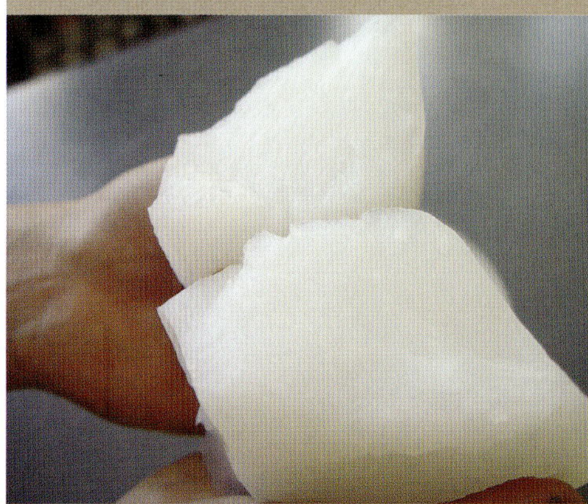

STARCH THAT IS TOO FIRM WILL BREAK APART WITH CLEAN EDGES.

TIP *The mixture must gel before it can be made into paste. If you thin the hot starch with water before it gels, it will make a very smooth solution that is easy to apply but lacks strength and tends to soak into, and even through, the paper. If this happens, the paper stiffens and may stick to the printing surface without providing a good bond.*

7. **TEST THE STRENGTH OF THE GELLED STARCH**

   Press into a lump of starch with the tips of your thumb and forefinger until the surface tears. Then spread your thumb and finger to open a crack. The sides of the crack should be rough like cottage cheese. The gelled starch should have a firm consistency, but if it breaks smoothly, it is too firm. This does not affect the quality of the paste, but will make the final paste preparation more difficult. After producing a few batches, you will be able to estimate the amount of water to add after cooking, but before cooling, so that the mixture will set up to the proper consistency.

8. **STORE THE GELLED STARCH**

   Keep the starch submerged in clean water in a covered container in the refrigerator until you are ready to make it into paste. Depending on the quality of the water and the temperature of the refrigerator, the starch may last for weeks or even months. Do not freeze it.

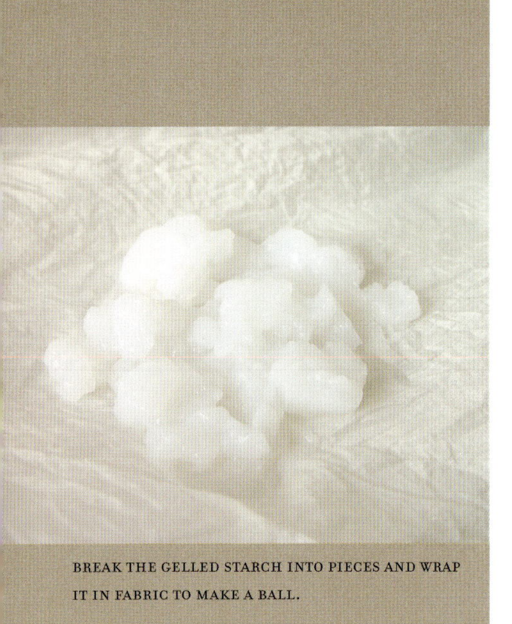



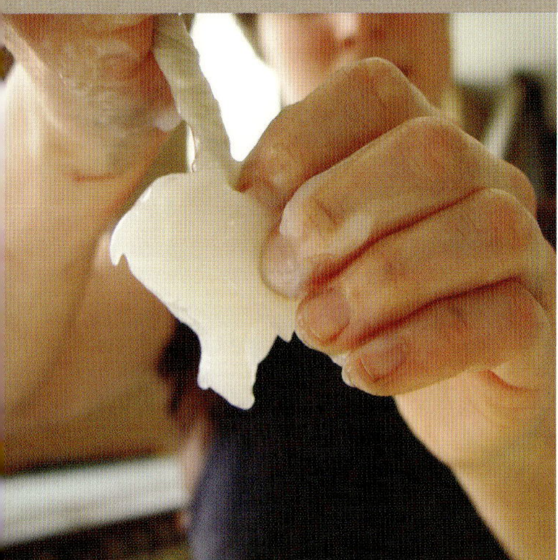



9. **PREPARE PASTE FROM THE STARCH**

When you are ready to use the paste, make enough for one day's work. Break off a lump of gelled starch. To turn it into small particles, I like best a method I learned in China: straining the gelled starch through a large square of fine silk. Put the lump of starch into the center of the square, and suspend it by taking all four corners of silk in one hand; then spin the lump to twist the silk until it tightens around the ball of gelled starch. Hold the spiral of silk and gently squeeze the ball until the starch is forced through the weave of the silk.

Another method, used by Chinese scroll mounters, is to mash the starch with the heel of the hand on the corner of a table and then work some water into it with a stiff brush made of coir, or coconut palm fibers.

The gelled starch can also be strained by forcing it through a #100 mesh stainless steel sieve procured from a ceramic glaze supplier. Use a plastic squeegee to press the mixture through the wire mesh. A wooden sieve with horsehair mesh is used in Japan.

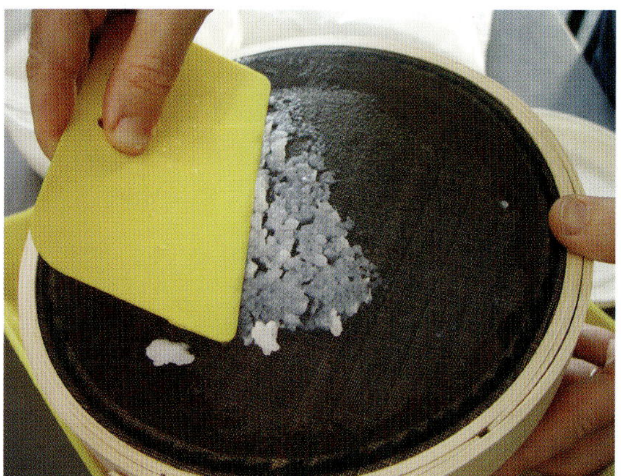

IN JAPAN THE STARCH IS STRAINED THROUGH A HORSEHAIR SIEVE.

A method that makes very fine particles, perhaps too fine for use on silk or very porous paper, is to put the mixture in a blender and run it on the lowest setting for a few seconds. If your gelled starch is too thick to strain, this might be the best approach.

*TIP Clean all the cooked starch from pans, sieves, and other equipment before it dries. Once dry, it will dissolve only in very hot water and can be difficult to remove.*

10. **THIN THE PREPARED PASTE**

Place the paste in a photo tray or flat pan. Add cold water, a little at a time, while gently working the mixture with a brush until it takes on the consistency of heavy cream. The paste you use for chine collé should be a slurry of tiny, rough particles of gelled starch suspended in water. Throughout your workday, be sure to keep the tray covered with a sheet of plastic or damp paper when you are not using the paste.

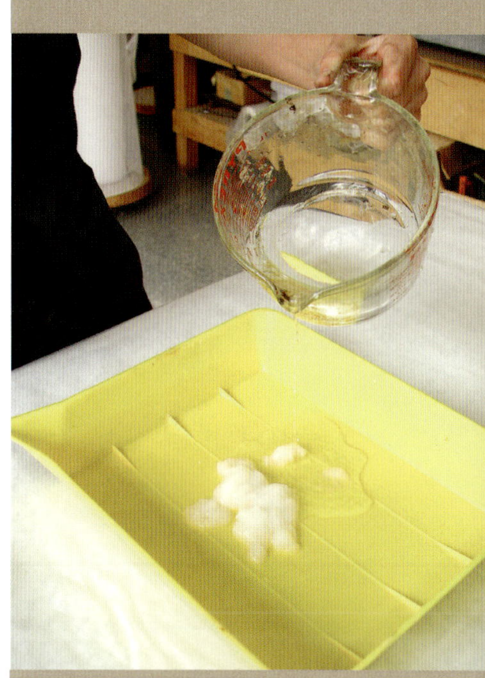
ADD WATER A LITTLE AT A TIME.

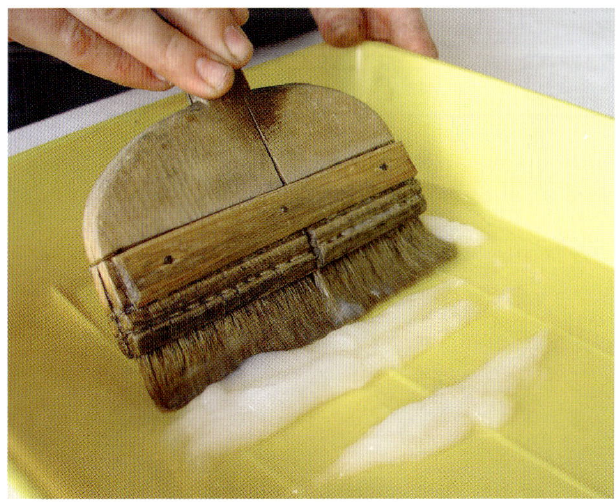
WORK THE MIXTURE WITH A BRUSH.

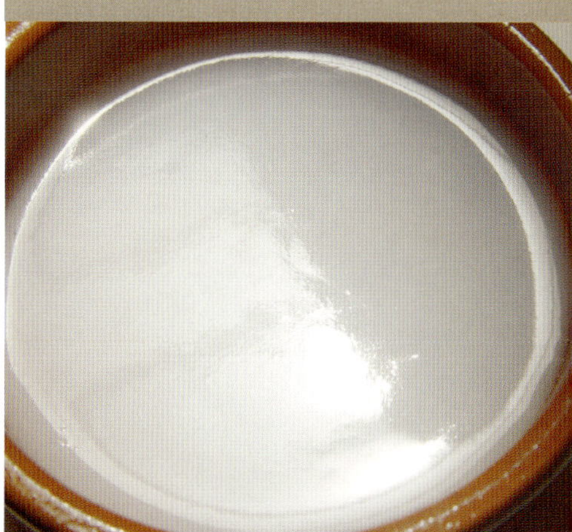
THE FINAL CONSISTENCY SHOULD BE A SLURRY OF TINY, ROUGH PARTICLES.

# Secret #2. SETTING UP

*The devil is in the details.*

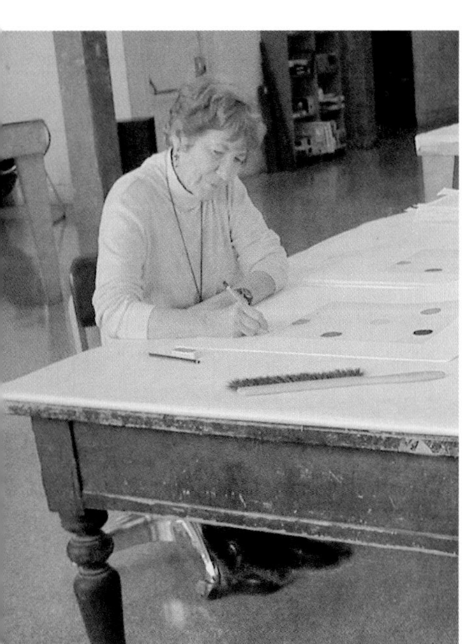

It's easy to overlook details in favor of the big picture, but the devil always lurks in the details, waiting to cause trouble if you don't realize that setting up properly is critical to a successful printing session. If you have to interrupt your proofing to rearrange your work area, find materials, or reset the press, you may never reach critical momentum so that the work flows smoothly. When you can get into a steady rhythm of inking and printing with the moisture level attended to and the pressure correctly set, you will experience the beauty of printmaking. All print processes *do* work beautifully once you set up the proper situation and then monitor it as you proceed. If you fail to notice one area that is not functioning—just a bit too much moisture, for instance—you may get a couple of good prints, but then everything slides out of balance. You begin to experience multiple problems such as wrinkling, lack of adhesion, and poor image quality. Usually there is more than one manifestation of an imbalance.

Mary Heilmann has been called "a virtuoso of nonchalance," so she may seem an odd choice to illustrate a chapter on the importance of details. I have chosen her because she skillfully achieves perfect balance in every work even though the work appears casually put together. As David Pagel wrote in a catalog essay for a 2005 exhibition, "Heilmann makes the complexity and difficulty of abstract painting look carefree and easy, part of the pageantry of everyday life that would simply slip by if not attended to with the devotion and focus made possible by passion."

Mary Heilmann's *Clear Day* (pl. 10) seems deceptively simple at first. It is a sugar lift aquatint with tonal variations created with spit bite aquatint, and it is printed in metallic silver ink chine collé on gampi paper that is tinted pale blue.

Because in an aquatint the ink is held below the surface of the plate in networks of little pits, the metallic ink cannot form an unbroken film on the paper's surface that will reflect light evenly. Instead, you see a kind of shimmer that appears now gray, now silver. The tonal variations within the marks are brought out by being printed on smooth tinted gampi paper, and the delicacy of the relationship between the changing grays and silvers of the image and the faint blue tone of the paper is complemented by the natural sheen of the gampi. The sheen and shimmer in the print contrast with the sturdy texture of the Somerset paper used as the support sheet.

Whether your matrix is an etching plate, woodblock, litho stone, or silkscreen, your paper is one of the key elements in your print. It must be properly prepared to most effectively receive the image. In chine collé, we have two types of paper: the impression paper and the support paper. I begin the step-by-step section of this chapter with instructions for making a damp pack for the support paper. The damp pack comes first because it must be made the day before you print. I believe that using a damp pack is essential for consistent success with chine collé in etching or any other form of intaglio printing, and it is important for working with chine collé in all the other print processes as well.

Another key element is your equipment: your printing press, baren, squeegee, or even your spoon—the vehicle you will use to transfer your image from the matrix to paper. In printmaking, these vehicles are simple, but the simplicity of a machine does not relieve you of the necessity to keep it properly maintained—in fact just the opposite is true. If you have ever taken apart a baren—the tool for printing a traditional Japanese watercolor woodblock—you will have noticed the care with which lacquered paper, braided string, and a bamboo leaf are fashioned into a tool that can be used with great precision as long as it is maintained properly. Proper maintenance includes frequent

application of camellia oil on the bamboo leaf to minimize
friction and wear, and replacement of this leaf from time to
time when it splits.

Steel etching and lithography presses, as low-tech in their
way as the baren is in its way, are capable of pressure far in
excess of what is required to produce an optimal impression.
If you apply excessive pressure, the top steel roller will flex and
temporarily distort. As a result, the pressure on the sides of
your plate will be excessive, and the pressure at the center will
decrease. You can noticeably degrade a copper etching plate
with one run through the press under excessive pressure, and
you can easily crack a litho stone by leaving a single dried bead
of gum on the bed beneath it. These simple machines require
continual attention to proper maintenance and careful use.
In the step-by-step section, I talk about setting up a press for
intaglio printing, including short discussions of blankets,
testing the pressure, and registration.

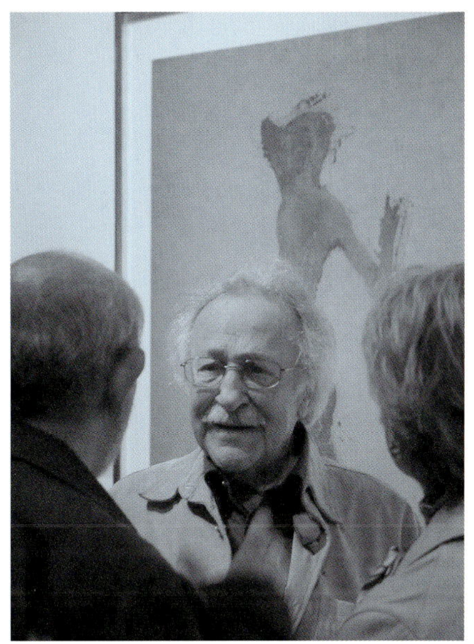

In the third and last step-by-step section, I deal with
assembling materials. I hope you will cultivate an appreciation
and enjoyment of the simple materials used in printmaking. In
intaglio printing, for example, no tool is more basic than the
tarlatan, and none so likely to cause you trouble if you ignore
the simple rules for using it. When a tarlatan pad is prepared,
folding it in layers and keeping it properly clean, it is capable
of extraordinary delicacy and precision.

In closing the introductory portion of this chapter, I'd
like to call your attention to *Copper Plate Nudes II (7)* by Nathan
Oliveira (pl. 11). It is a simple, single-plate image of moderate
size, printed in black ink on gampi paper chine collé. The
fidelity of the impression on the sensitive gampi allows the
tone in the figure, drawn with a sugar lift solution and then
enhanced with spit bite, to register an airy transparency. By
contrast, the background—the back of a discarded plate—is
full of strong, energetic scratches. The interaction between
these marks and tones, which paradoxically seems a reversal of

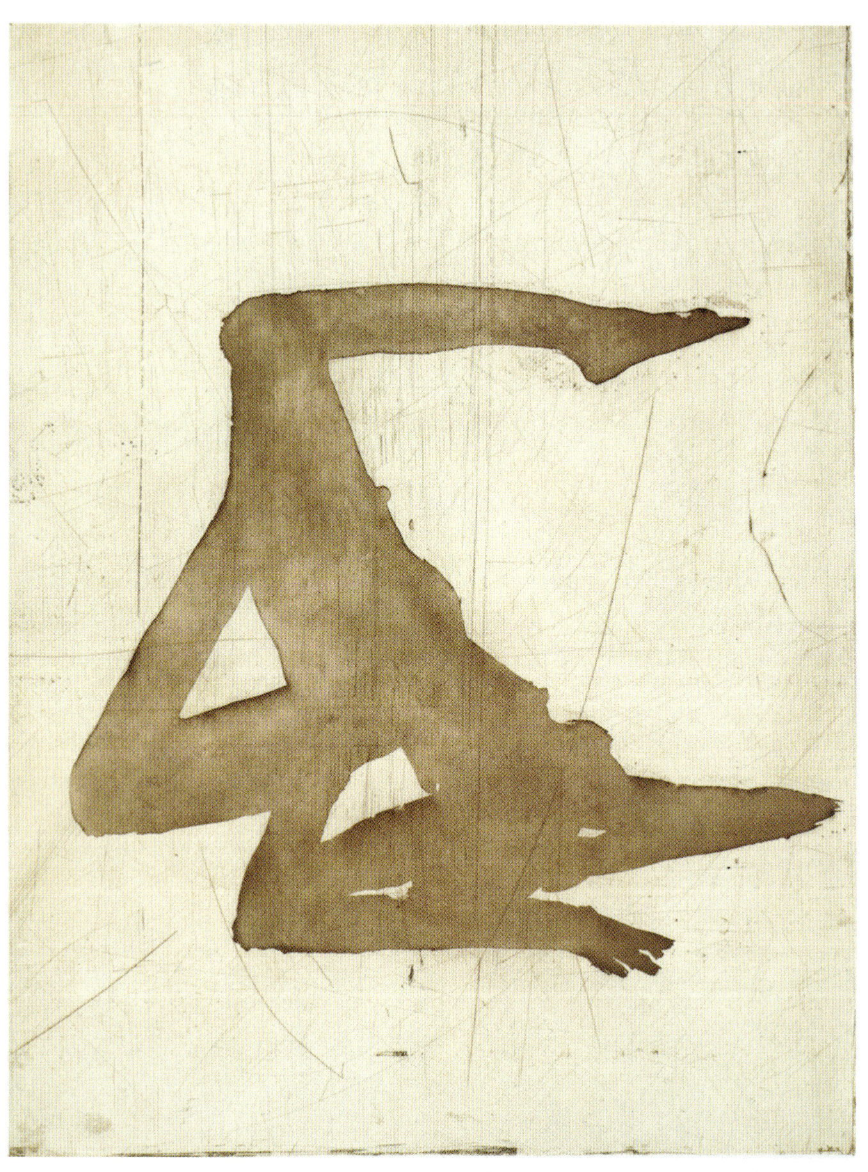

PLATE 11
Nathan Oliveira, *Copper Plate Nudes II (7)*, 2001.
Color sugar lift and spit bite aquatints with texture
from the back of a discarded plate printed on gampi
paper chine collé, 17 ¾ × 13 ¾ inches.

NATHAN OLIVEIRA  *The artists I most admire have had a relationship as painters to graphics, so I've always felt it essential to be a part of that. I made my first print in 1947.*

the standard figure-ground relationship, creates a wonderful openness. Every mark is distinct and crisp, and the tones are extraordinarily delicate. The light, transparent ink floats on the gampi in equilibrium with the way the gampi floats on the Somerset support paper.

We are given this image just as Oliveira put it on the plate because the printer, Dena Schuckit, was careful to use freshly washed blankets, a clean tarlatan pad that didn't mar the aquatint with flecks of dried ink, proper pressure, and an optimal moisture level. She transferred every nuance of the image onto the paper.

Thus, careful attention to setup helps you achieve beautiful prints. It also saves valuable time and materials and lets you focus attention on the work itself rather than being constantly distracted by technical problems. It is much easier to avoid problems with a good setup than to try to remedy them once they have begun to interrupt the flow of printing.

# Setting Up

This section contains three parts: setting up your support paper in a damp pack, setting up an intaglio press, and assembling the materials for working with chine collé. If you are working with lithography, you will find notes for press setup on page 91. Damp pack assembly and the materials you will use are the same as for intaglio. You can find sources for blankets, brushes, plant misters, and other supplies at www.magical-secrets.com.

# Making and Using a Damp Pack Step-by-Step

Paper is made of cellulose fibers; humidifying them makes them flexible. The support paper must be damp all the way through, but it must not be wet. Realize that the paste is moist, and you will be adding moisture to the impression paper. Controlling moisture is one of the keys to success in chine collé printing.

Prepare a damp pack for your support paper the day before you intend to print. In printing chine collé, the support paper is the sturdy sheet on which the thin impression paper (or fabric) is mounted. When you are ready to print, the support paper should already be evenly moist. If you print without a damp pack, you generally need prolonged soaking of the support paper, which causes it to absorb too much moisture. Even if you blot the surface just before printing, the fibers will probably still be too wet. A damp pack stabilizes moisture content, a crucial variable in the process. This is essential for reliable results in printing chine collé in intaglio and is desirable for lithography and other processes.

1. **FILL A LARGE TRAY, SINK, OR BATHTUB WITH WATER**
   Use cold water. Hot water can dissolve the sizing and weaken the paper. It is ideal, but not necessary, to have a water bath large enough to fully submerge a number of sheets at the same time.

FILL THE WATER BATH.

LAY OUT PLASTIC SHEETING NEAR THE WATER BATH.

 *If your paper is unsized, or waterleaf, do not use a water bath. Unsized paper, like blotter paper, immediately absorbs too much moisture and goes to pieces in water. Instead of soaking it, lightly brush or spray individual sheets with water and stack them on plastic sheeting, alternating wet sheets with dry if the paper becomes very wet.*

2. **SPREAD PLASTIC SHEETING NEXT TO THE WATER BATH**
   Greenhouse plastic is the best. The sheeting must be large enough to fold over your paper sheets while they are lying flat.

3. **DIP THE PAPER SHEETS**
   The easiest way to prepare a quantity of paper is to work with about ten sheets at a time. Place the paper in the water either by adding sheets one by one to the bath or by immersing several at once and then separating them as they float. Be sure all the sheets are wet on both sides, but do not soak them.

4. **REMOVE THE SHEETS FROM THE BATH**
   Without allowing the sheets to soak, align their edges. Firmly grab two corners of the entire stack and lift the stack in a block. Hold it above the tray until the water stops running and begins to drip. Then place the entire stack on the plastic sheeting.

   *TIP If you do not have a water bath, you can spray, sponge, or brush water on the individual sheets and stack them on the plastic. If your water bath is much smaller than your sheets, dip each sheet and remove it individually. Let the excess water run off and stack the sheet on top of the previous sheet.*

5. **REPEAT THE PROCESS IF NECESSARY**
   If you will need more than ten sheets for the next day's printing, cover the first ten sheets with a blotter or a dry sheet of paper and add another set of ten. Keep adding sets of ten to the stack until you have enough paper.



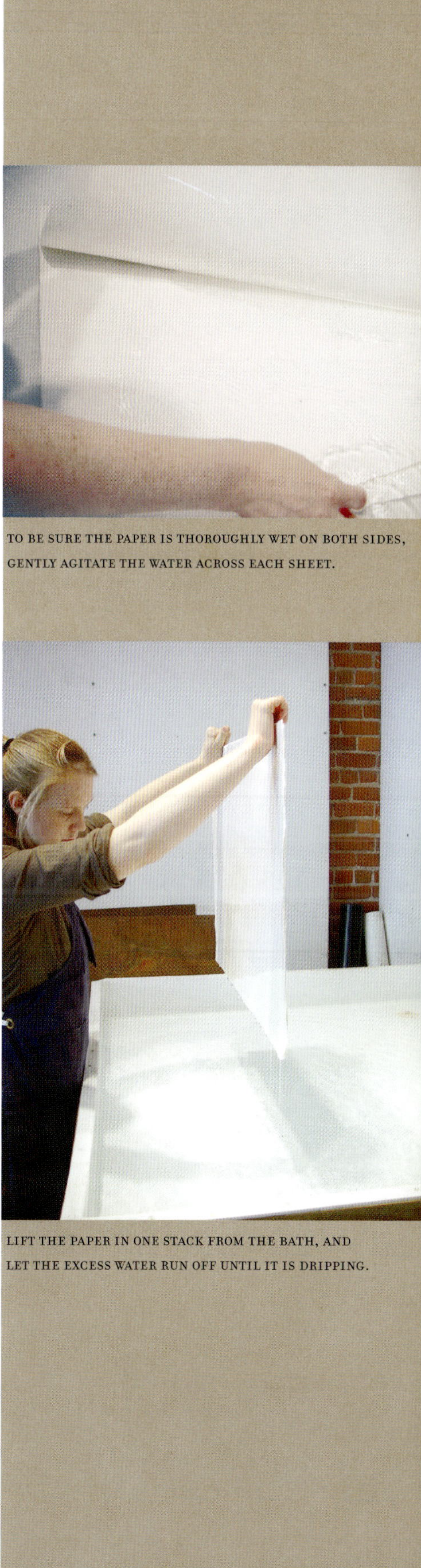

TO BE SURE THE PAPER IS THOROUGHLY WET ON BOTH SIDES, GENTLY AGITATE THE WATER ACROSS EACH SHEET.

LIFT THE PAPER IN ONE STACK FROM THE BATH, AND LET THE EXCESS WATER RUN OFF UNTIL IT IS DRIPPING.

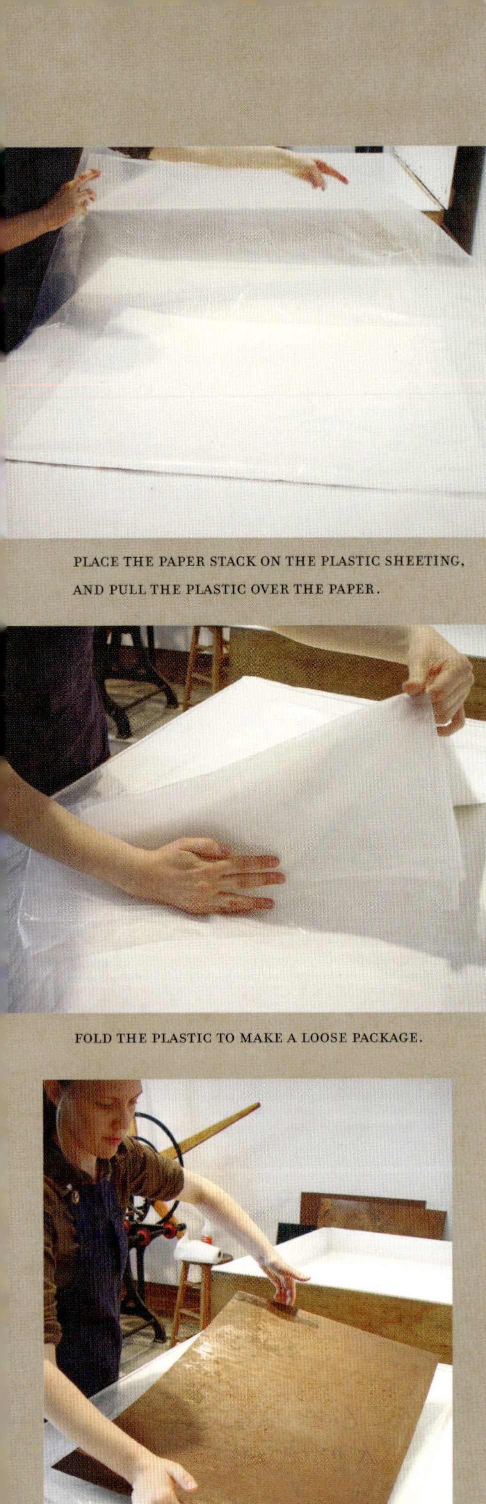

PLACE THE PAPER STACK ON THE PLASTIC SHEETING,
AND PULL THE PLASTIC OVER THE PAPER.

FOLD THE PLASTIC TO MAKE A LOOSE PACKAGE.

LAY A WEIGHT ON THE PACKAGE AND
LEAVE IT OVERNIGHT.



6. **FOLD THE PLASTIC SHEETING AND ADD WEIGHTS**

   Pull the sheeting over the stack of paper sheets and tuck the loose edges underneath to make a closed package. Weight the package with an intaglio plate, a sheet of glass, or other weights, and leave it overnight. The water will equalize through the stack; any excess will accumulate at the bottom.

   TIP *Once the water has permeated the paper, you can roll the damp pack and carry it to a studio if you like. Lay it flat on a table near where you will be working.*

7. **BEFORE PRINTING, TURN OVER THE DAMP PACK**

   Carefully turn the entire pack. Open the pack and use paper towels to blot the top sheet, which accumulated excess moisture when it was at the bottom of the pack. Before using each sheet of paper from the damp pack, check to be sure it is cool, flat, and flexible, without the shine that indicates surface moisture. If there is surface moisture, you must blot the sheet before you use it.

   TIP *Crown Point printers keep a roll of paper towels next to the damp pack. They use the whole roll for blotting, and pull off the outside sheets of paper as they get damp.*

8. **KEEP THE DAMP PACK CLOSED DURING THE PRINTING DAY**

   You can leave the weights off, but get in the habit of closing the pack each time you use it.

9. **USE THE DAMP SHEETS OR DRY THEM BEFORE THEY GROW MOLD**
Depending on your climate and whether the plastic you
used was scrupulously clean, you may be able to keep
the damp pack three or maybe even four days. After the
first day, smell the pack before starting work and discard
the paper if it has the slightest hint of a musty or moldy
odor. The safest approach is to dry the paper after each
day or two of printing and use fresh sheets in a new pack
if your printing continues into the next day. Spread the
unused sheets out on any flat surface to dry. They will not
dry completely flat, but at some future time when you
redampen them, the ripples will come out.

TIP *Avoid fungicides. Years ago the printers at Crown Point used
a drop of formaldehyde in the water to guard against mold, but
we stopped using it when we learned formaldehyde is extremely
toxic and in time may cause discoloration of the paper. Even
when we used formaldehyde, fungus still grew in the damp pack
after a few days, and it became stronger and less susceptible to
the formaldehyde over time.*

## Preparing the Press Step-by-Step

This section deals with setting up a press for intaglio printing.

1. **USE CLEAN WOVEN BLANKETS**
Woven wool blankets are far superior to the pressed felt ones
seen in many schools and workshops. You will need at least
two, one thick and one thin. Although more expensive than
pressed felt, woven wool blankets have a uniform thickness
that allows the ink to transfer with greater sensitivity. They are
also easy to keep clean. Pressed felt does not hold up well in a
washing machine, but woven blankets can be machine washed
in cold water with mild detergent. Air-dry them, or dry them
in a dryer on the delicate setting. Remove the blankets from
the dryer while slightly damp and pull them into shape.

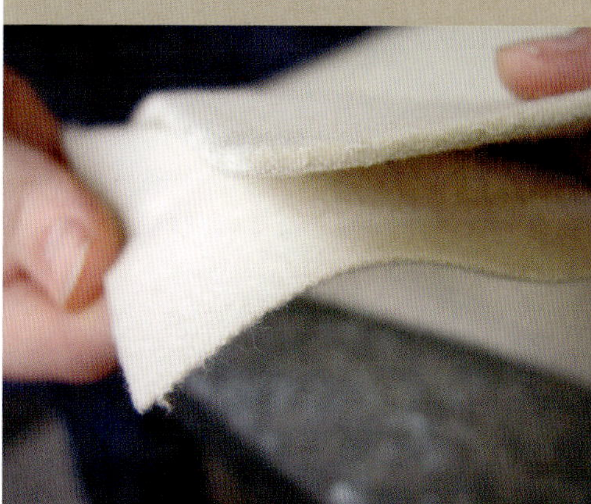

USE TWO WOVEN WOOL BLANKETS; ONE IS THICK, THE
OTHER THIN.

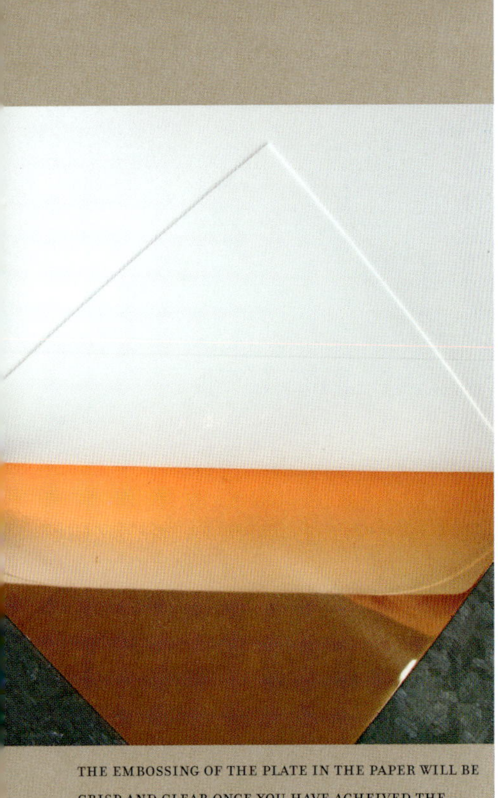



THE EMBOSSING OF THE PLATE IN THE PAPER WILL BE CRISP AND CLEAR ONCE YOU HAVE ACHEIVED THE CORRECT PRESSURE.

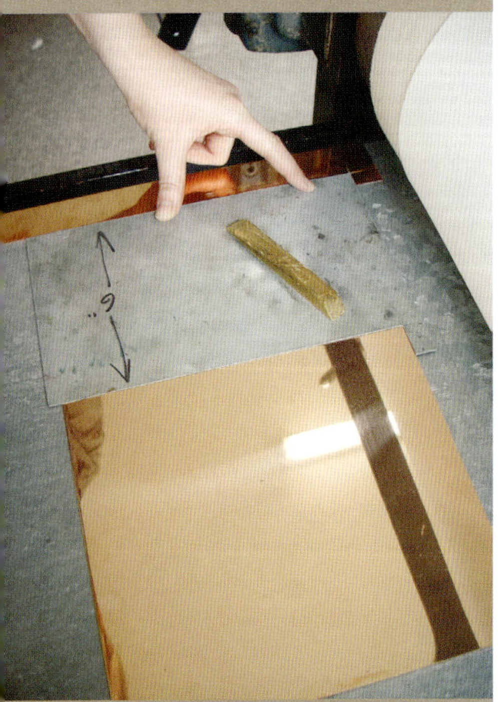

THE CROWN POINT REGISTRATION SYSTEM. A PLATE IS SET INTO A REMOVABLE NOTCHED JIG WITH A HANDLE. THE JIG RESTS IN THE NOTCHED REGISTRATION BAR.

2.  **SET THE PRESSURE AND TEST IT**

Dampen some scraps of your support paper and run one scrap through the press on your clean uninked plate, at first with light pressure. Repeat this, using new scraps and adding pressure until the embossing is crisp and clear. If you see shine in the plate area, you have gone too far. If you use excessive pressure, the plate area tends to stretch, and you are liable to see buckling and an unnatural glaze in the plate area of the print. After testing and achieving the right pressure for the support paper, you may need to lessen the pressure slightly if your impression paper is heavy.

TIP *New or freshly washed blankets compress as they are used. You may need to adjust the pressure occasionally as you proceed with printing.*

3.  **SET UP THE REGISTRATION**

Even a single-plate print should be registered so the plate will be positioned properly within the margins of the support paper. You can use whatever registration system you normally use, but I recommend the Crown Point system, which employs a strip of metal, or registration bar, attached to the press bed and a removable notched metal jig into which you place the plate. This gives almost foolproof registration. See www.magical-secrets.com for more details.

# Assembling the Materials Step-by-Step

Cook the wheat starch for making paste at least one day before
you need to use it (see pages 33–37). Also, prepare a damp pack
containing your support paper one day in advance (see pages 44–47).

1.  **WHEAT STARCH PASTE**

    Have ready just enough paste for the day's work. It is thinned to
    the consistency of heavy cream and is contained in a phototray
    or flat pan. Keep the tray covered when not in use.

2.  **BRUSH**

    Any brush suitable for pasting will do. I often use an Italian
    wallpaper-paste brush with stiff hog bristles. House-painting
    bristle brushes also work well. Japanese brushes are of
    consistently high quality but are expensive. At Crown Point we
    use a Japanese joining brush, the *Tsukemawashibake*. It is about
    6 inches wide and made of goat hair or horsehair (horsehair
    is stiffer). It smoothes out the paste very well and will last a
    long time with care. The traditional Japanese paste brush, the
    *Noribake*, has almost three times as much hair as the joining
    brush. It tends to hold too much paste but works beautifully if
    you don't load it up. The equivalent size Chinese paste brush,
    which is very inexpensive, is the familiar flat brush with a
    composite handle made of many joined small bamboo tubes.
    It is usually of goat hair. It tends to hold too much paste and
    to lose hair constantly. The hairs don't cause discoloration
    over time, and although they transfer to the paper and remain
    there, the Chinese printers and mounters I met did not find
    them disturbing.

    TIP *Be sure not to let paste dry into the bristles of your brush. If you do
    not clean your brush before it dries, it is very difficult to soften it again
    without damage. While you are working, keep your brush in the paste
    tray covered with plastic. Check it often to be sure it is not getting dry.*

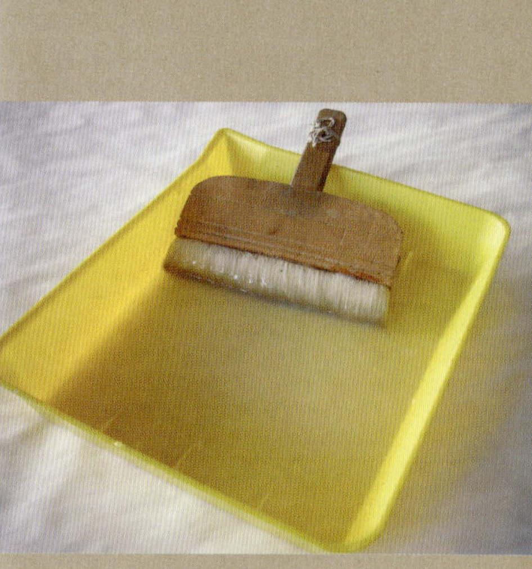

WHEAT STARCH PASTE AND BRUSH.

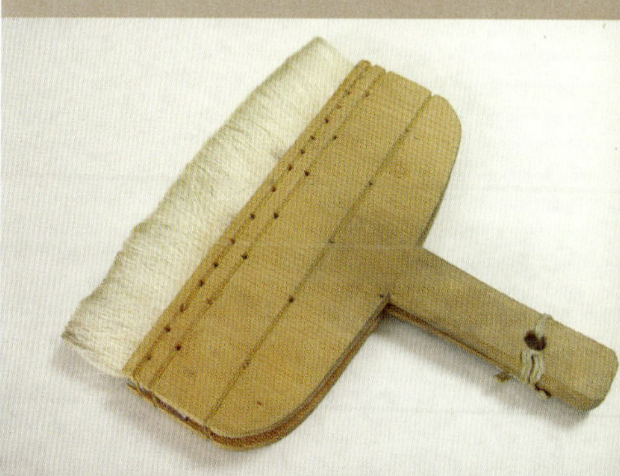

THE TSUKEMAWASHIBAKE.

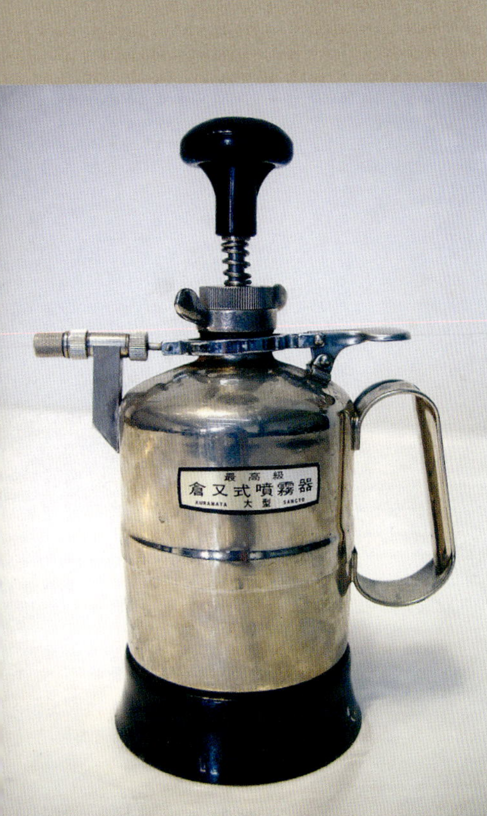


THE PLANT MIST SPRAYER USED AT CROWN POINT PRESS.

3. **PLANT MIST SPRAYER**

A large plastic bottle with a spray nozzle attachment will do. Professional stainless steel plant misters are the best because they provide a very even, fine mist. They are expensive but worth the investment. Fill the sprayer with water, preferably distilled or purified.

4. **BLOTTING TOOL**

Crown Point printers use a roll of paper towels or a clean sponge.

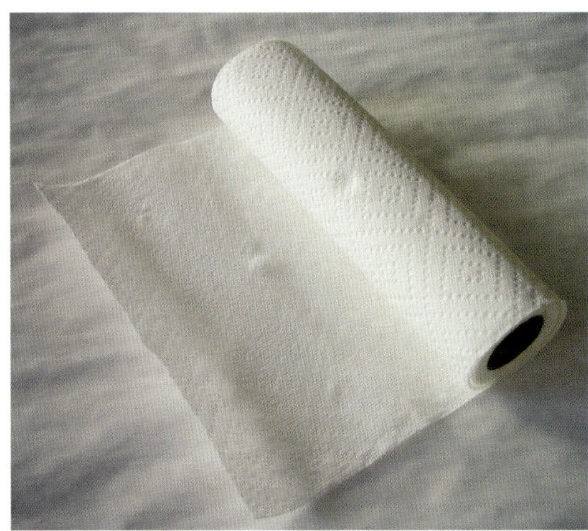

PAPER TOWELS.

5. **DRYING TOOL**

An electric hair dryer or a handheld fan works well.

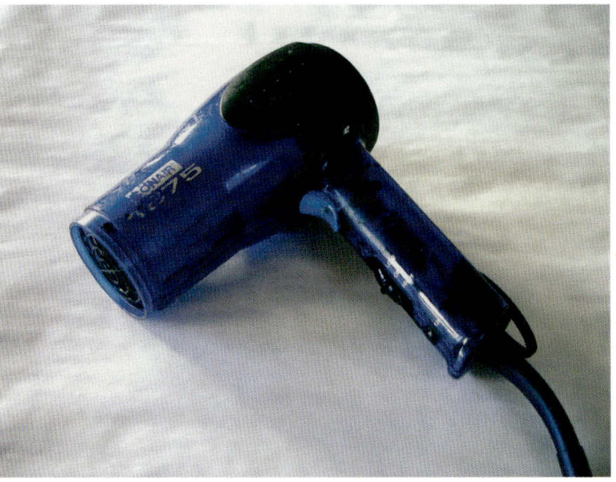

HAIR DRYER.

6.  NEW SINGLE-EDGE RAZOR BLADES

7.  BOX OR PEDESTAL SMALLER THAN YOUR PRINTING PLATE.
    At Crown Point we usually use a container—a can of liquid
    ground or lump asphaltum. If you put your plate on a
    pedestal with the plate edges overhanging, it is easy to work
    around and under the edges of the plate.

8.  IMPRESSION PAPER ON WHICH TO PRINT YOUR IMAGE
    Japanese gampi has a beautiful surface and takes a fine
    impression, but almost any thin paper will do. Your
    impression paper must be at least ¾ inch (2 centimeters)
    larger than the plate on all sides so that you can trim it
    exactly to fit the plate area. You will be dampening it just
    before printing.

9.  SUPPORT PAPER IN A DAMP PACK
    See pages 44–47 for instructions on making a damp pack.

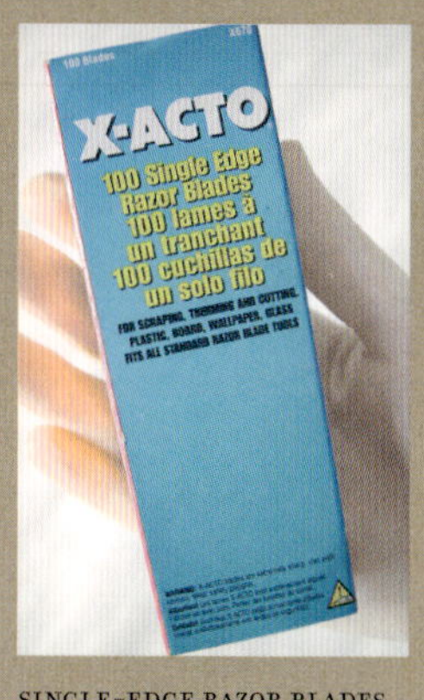

SINGLE-EDGE RAZOR BLADES.

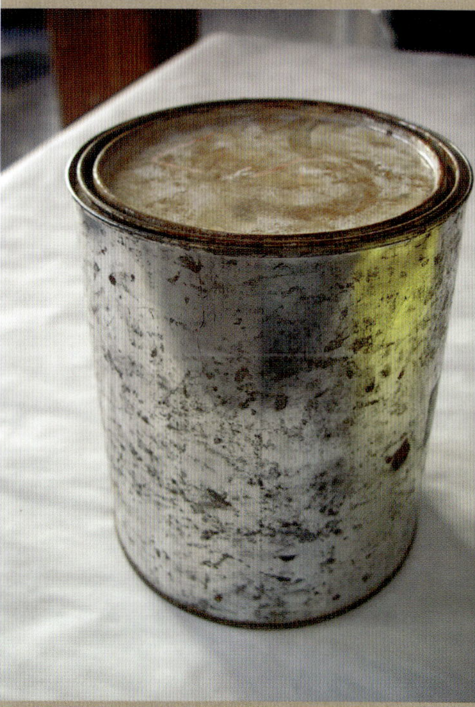

A PEDESTAL.

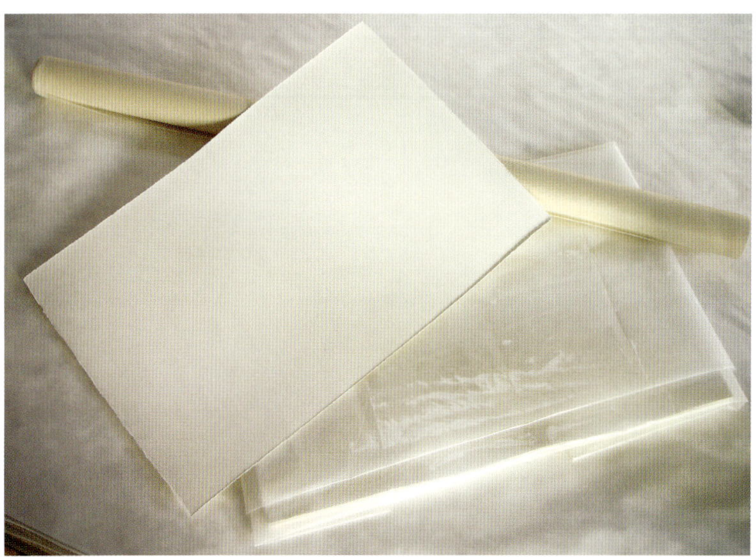

A ROLL OF GAMPI IMPRESSION PAPER, AND FLAT SHEETS OF SUPPORT PAPER IN A DAMP PACK.
A SUPPORT SHEET HAS BEEN REMOVED.

# *Secret #3.* PRINTING WITH CHINE COLLÉ

*Control moisture as you print.*

This chapter is the heart of the book, and the secret is the heart of understanding how to print chine collé successfully. The chapter gives instructions for printing chine collé in intaglio on paper, intaglio on fabric, intaglio with prepasted shaped papers; and lithography. No matter which technique you are using, "control moisture as you print" should run through your mind like a mantra as you work. Chine collé is an exacting process, but once you understand this secret, you will be able to work with it successfully. To lithographers, who do not necessarily print on damp paper, thinking this way may take practice. To printers in the Crown Point Press studio, it is second nature. We always prepare a damp pack in advance of printing—this is fully described in each book in the Magical Secrets series—because we realize that paper must be moistened and softened if it is to receive ink fully and evenly from an intaglio matrix. In printing chine collé, we are adding a second piece of paper, or perhaps fabric, and a layer of paste, so the possibility of problems increases exponentially. In intaglio printing, excess moisture causes a range of problems from mottled uneven impressions to poor adherence. Controlling moisture as you print will allow success, even in a studio situation as fast-paced and experimental as Crown Point's project with four teenage boys brought to our studio by Tim Rollins in 1989.

Rollins, who was trained as an artist, worked as a junior high teacher and in 1982 founded an afterschool group called the Art and Knowledge Workshop. In it, young people, many classified by the schools as "learning disabled," would read and, working with Rollins, record their responses to powerful allegories such as Franz Kafka's *Amerika* or Nathaniel Hawthorne's *The Scarlet Letter.* The kids named their group K.O.S., Kids of Survival. In their studio, members of the group would draw directly on book pages that they later mounted in series on canvases to become large paintings. Tim Rollins + K.O.S. paintings are now in the collections of the Museum of Modern Art in New York, the Art Institute of Chicago, and the Tate Gallery, London, among other musuems.

Working in the Crown Point studio with Rollins were Richard Cruz, George Garces, Carlos Rivera, and Nelson Savinon, four of the fifteen or so teenagers who were part of the group at the time. Although they may have been inattentive in school, they were very focused in the studio. Three printers, including myself, assisted them, and over the period of a week we produced the portfolio *The Temptation of Saint Antony* (pls. 12, 13, and 14), fourteen etchings based on Gustave Flaubert's 1874 prose-poem of the same title. Rollins and the kids made about 250 plates, drawing images using medical instruments and other

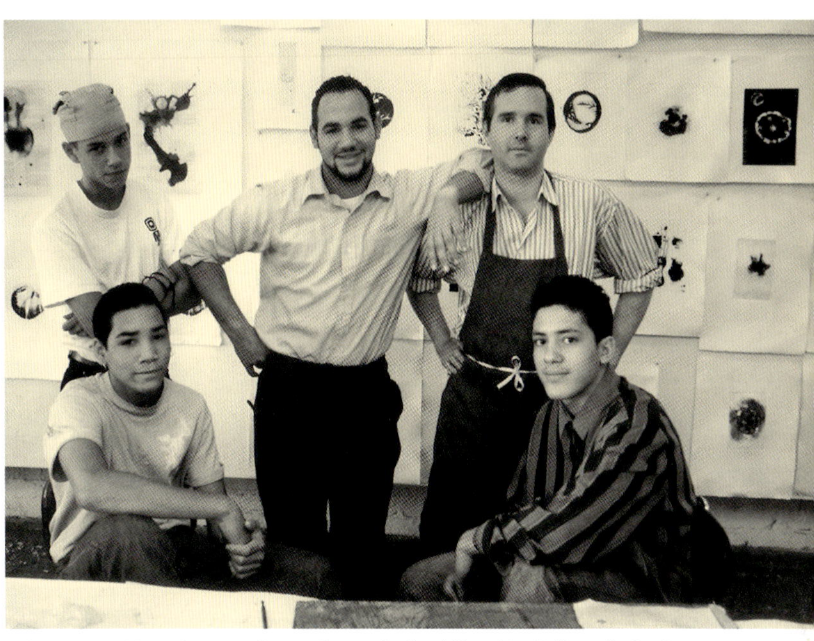

Left to right: Nelson Savinon, George Garces, Richard Cruz, Tim Rollins, Carlos Rivera

unconventional tools as well as traditional spit bite aquatint
and washes of plasticized carbon toner from a photocopier
ink cartridge. Then, in an intense daylong group critique, they
edited the 250 plates to 14.

The images are monsters and visions, developed as
metaphors for the evils that plague the childhoods and family
lives of many who grow up in the disadvantaged circumstances
typified by the South Bronx. The group was inspired in
their response to the text by several visits to the Prints and
Photographs Study Room of the New York Public Library in
preparation for the project at Crown Point. In using the collé
process, they pay homage to a portfolio of prints by Odilon
Redon based on the Flaubert text. Redon's portfolio was
published by Ambroise Vollard in Paris in a deluxe chine collé
edition in 1896.

Chine collé was especially appropriate for this project
because of the group's working method of drawing on
pages of the texts they were studying. Rollins wanted text to
appear behind all the *Temptation* images. The publisher of

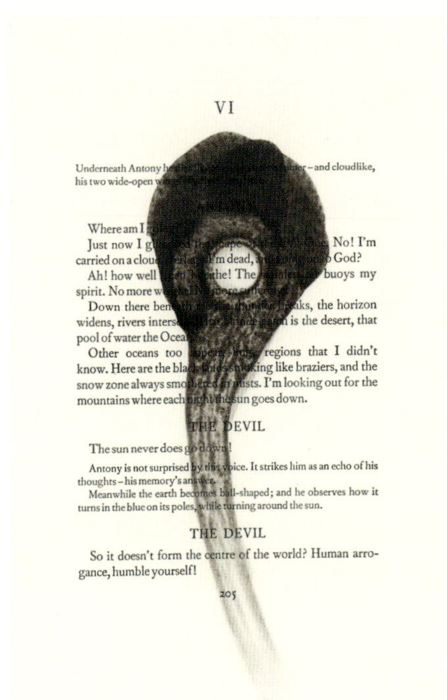

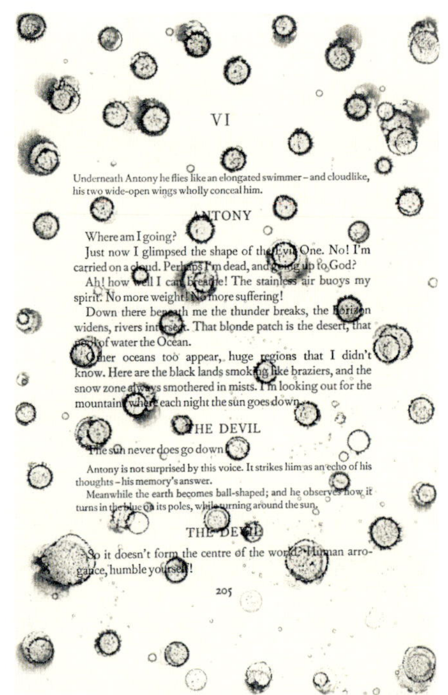

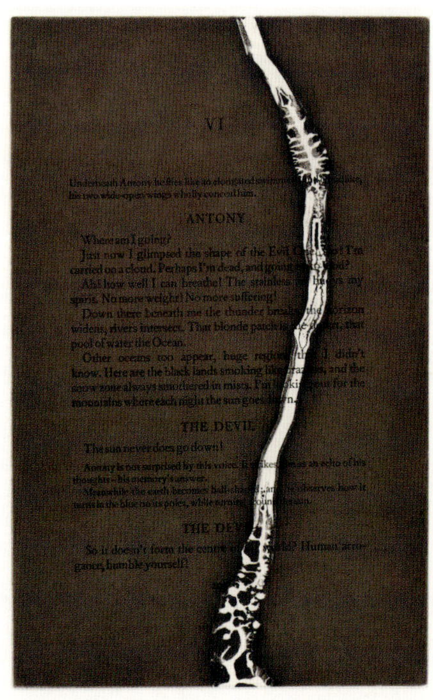

**PLATE 12 (TOP LEFT)**

Tim Rollins + K.O.S., *The Temptation of St. Antony I*, 1989.
Spit bite aquatint with xerographic text printed on Rives
Lightweight White chine collé, 8¼ × 5¼ inches.

**PLATE 13 (TOP RIGHT)**

Tim Rollins + K.O.S., *The Temptation of St. Antony XI*,
1989. Aquatint with xerographic text printed on Rives
Lightweight White chine collé, 8¼ × 5¼ inches.

**PLATE 14 (RIGHT)**

Tim Rollins + K.O.S., *The Temptation of St. Antony VII*,
1989. Aquatint with xerographic text printed on Rives
Lightweight White chine collé, 8¼ × 5¼ inches.

the translation of Flaubert that the group had studied didn't have enough loose pages available for our project but gave us permission to use photocopies. This also eliminated the conservation problem we would have faced if we had used the acidic pulp paper on which the book had been printed.

For the impression paper, which had to work perfectly in the photocopier as well as for intaglio printing, we chose a thin Lana book paper. The support paper is Somerset Satin. The printing was straightforward; in most cases the image was created on a single plate. In *The Temptation of St. Antony I* (pl. 12), the cobralike form has a window made by laying a circular glass slide cover on the center of the plate before applying acid for spit bite. The text reads "I'm dead" through the window. Rollins and the kids had already decided that a single text page would be used for all the images, and they liked the chance highlighting of "I'm dead" so much that this text page was chosen.

The bubbles or cells floating across the page in image *XI* (pl. 13) were made using drops of a thin oil, kept handy to lubricate our sharpening stone, combined with drops of a strong nitric acid spit bite solution. Image *VII* (pl. 14) is composed of a transparent background aquatint under a tendon or sinew shape made by floating toner in alcohol. When the alcohol had evaporated, we melted the toner powder onto the plate to form a resist, then aquatinted the plate and etched it in an acid bath.

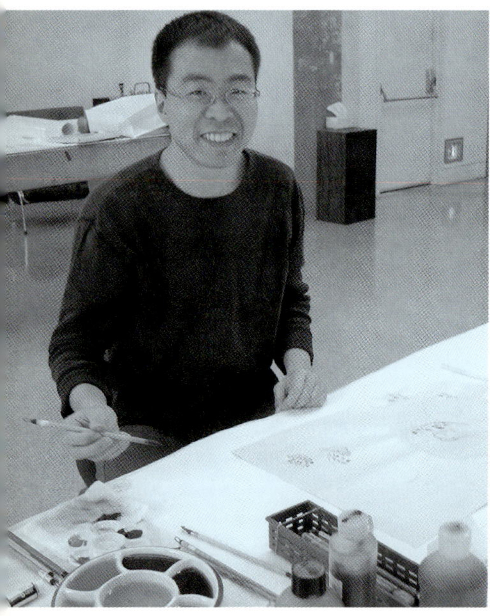



Wilson Shieh's *Three Angels* (pl. 15) is an example of a more traditional use of chine collé. It is printed on gampi, a Japanese sheet so smooth and fine that it registers even the most fragile tone or mark. Moisture control in Shieh's delicate work was paramount. Even the slightest air bubble under the impression paper would be so obvious as to necessitate a print being discarded. This 2005 work was printed from four plates by Catherine Brooks at Crown Point Press. The reflective surface of the gampi complements Shieh's finely drawn brush lines and whisper-light tones.

Shieh was born in 1970 in Hong Kong and continues to live there. He works in *gongbi*, a fine-brush Chinese painting style developed over a thousand years ago that requires a great deal of skill in executing meticulous lines. For this print, Shieh drew the outlines of the image on Mylar using his own brushes and Chinese ink. Brooks transferred the drawing to a copper plate using a variant of the photogravure process called direct gravure. Shieh added the colors on additional plates with aquatint.

Traditional photogravure, in which an image from a camera is transferred to a copper plate and etched and printed in intaglio, is not simply a method of photomechanical reproduction, but a distinct, continuous-tone photographic process with unique visual characteristics achieved with careful control of film density and a multi-bath etch. Many printers feel that printing photogravures on gampi paper or silk enhances the range of tones. Both gampi and silk are so thin that in order to print on them successfully the chine collé process must be used.

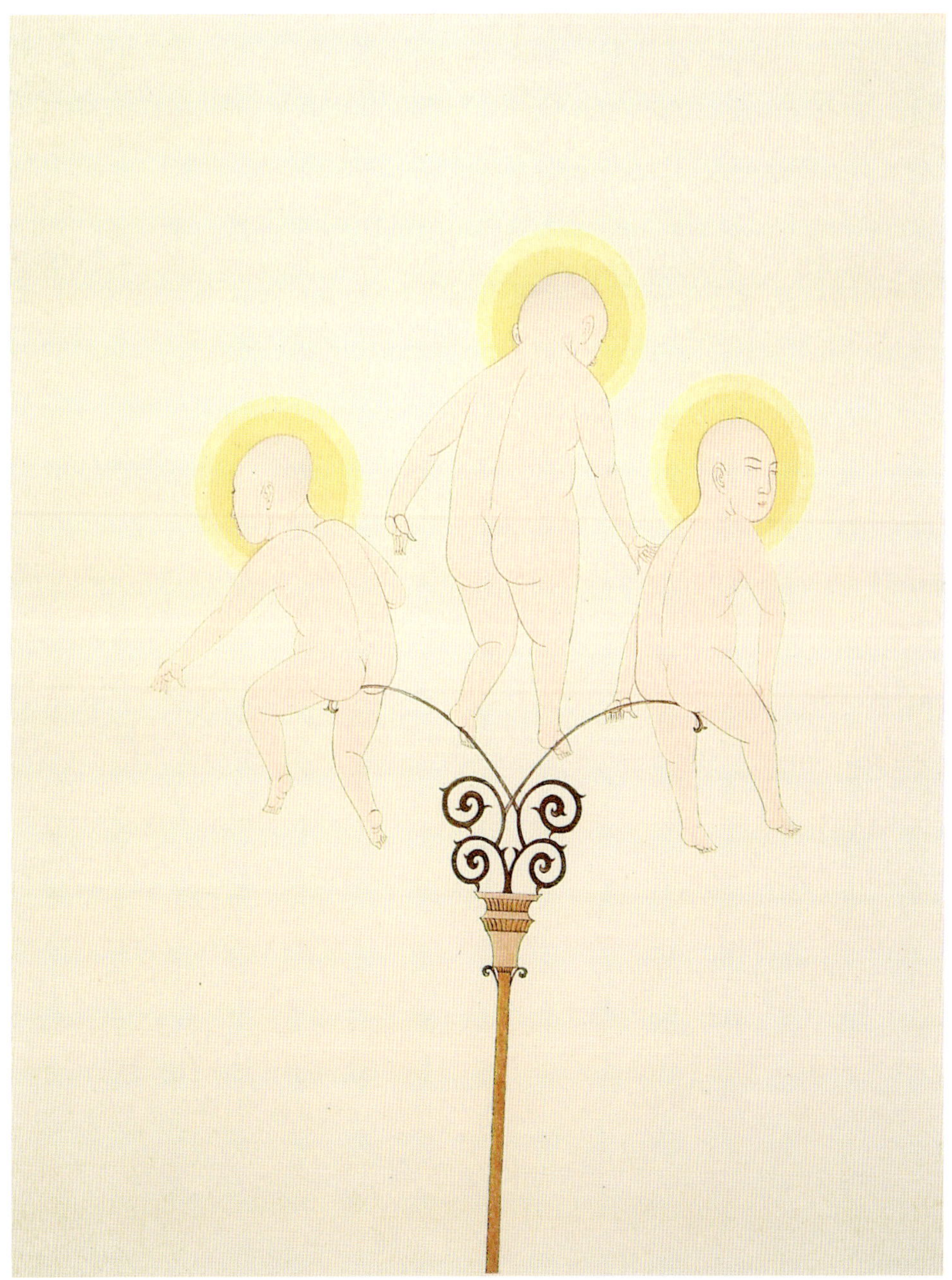

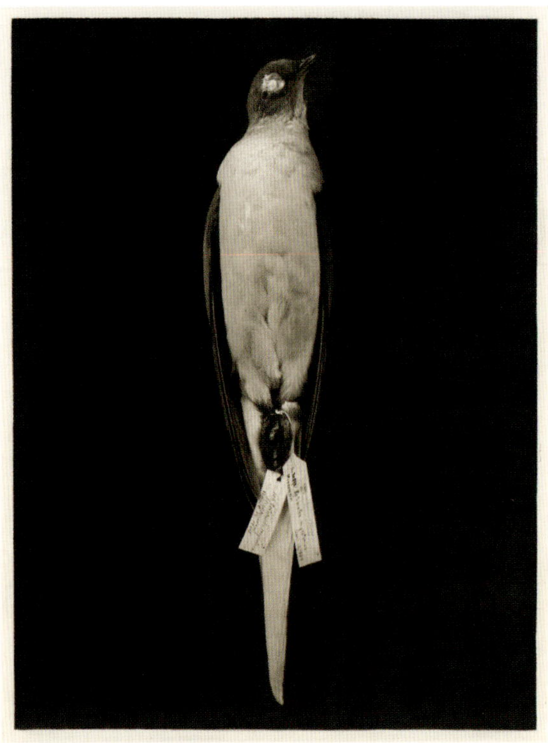



*Passenger Pigeon* (pl. 16) by photographer Susan Middleton was printed at Crown Point Press on gampi chine collé by Asa Muir-Harmony in 2008. The passenger pigeon was once the most common bird in North America but is now extinct. Middleton's photogravure from a digital photograph of a labeled specimen at the California Academy of Sciences demonstrates the tonal capacity of photogravure when it is printed chine collé on gampi. The physicality of the deep black background contrasts with subtle tones in the bird's feathers.

The late photographer Robert Mapplethorpe produced three photogravures of flowers printed chine collé on silk by Deli Sacilotto at Graphicstudio at the University of South Florida in Tampa. *Hyacinth* (pl. 17) is shown here. Quality of light is an important element in Mapplethorpe's work, and the hyacinth in this image is bathed in a soft light that is enhanced by the warm tonality of the silk on which it is printed. Silk

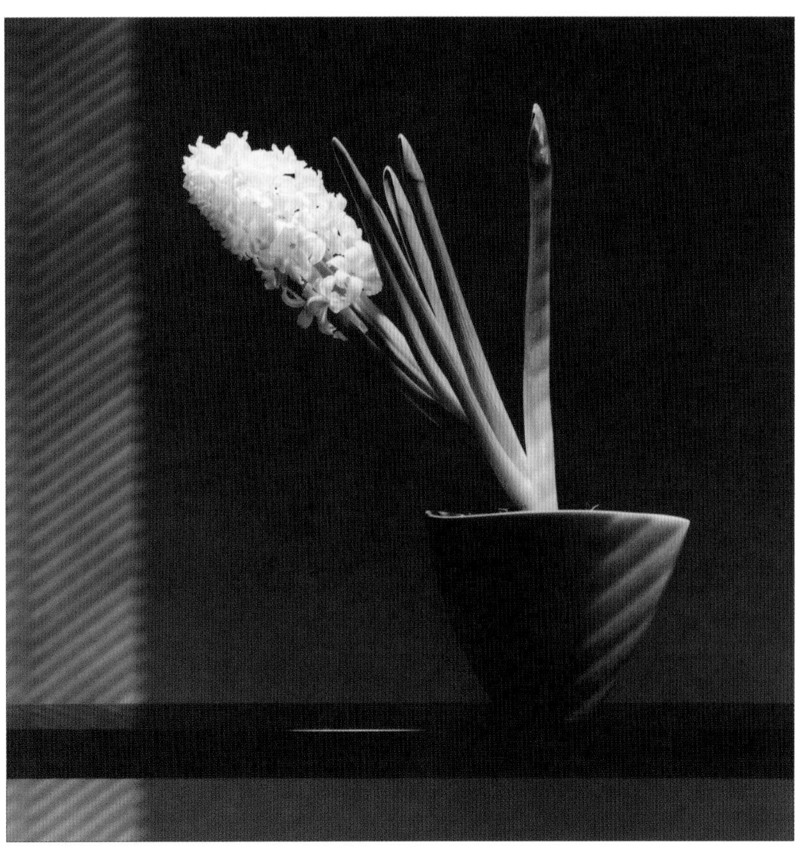

can absorb more ink than most papers, so that in this image
Mapplethorpe was able to fully exploit the extended tonal range
uniquely possible with photogravure.

This print is a technical tour-de-force in its size, its
range of tones, and the application of the silk layer during the
printing process. The silk collé process used is almost identical
to what I describe in the step-by-step section of this chapter. It
involves an extra run through the press during which the fabric
is applied to the paper as a separate step in advance of printing
the image. This technique, developed to combat problems
of stretch, and of paste bleeding through thin fabric, has
prompted me to extend the traditional definition of chine collé
to works in which the collé layer is applied with a press, but the
image is not printed at the same time.

PLATE 17
Robert Mapplethorpe, *Hyacinth*, 1986.
Photogravure printed on silk chine collé,
32¾ × 32½ inches. Published by Graphicstudio,
University of South Florida.

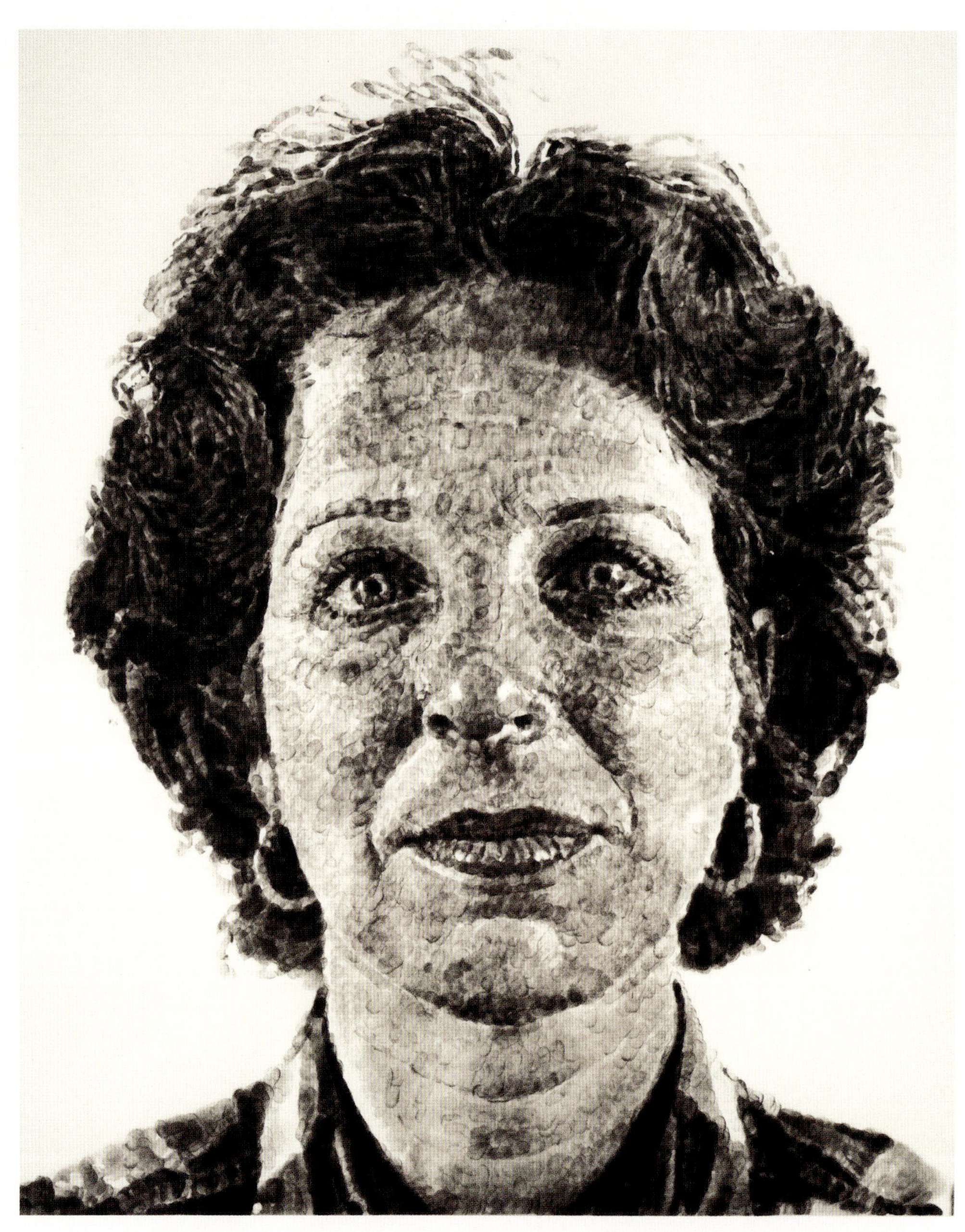

The Graphicstudio technique differs from my step-by-step
section only in the adhesive used. Sacilotto told me that he and
Patrick Foy, the printer who helped devise their method, feared
problems with air bubbles and delamination, so they used a
mix of polyvinyl acetate and wheat starch paste. The synthetic
addition did not cause problems, but I believe wheat starch
paste alone also would have been fine.

A second example of chine collé on silk from Graphicstudio
is Chuck Close's *Leslie/Fingerprint/Silk Collé* (pl.18). Patrick
Foy was the lead printer. Close has created detailed portrait
heads in mezzotint, traditional etching, paper pulp, woodcut,
hologram, daguerreotype, Polaroid photography, and painting
styles that range from airbrush to dabs and dots. He made this
image of his wife in fingerprints, using the process of direct
gravure printed chine collé. Over and over, Close pressed his
thumb into lithographic ink and transferred the ink to Mylar.
He made shadows by pressing more ink onto the sheet, and
lighter areas by pressing lightly, sometimes removing some
of the ink with an eraser. Because of the capacity of gravure
for varying depths in the bite, a proportionately deeper bite
occurred on the plate wherever there was more ink on the
Mylar. The Mapplethorpe and Close works were printed on
Chinese silk presized for painting, a product available at
Chinese art supply stores (see www.magical-secrets.com for
specific information).

*Textbook Comic Devices* (pl. 19) by Brad Brown demonstrates
a different procedure, that of prepasting. Prepasting is a
chine collé technique developed in the nineteenth century for
printing lithographs or engravings on Chinese paper. You must
use prepasting in lithography because the matrix is larger than
the image. You cannot trim and paste the impression paper as
you would if you were working in intaglio. You may want to use
prepasting in intaglio if your work incorporates cutout shapes
or found material; positioning shapes is easier if you are not
applying paste in the same step. You might use prepasting



PLATE 18 (OPPOSITE)
Chuck Close, *Leslie/Fingerprint/Silk Collé*, 1986.
Direct gravure printed on silk chine collé,
54¼ × 40¼ inches. Published by Graphicstudio,
University of South Florida and Pace Editions.

simply for convenience. You can prepaste impression paper, let it dry, and store it until you are ready to print.

In Brad Brown's *Textbook Comic Devices*, shaped pieces of thin cream-colored Japanese hosho paper are integral tonal elements that have equal visual weight to the drawn marks. Brown worked with master printer Case Hudson at Crown Point Press on this image.

*Textbook Comic Devices* marked a turning point in Brown's approach to his work, which is mainly drawing. For years, he had cut up his drawings and used them as collage material to make new drawings, often incorporating fragments from several time periods into a single piece. He thought of his work as a circle, he said, turning back on itself. With this intaglio print he began to think of his work as a line composed of discrete pieces, though the pieces continued to be fragmentary.

Brown developed this image as a whole, on three plates printed one over the other in different colors. After finishing the drawing, he cut up the plates but kept the image intact. The feeling of fragmentation comes from the cuts and from the chine collé shapes. The inspiration for the work was a scene in a Buster Keaton movie in which Keaton's automobile falls apart in slow motion, a wheel falling off here, an engine part there. "I loved the idea of something fragmented that stays visually whole," Brown said.

After an artist develops an image in a professional print shop like Crown Point, finished proofs are made for the printers to use as a model in printing an edition without the artist present. Brown wanted to cut the hosho shapes himself but did not want to be at the press for the entire lengthy printing process. This was easy to accomplish with prepasting.

The printer, Case Hudson, began by applying wheat starch paste to full sheets of hosho paper and leaving them to dry. The artist returned to Crown Point to cut the shapes out of the prepasted paper with scissors, many at a time, using patterns but working loosely. The shapes vary somewhat from print to

PLATE 19 (OPPOSITE)
Brad Brown, *Textbook Comic Devices*, 2001. Color sugar lift and spit bite aquatints with drypoint printed on hosho paper chine collé, $23\frac{1}{2} \times 30\frac{3}{4}$ inches.

BRAD BROWN   *My work deals with fragmentation and unity and repetition and variation, and that's where printmaking really lives.*

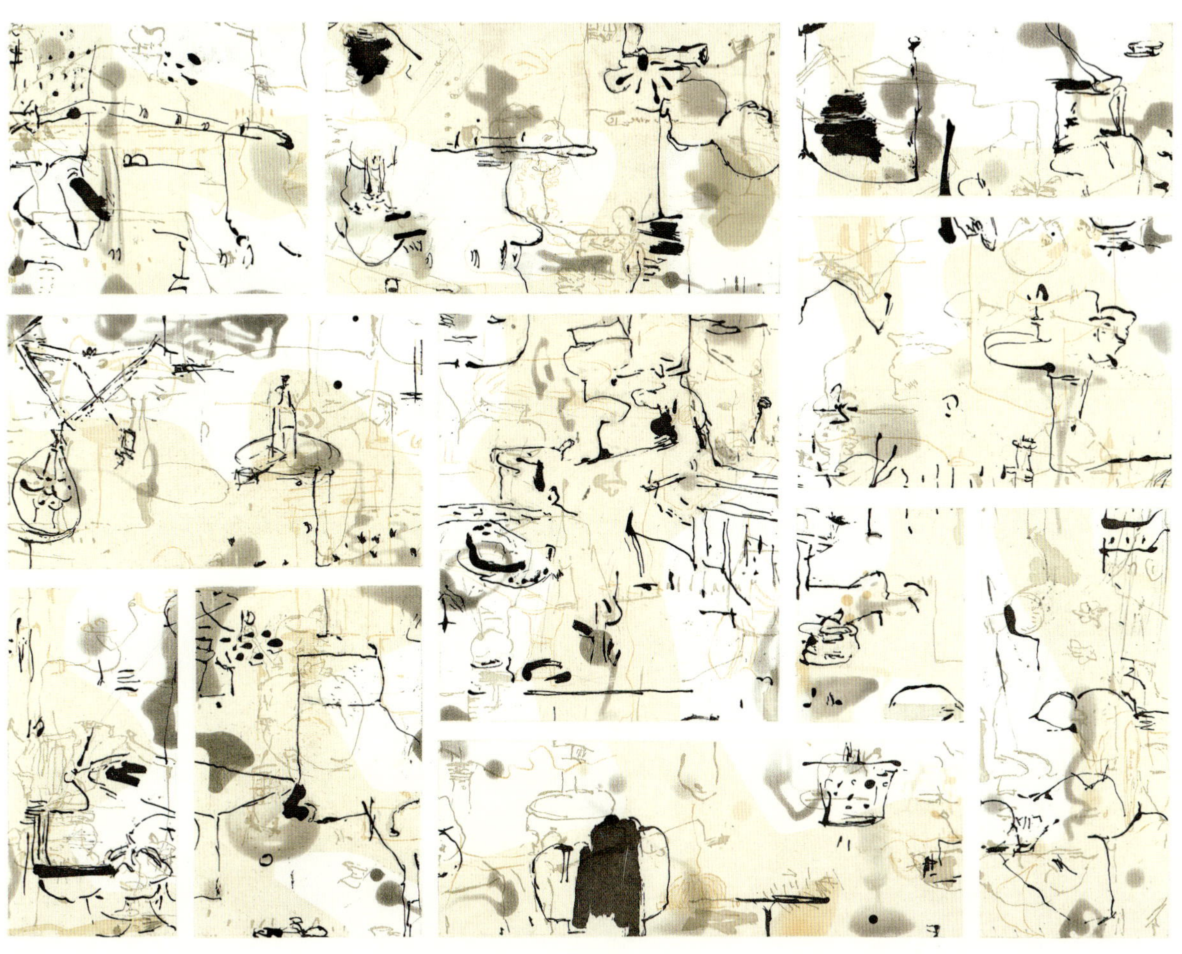

print. Brown cut each shape with a right angle that Hudson could align with a designated plate corner. Before printing, Hudson used a damp pack to reactivate the paste on the cut shapes. For each print in the edition, he inked all the plates and started by arranging on the press bed the plates carrying the darkest color. Then he printed the dark ink and colléd the gampi shapes on one pass through the press. With the hosho paper cutouts pasted in place on the support paper, he continued with two more runs, using different plates to add the gray and yellow marks.

I conclude this chapter with two examples of chine collé in lithography, a lithograph of my own as an example of a traditional chine collé approach, and one by Enrique Chagoya that is much more complex.

My lithograph, *Museum Steps* (pl. 20), is the image I used to demonstrate the chine collé process in lithography step-by-step (pages 88–94). It is printed on tea-toned handmade Indian paper supported by a white sheet of Rives BFK. I made the drawing on transfer paper and then transferred it to a freshly grained stone at the Rhode Island School of Design.

Transfer paper was developed along with the invention of lithography, and its composition and use are related to the chine collé process. Transfer paper is a sheet of tissue-thin cotton vellum mounted on a thicker backing sheet. The adhesive is a gelatin-starch mix. A thicker, shiny layer of the same paste coats the vellum and provides the surface on which you draw. The drawing

is reversed during transfer to the litho plate or stone, so that the printed image reads the same way as the drawing. This is useful for music, text, portraits, landscapes, and cityscapes, which can be problematic to draw in reverse. See www.magical-secrets.com for recommended brands and for instructions for making transfer paper yourself.

*Museum Steps* is a study of about sixty figures in an illusionistic architectural space. My drawing process involves discovering the image slowly by reworking and redissolving tusche, a solvent-based drawing medium for lithography. If I had drawn directly on the stone, where every mark chemically transforms the surface, the result would have been a solid black rectangle. The thick paste layer on the transfer paper prevented the tusche from soaking into the vellum.

After the drawing was done and the solvent had completely evaporated, I placed the sheet in a damp pack for a few minutes to humidify the backing paper. Then I laid the transfer sheet in register face down on the stone with a piece of slightly damp paper on top and ran it through the press.

The pressure forced the tusche into tight contact with the stone and also drove the moisture through the papers and paste, sticking the drawing and the paste film to the stone. I gently peeled the backing sheet away from the vellum, then laid a second damp sheet over it and once again ran it through the press, with lighter pressure, forcing more moisture into the vellum so I could peel it from

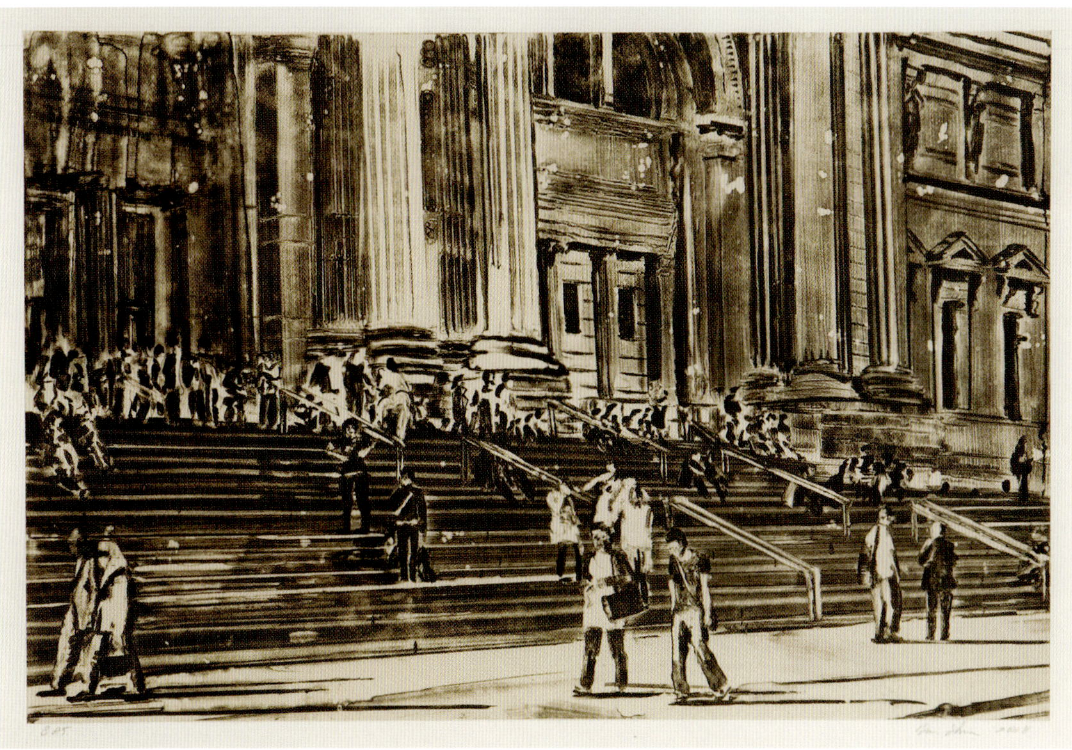

the stone. The image had released from the softened coating
and transferred to the stone, leaving it ready to be processed
and printed.

Enrique Chagoya's *Abenteuer der Kannibalen Bioethicists*
(pl. 21) was printed by Bud Shark at Shark's Ink in Lyons,
Colorado, and published by Shark's Ink. The accordion-fold
codex format Chagoya used was the standard Mesoamerican
format for centuries. The title is in German because the work is
based on a Mayan codex that is in Dresden, Germany.

Of thousands of codices that had recorded more than
eight hundred years of Mayan history, it seems only three and
a half survived systematic destruction by clergy accompanying
the Spanish conquistadors to the Yucatán in the sixteenth
century. All precolonial Aztec codices in Mexico were also
destroyed, but painters continued the tradition under Spanish

rule, and about five hundred colonial-era Aztec codices exist. These describe daily life and, in one copy of a destroyed earlier codex, the history of the Aztec peoples.

Chagoya wrote to me that in reading about the destruction of Mayan and Aztec books, he realized that "history is written by the victors of war, and from that perspective, written history can be more of an ideological construction than a science." He then decided to make books following the pictorial (nonalphabetic, nonphonetic) language of the ancient indigenous books. His codex is a nine-color lithograph and woodcut with chine collé and collage printed from seven plates and a single woodblock. The support paper is a handmade ivory amate paper from Mexico, with three thinner papers from Thailand and Japan chine collé. The work is one long accordian-folded codex, shown here in two sections. In both the form and the choice of paper, Chagoya reaches back into history.

Amate paper was used in Mesoamerica beginning at least as far back as the first millennium BCE. Not a true paper because it is not formed from pulp, it was originally made by using stones to pound the inner bark of various trees into sheets. The term *codex* generally refers to handwritten books from late antiquity up to the introduction of printing at the end of the Middle Ages in Europe.

*Abenteuer der Kannibalen Bioethicists* was printed on a 23-by-30-inch sheet that the printers tore into four strips that they glued together end to end, then scored and folded.

The adhesive is a pressure-sensitive acrylic emulsion made by Rhoplex. The printers cut the thinner papers into specific shapes, then sprayed them with adhesive on the reverse, applied them to the amate sheet, and adhered them in a run through the press.

Wheat starch paste would have worked, and because—like paper—it continually responds to humidity changes, the possibility of the paper's curling over time might have been lessened. However, I understand why Shark used Rhoplex. Damp packs are not frequently employed in professional lithography shops, so an adhesive activated by pressure rather than moisture is convenient for lithographers. Also, working this way permitted the printers to focus on registering the papers properly without having to worry about keeping the lithographic image stable during the time it would take to handle and register papers prepasted with wheat starch paste. Shark's approach, in which adhesion occurs in runs through the press separate from printing, increases the number of runs but simplifies those runs, making the approach an efficient way to print the edition.

Because Shark used a synthetic, pressure-sensitive adhesive, his approach to printing chine collé is the only one in this chapter not dependent on the secret with which I began: control moisture as you print.

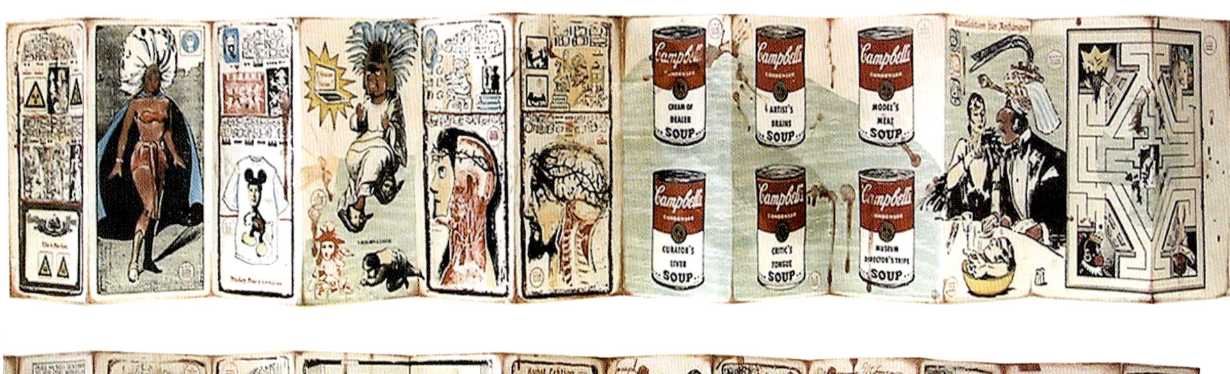

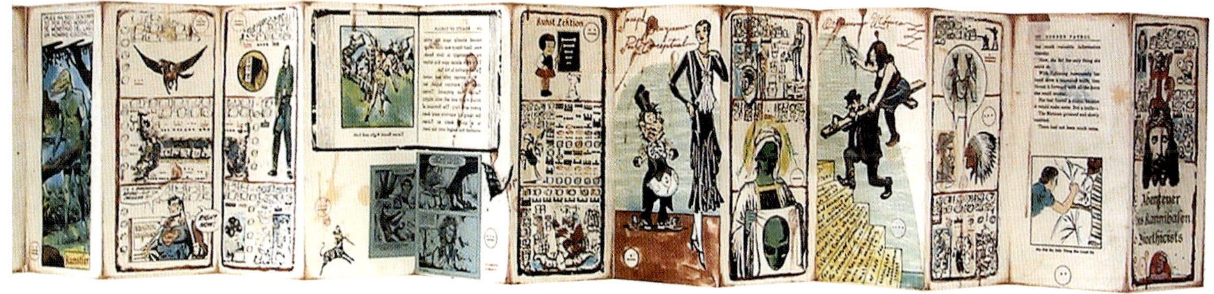

PLATE 21

Enrique Chagoya, *Abenteuer der Kannibalen Bioethicists*, 2001.
Color lithograph with woodcut and collage on natural Thai
mulberry, white Thai mulberry, and Moriki paper chine collé,
19 × 61 inches. Published by Shark's Ink.

# Printing with Chine Collé

This section deals with chine collé using a press. It includes intaglio printing and lithography, and you can also use these techniques for monotype. The fourth common printmaking method, relief printing (woodblock), is not discussed here. For block printing, the impression sheet must be mounted on a backing sheet, before (or after in a separate step) the image is printed (see pages 110–113 on mounting.) A woodblock comes into contact with the paper only in the image area, so even if a press is used, an impression sheet cannot be properly adhered to a support sheet during printing.

I recommend that you read this chapter even if your main interest does not involve using a press. This is the foundation section and will acquaint you with approaches that we will change and adapt as the book continues. The intaglio step-by-step begins with discussions, not repeated elsewhere, of paper grain and the printing side of the impression sheet, and continues with a straightforward chine collé method to use in printing from a single plate or multiple plates. The section continues with a brief discussion of multiple-plate printing and step-by-step instructions for using fabric instead of paper as the impression sheet.

Finally, in this chapter, I detail an alternate method of printing chine collé using prepasted paper. Prepasting is necessary for chine collé in lithography, and the step-by-step on prepasting is followed by instructions for lithography.

# Printing an Intaglio Print
# Chine Collé Step-by-Step

You have already set up the press and assembled the materials, including lightweight impression paper and heavier support paper. The support paper is contained in a damp pack.

1. **INK AND WIPE THE PLATE**

   Be sure to wipe the plate edges, which should be smooth. If they are not, carefully burnish out even tiny nicks, which may catch the blade used to trim the impression sheet and slow that step down unnecessarily.

   *TIP A beveled plate is not necessary if its edges are smooth and the pressure on the press is set correctly. Crown Point printers pull a deburring tool along each plate edge to smooth it and take off any sharp angles that may cut the paper during printing. A fine file, used perpendicular to the plate surface, works well.*

2. **DETERMINE THE PRINTING SIDE OF THE IMPRESSION PAPER**

   In most cases you will want to print on the smoother side. The back of Western papers—also called the verso or screen side—generally shows a pattern from the wire mesh screen on which the sheet was formed. The face—also called the recto or felt side—has a smoother, less mechanical texture created by felt that pressed the moisture out of the sheet after it was formed. In Asia, paper is often dried against a plaster wall, a board, or a heated metal sheet, so it may be very smooth and shiny on its face. The back is rougher and may carry brush marks from being brushed against the drying surface. Because Asian paper is stacked without felts when the water is pressed out, it does not have texture from felt. Chain or laid lines may show on the face of the paper, even if it is smoother than the back. If in doubt about which side to print on, hold the paper so that you can see across the surface in a raking light. Print on the side with fewer fibers sticking up.

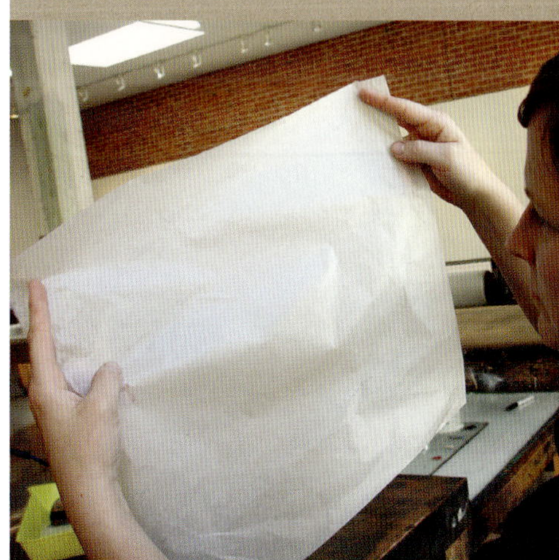

HOLD UP THE IMPRESSION PAPER TO DETERMINE THE PRINTING SIDE.

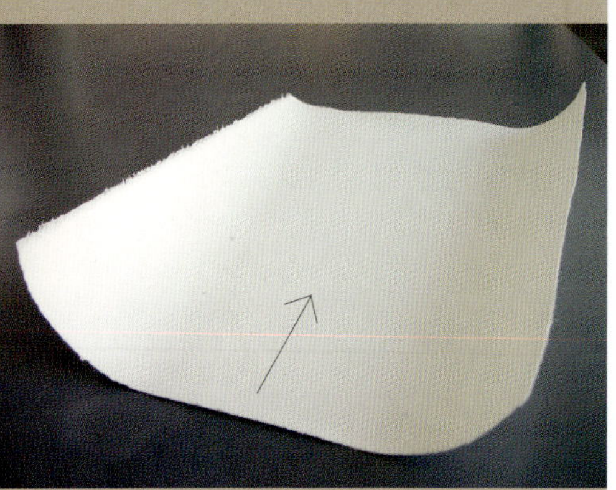



*TIP If there is a visible watermark, it is usually, but not always, readable correctly from the face side. Rives heavyweight is one exception: the watermark reads correctly on the wire side.*

3. **DETERMINE THE DIRECTION OF THE GRAIN IN BOTH THE IMPRESSION PAPER AND THE SUPPORT PAPER**

Expansion due to moisture is always greatest across the direction of the grain, so the grain of the support paper should run in the direction the press bed travels to minimize stretch and avoid wrinkling. This is especially important for large images and multiple-plate prints.

To prevent the print from curling over time, orient the two papers with the directions of grain perpendicular to one another. Many thin handmade impression papers have little noticeable grain, but if you use an impression paper in which you can easily find the grain, you should try to orient it at right angles to the grain in the backing paper.

To determine grain, moisten one side of the paper and note the direction of curl. The paper will curl parallel to the grain, not against it, and it will tear more readily with the grain as well. Even without moistening the paper, you can probably feel the grain by rolling an edge in each direction. The paper will resist rolling against the grain but will roll easily with the grain.

Grain is most prominent in machine-made papers and runs in the direction in which a continuous roll of paper is formed. Machine-made papers have only two deckles, since a continuous roll is torn into sheets after production. The deckles will always be on the edges that run with the grain of the paper, usually (but not always) the length rather than the width of the sheet.

 MOISTEN THE IMPRESSION PAPER AND POSITION IT ON
THE PLATE

Papers used for intaglio printing must be moistened to
make the fibers flexible so that they can mold into the
intaglio plate, transfer the ink, and take a good impression.
A very thin paper used for chine collé might receive enough
moisture from its backing sheet to make its fibers flexible,
but if you don't moisten the impression paper in advance
it may wrinkle from expansion during printing. Moisture
also helps keep the impression paper from sticking to the
ink while you are positioning it on the plate. After you
have positioned the paper, an extra ¾ inch or so should
be hanging over the edges of the plate on all sides. Use
one of three basic methods to moisten and position the
impression paper: (A) spray the paper, (B) spray the plate,
or (C) immerse the plate and paper in water.

**METHOD A:** Spray the paper. This method works well for
strong sheets like gampi.

### SET UP THE PLATE

Start by placing the inked and wiped plate on a pedestal or
box smaller than the plate. The plate should be stable but
should overhang the pedestal on all sides.

### SPRAY THE PAPER

Using a plant mister, drench the paper with a water mist.
Hold the sheet by a corner with the opposite corner between your lips, or ask someone to help you. For a large or
especially fragile sheet, wet a clean ruler or strip of wood,
place it against an edge, and use it to hold the sheet flat as
you spray. Gently mist both sides of the sheet.



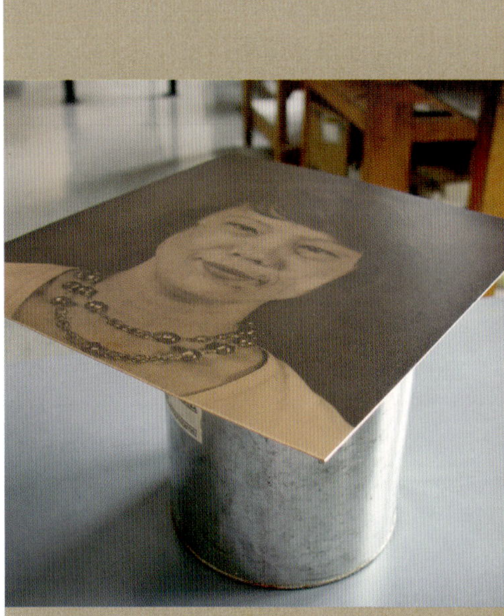

THE INKED PLATE SITTING ON A PEDESTAL.

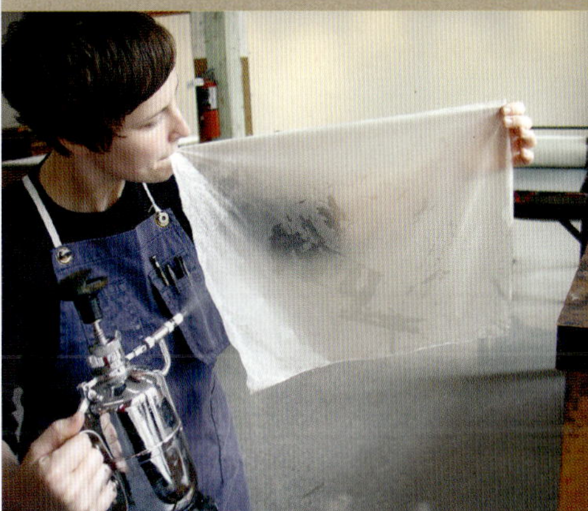

SPRAY THE PAPER. KEEP THE PAPER TAUT BY HOLDING ONE
CORNER WITH YOUR LIPS, OR ASK SOMEONE TO HELP YOU.

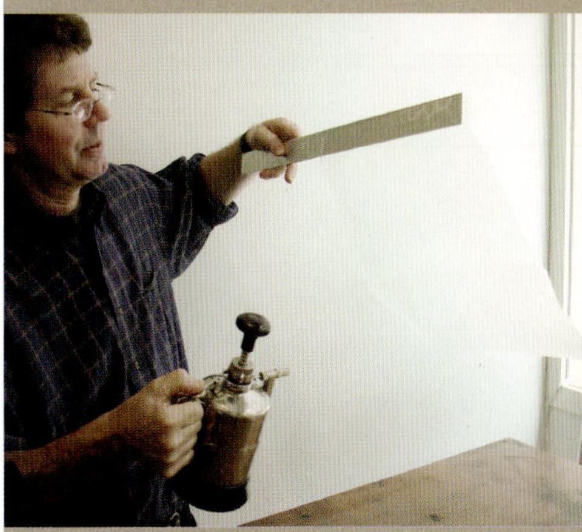

FOR A LARGE SHEET, PRESS A WET RULER AGAINST AN EDGE
BEFORE SPRAYING.

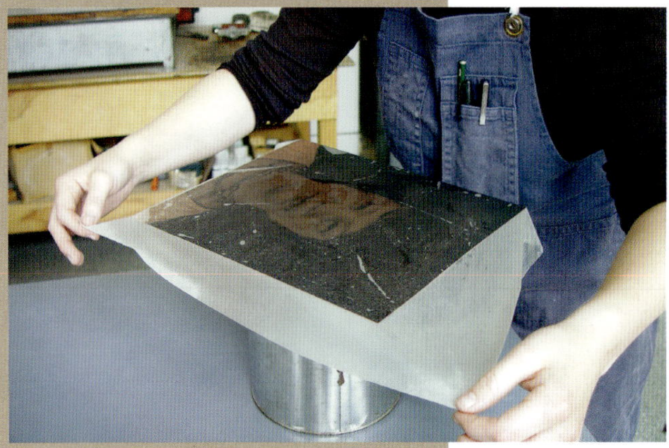

LAY THE MOISTENED IMPRESSION PAPER ONTO THE INKED PLATE. THE SHEET SHOULD BE BIGGER THAN THE PLATE SO THAT EXTRA PAPER HANGS OVER EACH EDGE.

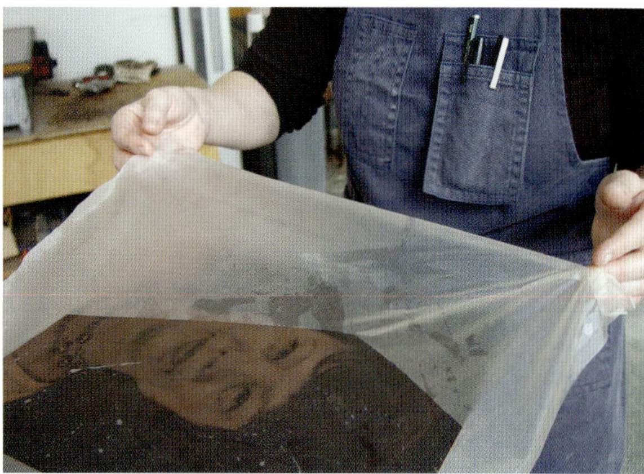

LIFT THE EDGES OF THE PAPER AND PULL THE PAPER UP AND AWAY FROM THE PLATE TO GET RID OF WRINKLES AND AIR BUBBLES.

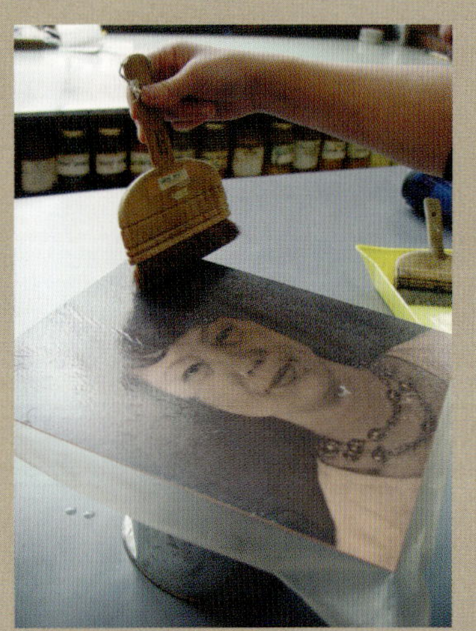

BRUSH OUT REMAINING AIR BUBBLES.

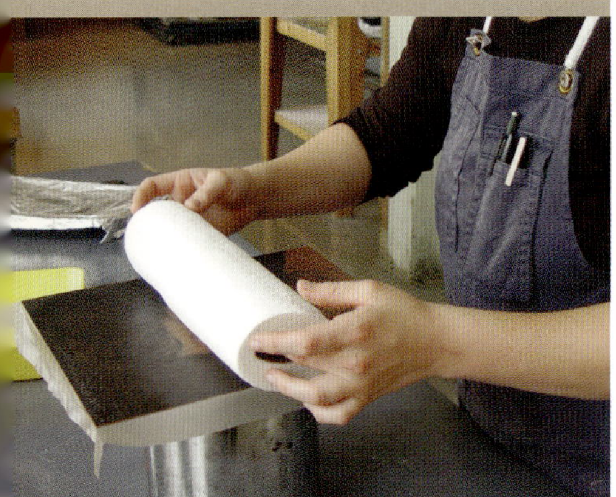

BLOT THE EXCESS WATER WITH A ROLL OF PAPER TOWELS.

## PLACE THE PAPER ON THE PLATE

As the paper relaxes, hold it loosely by one edge and drop it face down on the plate with its edges overhanging all around the plate. If possible, place the paper so that the grain will be at right angles to the grain of the backing paper. There will be ripples and pockets of air at this stage. Carefully lift the edges of the paper and pull gently to flatten it and get rid of large wrinkles and air pockets. The paper should be very wet—spray it again if necessary.

## REMOVE EXCESS MOISTURE AND AIR BUBBLES

Blot the excess moisture and at the same time chase air to the edges. First use a clean brush, then a squeezed-out sponge or a roll of paper towels tpulling off the outer towels on the roll as it gets wet.

TIP *Do not fuss over every small air pocket. The little ones will come out without wrinkling as the plate goes through the press.*

METHOD B: Spray the plate. This method works well if your impression sheet is too large or too delicate to move when wet.

### SPRAY THE INKED PLATE ON THE PEDESTAL
Be sure the plate is very wet.

### POSITION THE PAPER
Lay the dry impression sheet face down on the plate and gently pull on the edges of the paper.

### MIST AGAIN AND FLATTEN
Spray water heavily on the sheet. Then remove air bubbles and blot excess water as shown on page 72.

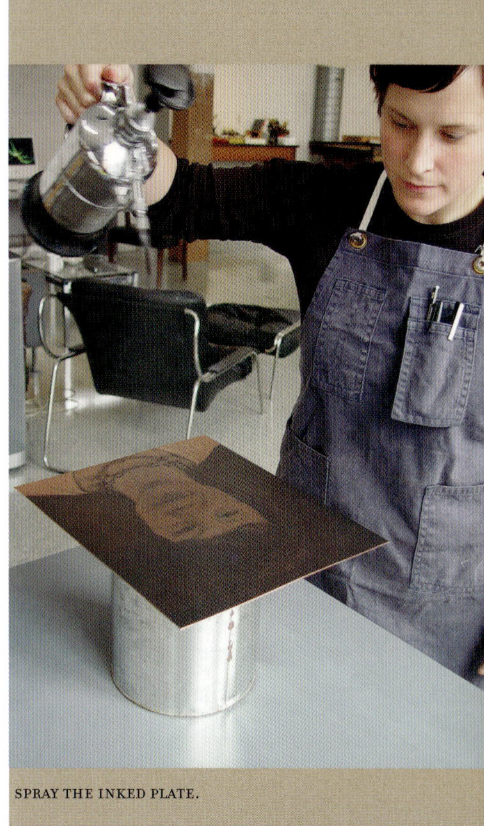
SPRAY THE INKED PLATE.

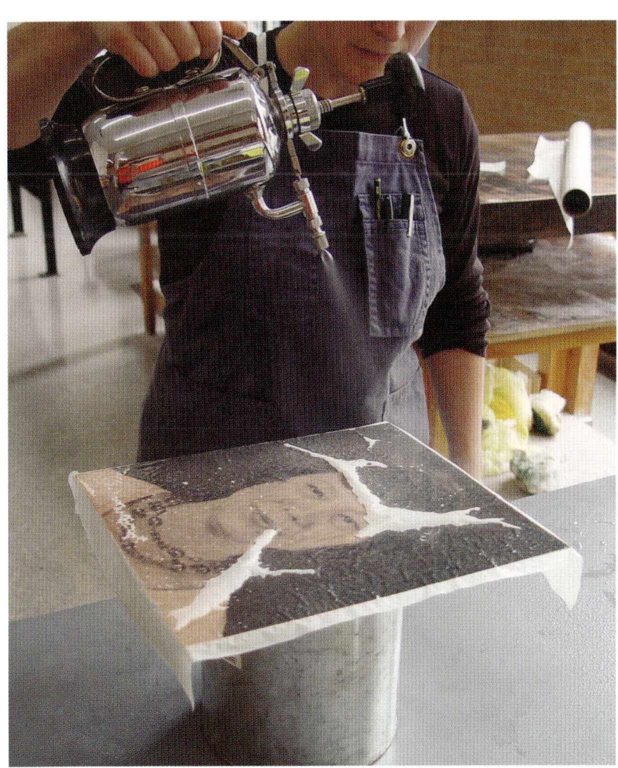
MIST THE PAPER AGAIN.

LAY THE DRY PAPER DOWN OVER THE WET PLATE.

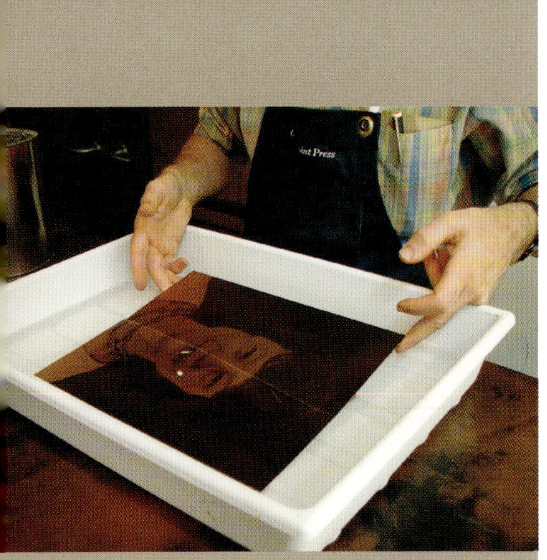



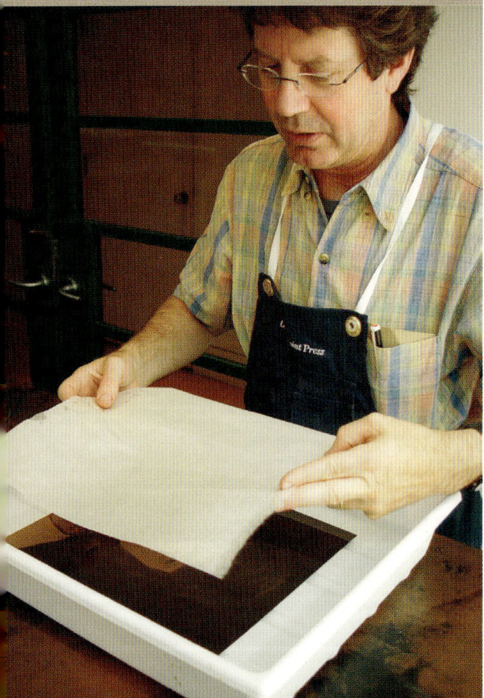



METHOD C: Immerse the plate and paper in water. The Crown Point printers learned this method from the Japanese artist Shoichi Ida. It is the most foolproof method for small plates and is especially useful for images with heavy surface ink that might smudge and for very thin paper or cutout shapes that are difficult to handle and position.

### IMMERSE THE PLATE AND PAPER

Fill a tray with water and submerge the inked plate in it. Float the impression paper face down on the surface of the water and wait until it has expanded evenly and looks flat.

### REMOVE THE PLATE AND PAPER

Gently raise the plate while keeping it centered under the paper. You can easily push even irregular fragments of paper into place if someone else raises the plate while you manipulate the paper into position.

Let the water run off and then blot the reverse side of the plate. Set the plate on the platform. The paper will be flat and ready to paste after very gentle blotting.

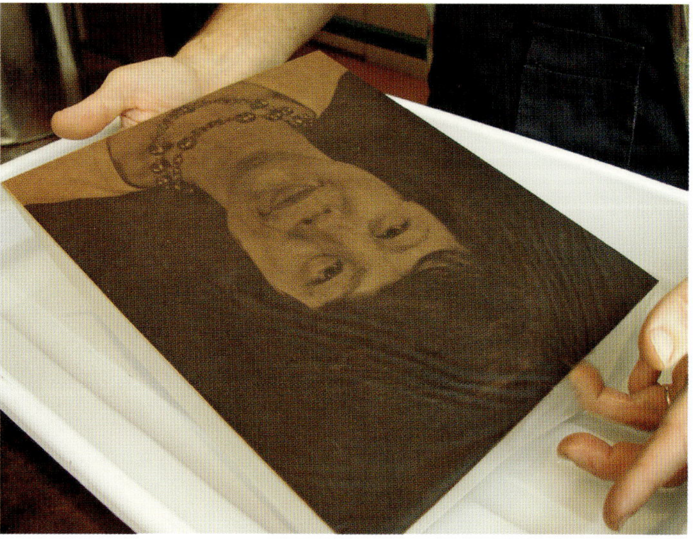

KEEPING THE PLATE CENTERED UNDERNEATH THE IMPRESSION PAPER, LIFT IT FROM THE WATER BATH ALONG WITH THE PAPER.

5. **APPLY THE PASTE**

Brush a thin layer of paste evenly over the paper. The water
in the paste slurry will be absorbed into the paper, leaving
a very thin, even layer of paste particles on the surface.
Carefully brush out these particles, using a firm movement
of your selected paste brush (see page 49) across the
surface of the paper in all directions. This causes the
particles to lock into the paper fibers and provides a bond
that is stronger than either of the papers being joined, yet
has no appreciable substance of its own.

TIP *It is very important that the paste coating be thin. More
paste does not make the bond stronger, and curling or buckling
can result from using too much paste. (Curling is likely to
become more noticeable over time.) The thinner the coating of
paste, the better.*

Observe the surface obliquely, and you will be able to see
your brushstrokes and areas that were missed by the paste.
Brushstroke marks may show in the print if the paper
is unevenly wet and absorbs ink unevenly. If you detect
missed areas or prominent brushstrokes, mist the surface
lightly and brush in all directions until they disappear. Do
not add more paste. Slight brushstrokes will disappear as
the paste dries.

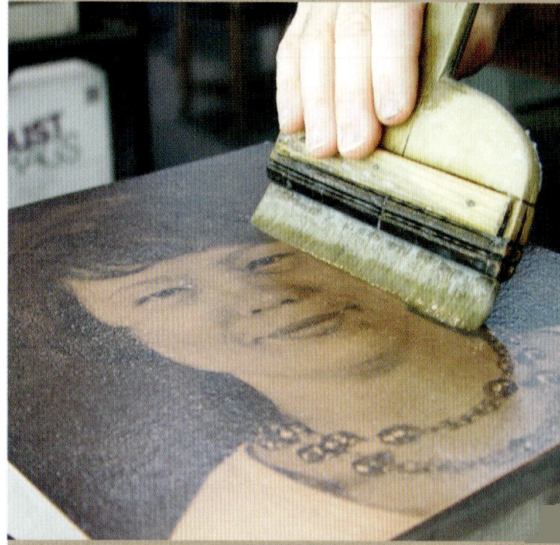

BRUSH ON A THIN LAYER OF PASTE.

EXAMINING THE PAPER FROM AN OBLIQUE ANGLE, LOOK FOR MISSED
AREAS. BRUSHSTROKES LIKE THESE WILL DISAPPEAR. THE TEXTURE AT
RIGHT IS PART OF THE IMAGE.

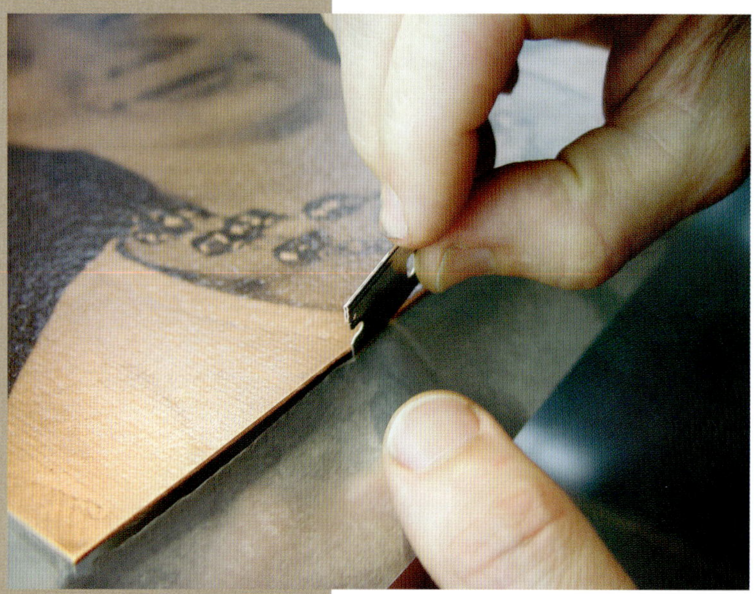



6. **TRIM THE PAPER**

Trim the excess paper exactly at the plate edges so that after you have printed your image, the chine collé will be in the plate area, and the support paper will provide the margins. Trim with new single-edge razor blades.

Gently grip the paper overhang and cut into it, sliding the blade in short strokes against the plate edge. If it does not cut cleanly, the paper is probably too wet; partially dry it with a fan or hair dryer and try again.

TIP *Each time the blade catches against the plate edge, the blade gains a nick that impedes it from cutting cleanly. Have a plentiful supply of new blades handy. Often it takes several blades to trim each sheet. X-Acto brand makes razor blades that are sharper than others I've tried and can be purchased in packages of one hundred.*

7. **CHECK THE EDGES**

After trimming, slide your fingers gently around the edges of the plate with an upward motion to dislodge any loose fibers that may have curled underneath. If these are not brought up off the edge, they can catch and cause the paper to tear when you remove it from the plate after printing.

8. **DRY EXCESS MOISTURE**

The final step before printing is to remove excess moisture from the pasted impression sheet. The timing of this step is crucial and is subject to the humidity and temperature of the room. The paste is hygroscopic; that is, it readily absorbs moisture and traps it in the paper. If the moisture is uneven, the impression will print unevenly.

As the paste dries, the paper becomes less translucent. There is a tendency for the edges to dry first and begin to curl back from the plate, causing wrinkling. Accelerate the drying with a hair dryer or handheld fan and aim the air at the center of the paper.

When the paste has given up enough moisture, it shrinks. Any visible brushstrokes should disappear, and the surface will feel cool to the touch but not sticky. If there is excess paste in places, gently wipe it away with your finger. When you are ready to print, the pasted surface should have a dull, leathery look and feel.

TIP *Once the paste has shrunk, it absorbs moisture more slowly, so you can rehumidify it if necessary. If the paste begins to look hard and dry or if the edges curl or wrinkles appear, mist the paper lightly, then gently sponge or brush the surface. If the paper seems to be drying uncontrollably, add humidity to the air by mopping the floor with a wet mop and misting the room with an atomizer.*

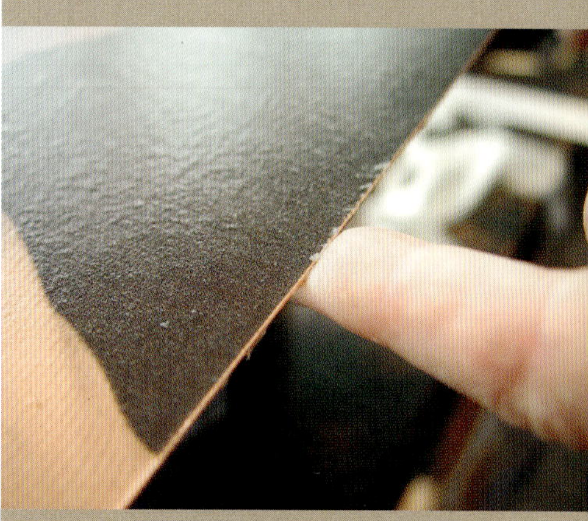

USE YOUR FINGER TO MAKE SURE THERE ARE NO LOOSE FIBERS ALONG THE EDGE OF THE PLATE.

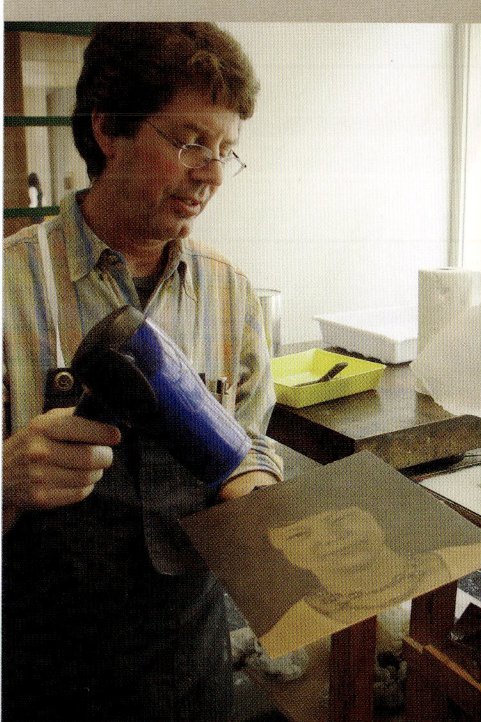

USE A HAIR DRYER TO SPEED UP THE DRYING PROCESS.

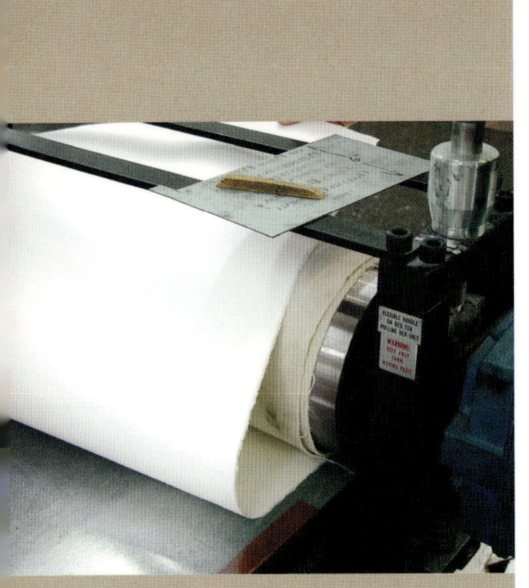

CATCH THE SUPPORT PAPER UNDER THE PRESS.

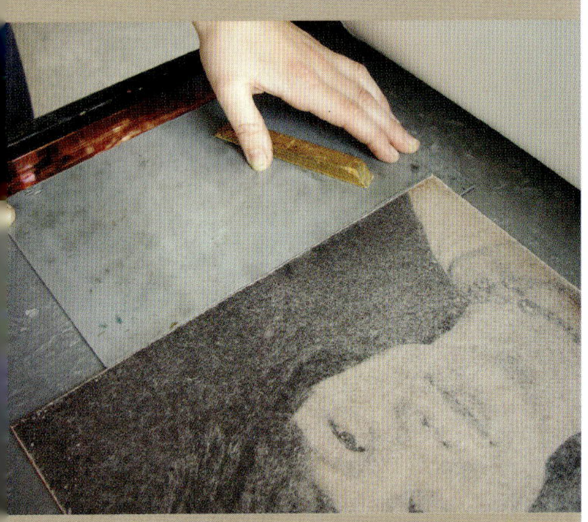

REGISTER THE PLATE ON THE PRESSBED.

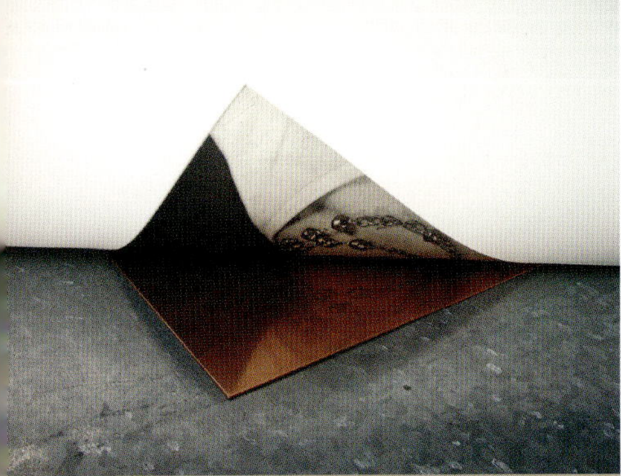

PULL THE PRINT SLOWLY FROM THE PLATE.

9. PRINT YOUR IMAGE CHINE COLLÉ

When the impression paper is almost at the right humidity, stop drying it with the fan or hair dryer and let it sit a moment while you set the support paper in the press. Remove a sheet of support paper from the damp pack, blot any surface moisture, catch the sheet under the blankets and roller of the press, and then pull the blankets and the sheet back over the roller to expose the press bed. Next, set the plate into the registration system.

TIP *If you are using gampi as your impression sheet, it will have turned from translucent to nearly opaque when the moisture level is correct. If the impression sheet is still a little damp, use the hair dryer to dry it further. If it is too dry, mist it slightly again just before printing. If in doubt, keep it on the dry side.*

Once the plate is registered, run it through the press. Pull the print off the plate slowly. The impression paper should be firmly attached in the plate area, with no bubbles.

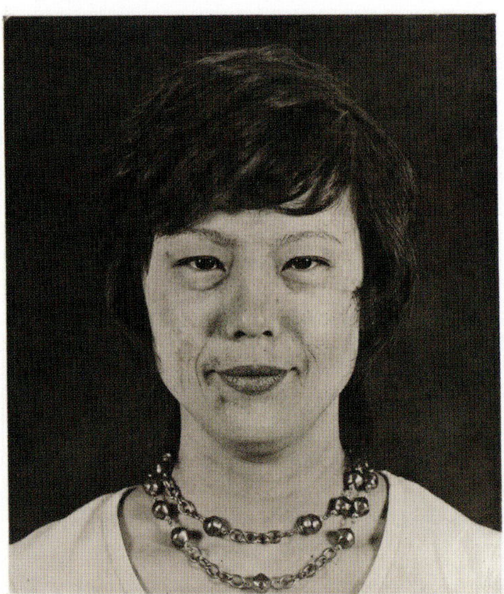

ATSUKO MORITA, *SELF PORTRAIT AS FEMALE, AGE 50*, 2008. PHOTOGRAVURE PRINTED ON GAMPI PAPER CHINE COLLÉ, 12 × 10 INCHES. CREATED IN THE CROWN POINT SUMMER WORKSHOP, 2008.

If the impression paper has bubbled, pulled away from the support paper, or stuck to the plate, you probably used too much moisture or too much paste. If there are just a few bubbles, you can try piercing them with a hypodermic syringe containing very thin paste and inserting a little paste below the surface. Blot with a soft tissue to absorb excess moisture. However, if either of those problems occur, they indicate that the bond is not stable and may not be trustworthy.

If a small area of the impression paper is not stuck down, you can pull it back, brush on a tiny bit of paste, and let the impression paper fall back against the support paper where it will adhere from capillary action.

If paste has squeezed out from between the sheets, there is no remedy but to try again. You most likely used too much paste, too much moisture, too much pressure, or some combination of the three. Perhaps the blankets are filled with moisture and sizing. Decreasing the pressure and changing the blankets will correct that problem temporarily, but it will recur unless you get the paper moisture under control.

TIP *If the print looks good but you are uncertain about the bond, you may want to sacrifice a print to be sure your procedure was correct before you print an entire edition. Scrape up a corner of the impression paper with a fingernail and peel it from the support paper. This should be difficult. Whichever paper is the stronger will pull fibers away from the other as you attempt to separate them. The presence of pulled fibers indicates that the bond is stronger than the papers and is, therefore, successful and will not loosen over time.*

# Working with Multiple-Plate Images in Intaglio

It is very important to take paper stretch into account. You can trim and file plates to compensate for the stretch, but that will be effective only if you keep their printing order consistent. Be sure to start with the bed on the same side of the press each time. Use a support paper with minimal stretch and remember to pay careful attention to paper grain. Control the moisture by using a damp pack for your paper and keep your chine collé method and timing the same each time you print.

> TIP *If you are having trouble with registration, you will need to slightly adjust all the plates by filing them after their printing sequence has been definitively established. In a large print, the first plates you print may need to be out of square for the image to end up square. To understand this, you can run a large rectilinear plate back and forth through the press and measure the plate mark each time. You will find you get a trapezoid as the paper stretches on the first run, and then a reversed trapezoid on the return.*

In large images, you may see multiple plate marks no matter what you do. An image 30 inches across can stretch ¼ inch during printing. Generally the paper stretches more on the first run through the press and less on each subsequent run.

> TIP *Run a blank plate through the press in both directions before you begin printing the image-bearing plates. This plate, called a prestretch plate, should be cut slightly smaller in both dimensions than the image-bearing plates.*

The extra runs through the press needed for multiple-plate printing force more moisture out of the paper, and it may wrinkle or take the ink poorly if it becomes too dry. You can lightly mist the back of the sheet between runs, but do not do this unless absolutely necessary. Too much moisture is worse than too little. Resist the tendency to mist unless you see the support paper beginning to wrinkle. If the ink is transferring properly as you print, there is generally enough moisture in the paper for chine collé.

If you are printing part of the image on the support paper, the paste on the back of the impression paper may not stick to the inked sections. If it does not stick, there is probably too much moisture present in the paste or in the impression paper. The wet ink decreases the absorption of the support paper, so the extra moisture has  nowhere to go. Be especially vigilant about the moisture level in your paste and papers if you are working with printed support paper.

If, with absolute minimum moisture, the paper still bubbles or pulls away, try using prepasted impression paper (see instructions on pages 85–88). Before printing, barely moisten the paper to reactivate the paste.

If using prepasted paper is not practical, gently brush a very thin preparation of paste onto the heaviest deposits of wet ink after printing the support sheet and before printing the impression sheet. Use a soft brush and be sure to blot off any excess paste. This is an emergency measure and may not produce consistent results. Before resorting to it, try reducing the dampness of the support paper even further. Has it been in a damp pack at least overnight? The problem is almost always excess moisture.

# Printing Chine Collé with Fabric Step-by-Step

The softness and absorbency of silk make it an excellent printing surface, and it is still widely used for printing in China. Chinese craftspeople print on the same fine, tightly woven silk that is used for painting. For printing, it is mounted on a thin backing paper to add dimensional stability. The paper-backed silk is available from Chinese art supply houses (see www.magical-secrets.com for sources). You might also wish to collé other fabrics, whether you print on them or not.

Silk and other fabrics, with or without sizing, can be printed on and pasted down successfully as long as the thickness and absorbency of the fibers are considered, and the pressure and moisture are properly adjusted. The primary problems to overcome when working chine collé with fabrics are their dimensional variability and their tendency to absorb too much moisture for the paste to stick.

1.  **CUT A SEPARATE BLANK PLATE TO USE FOR PASTING**
    The new plate should be slightly smaller than the image plate. You will use this plate to paste the silk, trim it, and transfer it to the support sheet. The plate must be smaller than the image plate because the fabric stretches proportionately more than the support sheet as they run through the press together, and the stretch may bring the fabric out beyond the plate mark. Set the new blank plate on your pedestal. Ink and wipe your image plate and set it aside.

    *TIP Be sure the edges of the blank plate are free of nicks. It is not necessary to bevel the edges, but smooth them with a file or deburring tool and then with a burnisher or fine steel wool. Nicks will catch and impede the razor blade when trimming.*

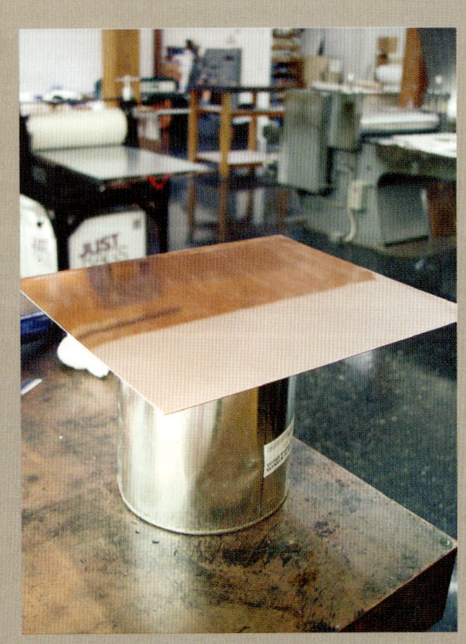

A BLANK PLATE USED FOR PASTING THE FABRIC AND TRANSFERRING IT TO THE SUPPORT SHEET. IT SHOULD BE SMALLER THAN THE IMAGE PLATE.

2.  **DAMPEN AND POSITION THE FABRIC**

    Use enough fabric so that it hangs over the edges of the
    plate by at least ¾ inch all around. This will allow you to
    comfortably grab the fabric when trimming. Mist the plate
    lightly and dampen the fabric by misting. Lay the fabric
    damp side down on the plate.

    Next, mist the fabric in place on the plate. Carefully lift and
    pull on the edges to remove bubbles. Adjust the fabric so
    that the threads run parallel to the edges of the plate. Silk
    will appear translucent and should be easy to manipulate
    when it is damp. Blot extra moisture with a sponge, tissue,
    clean cloth, or roll of paper towels.

3.  **APPLY THE PASTE**

    Brush a very thin, even layer of paste over the fabric. The
    paste will penetrate the fabric and adhere it to the plate.

4.  **DRY ALMOST COMPLETELY**

    Use a fan or hair dryer.

5.  **TRIM THE EDGES**

    Since the fabric is almost dry, it is stiff where it hangs over
    the plate and easy to trim with a sharp blade. Carefully trim
    off any stray threads so that they will not be caught under
    the plate and pull the fabric away from the support sheet
    when you lift the print after printing.

6.  **APPLY A SECOND LAYER OF PASTE**

    Dry the second layer of paste almost completely.

7.  **REGISTER THE SUPPORT PAPER**

    The support paper should be only barely damp. After plac-
    ing the paper in register on the press bed, trap the leading
    edge under the roller and blankets and lay the paper back
    over them.

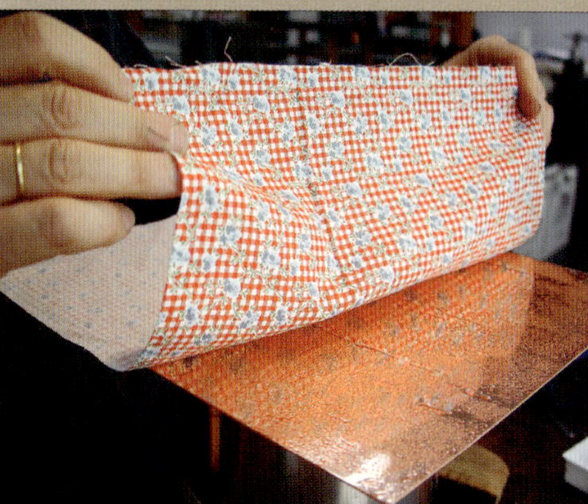

LAY THE DAMP FABRIC ONTO THE BLANK PLATE THAT HAS
BEEN MISTED LIGHTLY.

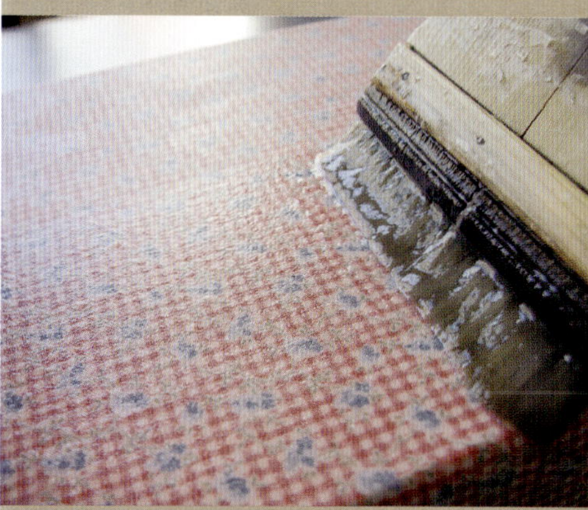

BRUSH A THIN LAYER OF PASTE OVER THE FABRIC.

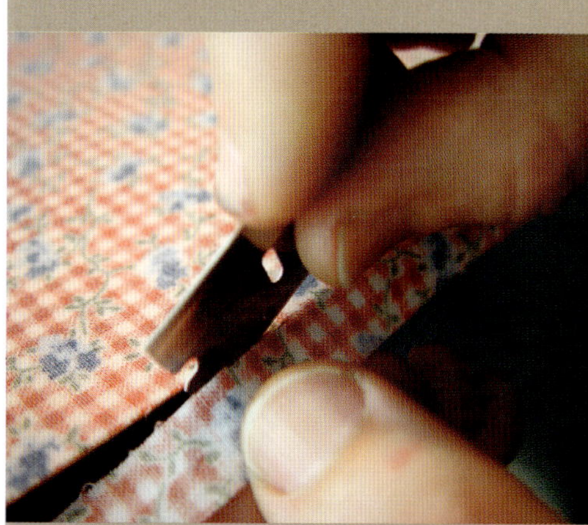

TRIM AGAINST THE PLATE EDGE WITH A SHARP RAZOR BLADE.

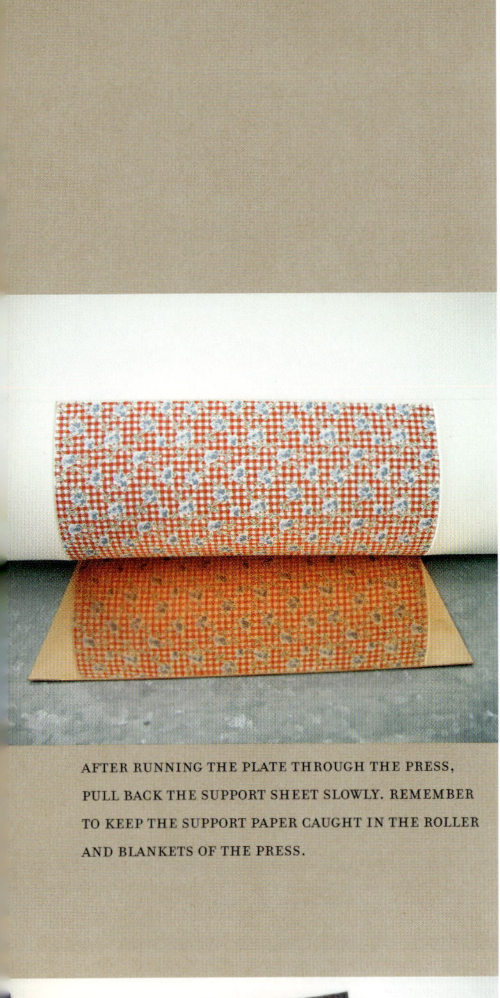

AFTER RUNNING THE PLATE THROUGH THE PRESS,
PULL BACK THE SUPPORT SHEET SLOWLY. REMEMBER
TO KEEP THE SUPPORT PAPER CAUGHT IN THE ROLLER
AND BLANKETS OF THE PRESS.

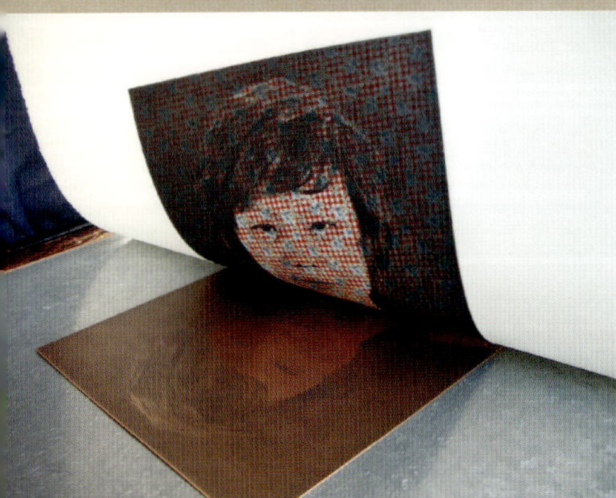

PRINT THE IMAGE PLATE OVER THE PASTED FABRIC.

8. **LIGHTLY MIST THE FABRIC**

   Introduce only enough moisture to soften the paste that is ad-hering the fabric to the plate. Brush out any large water droplets.

9. **REGISTER THE PLATE AND RUN IT THROUGH THE PRESS**

   This will transfer the fabric to the support sheet. Proper pressure will push the moisture from the support sheet into the fabric, reactivating the paste.

10. **LIFT THE SUPPORT SHEET SLOWLY**

    It may take a minute for the paste to soften and release the fabric from the plate. If fibers are caught under the plate, carefully cut them away as you pull up the sheet. Do not remove the support sheet from the registration system.

    TIP *If there are bubbles between the fabric and the support paper, they may come out when you print the image plate. If the bubbles are severe, you may be able to apply a small amount of thinned paste between the layers with a hypodermic syringe or slip some paste under the edge with a thin fan brush or palette knife. Do not use your fingers to press out the air bubbles, as fingerprints will probably show in the image.*

11. **REMOVE THE BLANK PLATE AND SUBSTITUE THE IMAGE PLATE**

    There will be a residual layer of paste on the blank plate. Wash this off before using the plate again or before storing it.

12. **PRINT THE IMAGE PLATE**

# Prepasting Impression Paper Step-by-Step

Prepasting involves applying paste to the impression paper
and allowing it to dry as a separate step prior to printing.
It is an efficient way to work in production printing and is
sometimes used in printing intaglio editions to save time.
It can also be useful to solve problems that occur when you
work in unusual ways. Prepasting is necessary for working in
lithography, where the matrix must be larger than the image,
and can be used for monotype if a press is used for printing.

If you intend to use different pieces of impression paper
on sections of the image, it is easy to use prepasted paper.
Using prepasting techniques, you can paste shaped pieces of
paper or fabric, add collage elements to a print, or paste collage
materials to an unprinted support paper.

You will be using paste prepared as described on pages 33–37.

1.  **SET UP FOR PREPASTING**

    A self-healing rubber or plastic mat is a good surface to use
    for cutting. A stack of damp newsprint is a good substitute.
    You will need very sharp blades.

    Start by cutting sheets of newsprint slightly larger than
    the impression sheets. You will need at least one sheet of
    newsprint or newspaper for each impression sheet you
    plan to prepare. If you are working large, cut a cardboard
    backing sheet to facilitate moving the wet sheets around.

LAY THE IMPRESSION PAPER ON THE NEWSPRINT.

2.  **CUT THE IMPRESSION PAPER LARGER THAN REQUIRED**

    In order to have the impression sheets fit the image
    precisely, cut them larger than necessary and trim them
    further later. If you try to cut the paper to size before
    pasting, it is likely that expansion caused by moisture in
    the paste will change the size. Also, in handling and during

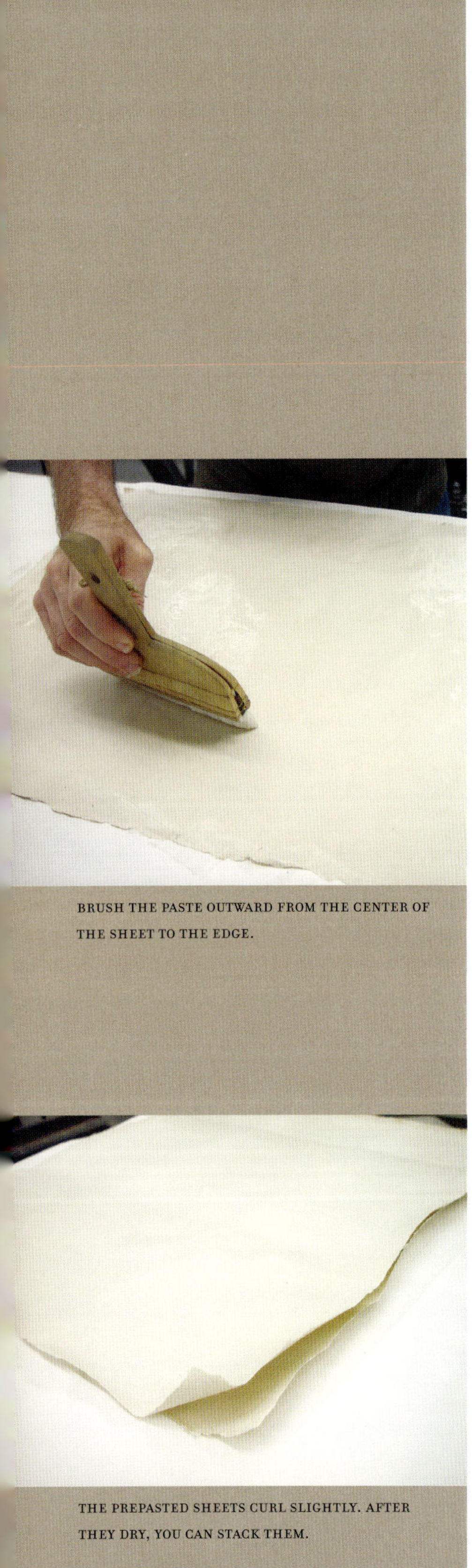

BRUSH THE PASTE OUTWARD FROM THE CENTER OF THE SHEET TO THE EDGE.

THE PREPASTED SHEETS CURL SLIGHTLY. AFTER THEY DRY, YOU CAN STACK THEM.

pasting, you might mess up the edges, or some paste might crawl onto the front at the edges when the paper stretches. Finally, there is a good chance that brushing out the paste will disturb the fibers on a cut edge and make it uneven and fuzzy. Leaving a little paper all around to trim just before printing will prevent these problems.

The problems above apply when cutting shaped pieces. In addition, it is tricky to apply paste to cut shapes. Generally it is best to prepaste sheets and cut your shapes out of them after they have dried. Keep in mind that the shapes will expand when they are remoistened for printing.

3. **APPLY THE PASTE**

Place a sheet of newsprint on top of the cardboard, then a sheet of impression paper.

TIP *You can apply the paste to wet or dry paper. Misting the sheet first makes it easier to even out the brush marks, but the drying time will be longer. If you are using dry paper, be especially sure the paste is thin and smooth.*

Keep the paste thin and even as you brush it on. Brush outward from the center of the sheet. I like to align two edges with a corner of the worktable. As each impression sheet is pasted, set it aside to dry, still on its sheet of newsprint. Paste the next sheet using a fresh sheet of newsprint.

TIP *Be careful not to get paste on the face or underside. If you do accidentally get paste on the face, you must put the sheet aside. Later, you can use the clean area of the sheet for a smaller image.*

4. **DRY THE PREPASTED SHEETS**

Let the prepasted papers rest until they are fully dry. As they dry, they might curl. Do not try to straighten them. It is natural that they should curl slightly, but if they curl excessively you have probably used too much paste.

After the sheets are completely dry, remove them from the
newsprint and stack them. Prepasted sheets can be stored
for years as long as they remain dry.

5.  **WHEN READY TO PRINT, REDAMPEN THE PREPASTED SHEETS**
    Mist the sheets one at a time very lightly with water and al-
    low them to relax. Then put them in a damp pack. Stack five
    or six pasted sheets, add a barely moist blotter, then add
    another group of pasted sheets. If you prefer, you can stack
    them between damp newsprint sheets. Wrap the stack in
    the plastic sheeting and weight it.

    TIP *Instead of making a new damp pack, you can insert the
    prepasted sheets into a damp pack that contains the support
    paper and has already been held overnight so that the moisture
    is equalized. The sheets will not stick together if they are not so
    wet that the paste is completely reactivated.*

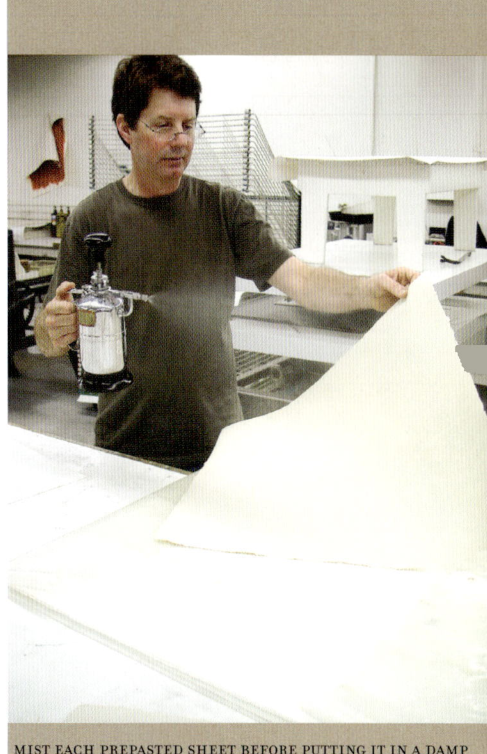

MIST EACH PREPASTED SHEET BEFORE PUTTING IT IN A DAMP
PACK PRIOR TO PRINTING.

6.  **CUT THE PREPASTED SHEETS**
    Cut only the number of sheets you can print in two or three
    hours. If you are printing in intaglio, you can use the plate
    you will be printing as a template. Lay the uninked plate
    face down on two or more of the damp impression sheets.
    Use a self-healing plastic mat as a cutting surface if you
    can, and be sure the blade is sharp.

    TIP *If you use your plate as a template, be sure it is face down.
    This way, if the blade slips it will not damage the image. It
    is best to cut the impression sheets with their unpasted sides
    against the image side of the plate, since plates are almost never
    truly square. If you do that, the paper and the plate can later be
    aligned properly for printing.*

    I usually begin by cutting two sheets together. If, after
    printing, the first one does not match exactly, I adjust the
    size of the second sheet and, with a straightedge to cut
    against, use the adjusted sheet as a template on a stack of
    the next few sheets to be printed.

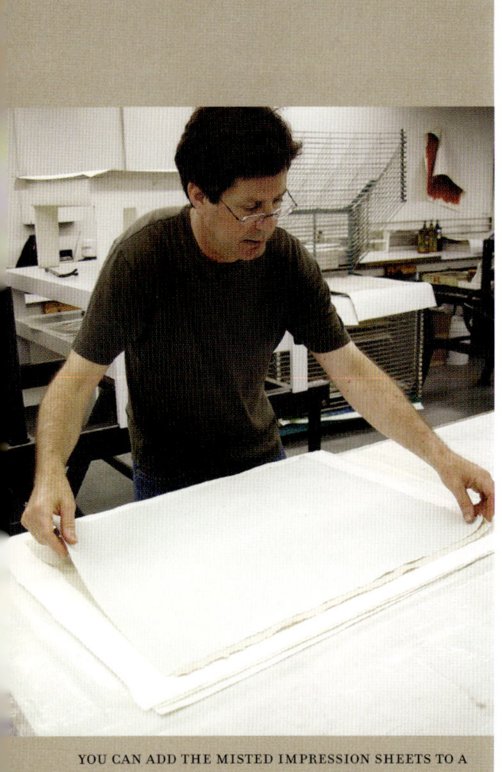



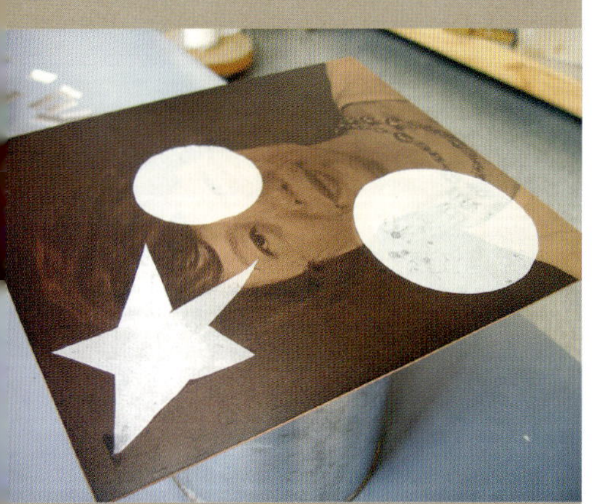



Put the cut sheets back in the damp pack until you are ready to print. If they do not sit long in the pack, they probably will not expand further. If they do expand, you may have to make another trim with a straightedge just before printing.

7. **PRINT IN INTAGLIO USING A PREPASTED IMPRESSION SHEET**
Register the support paper, fold it back over the roller and blankets, and set the inked plate on the press bed using your registration system.

Take a trimmed impression sheet or a set of precut fragments out of the damp pack and place paste side up in position on the inked plate.

The moisture level is probably correct if the sheet has been in the damp pack and has not stuck to other papers. It should feel cool to the touch but not sticky.

Run the print through the press, covering the impression sheet or fragments with the support sheet. Carefully pull the print away from the plate. The moisture in the support paper combined with the pressure of the press will activate the paste and create a secure bond.

TIP *At Crown Point we usually place the completed print in a damp pack in which we keep an entire day's printing moist until we are ready to put everything in the dryer at the end of the day. (See pages 163–168 on drying.)*

# Printing a Lithograph Chine Collé Step-by-Step

The techniques described here apply when the image is printed directly on paper from a stone or plate rather than first being offset onto a rubber blanket. These techniques will work for traditional lithography in which moisture is a major factor and

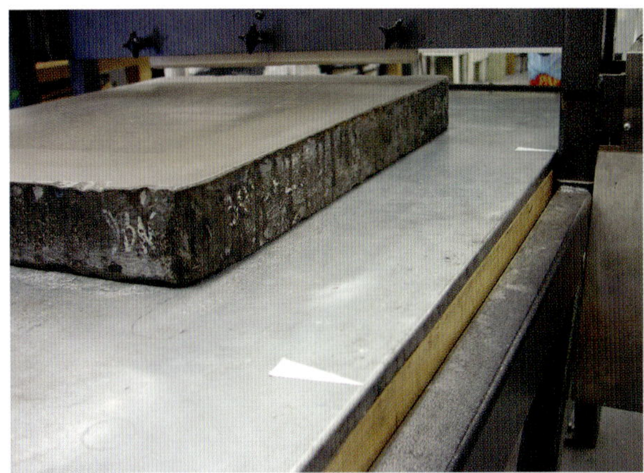

THE STOPS ARE MARKED ON THE PRESS BED.

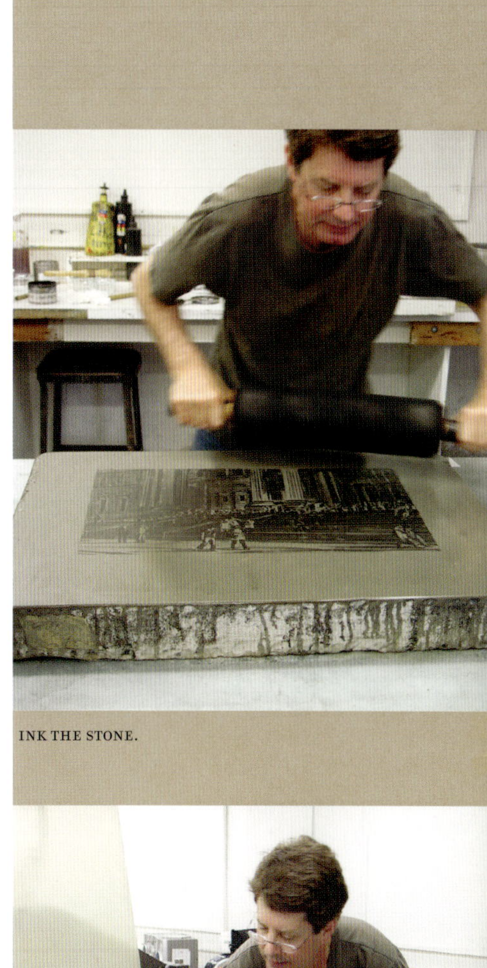

INK THE STONE.

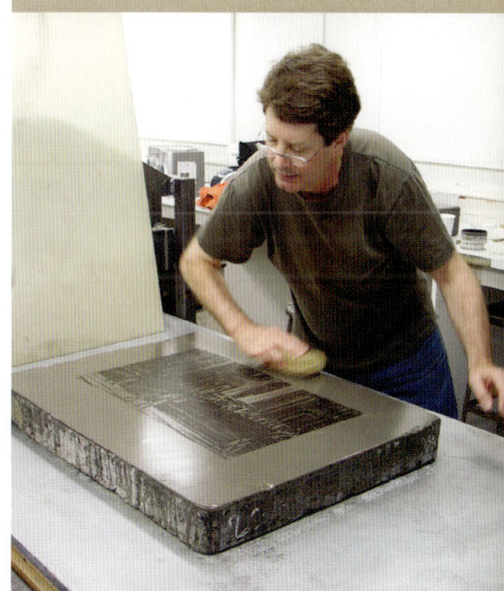

SPONGE-GUM THE STONE.

for the newer waterless lithography that has a silicon-based nonimage area. They will also work for monotype if a press is used for printing. These instructions assume that you already understand the basics of printing in lithography.

Unlike intaglio printing, lithographic printing requires that the image be on a plate or stone that is larger than the area to be printed. This is necessary because the surfaces of the tympan and scraper bar of the press must be absolutely smooth if they are to print a good impression. If you print the edge of the stone, it dents the scraper bar and will incise the tympan; the same is true of a plate trimmed to image size. You sometimes see prints that show the edges of the stone. Lots of good tympans and scraper bars have been wasted that way, and many stones chipped or broken.

In addition, traditional lithography requires careful maintenance of the chemical balance of the plate or stone during editioning. The gum film must be kept moist to protect the nonimage areas. This is best achieved by keeping the number of steps to a minimum so you can concentrate on inking and keeping the gum film moist.

Because it is necessary to maintain chemical balance and it is inadvisable to print the full plate or stone, prepasted

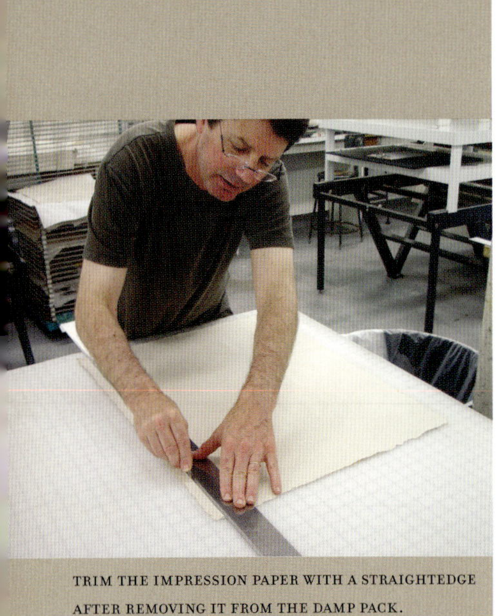
TRIM THE IMPRESSION PAPER WITH A STRAIGHTEDGE
AFTER REMOVING IT FROM THE DAMP PACK.

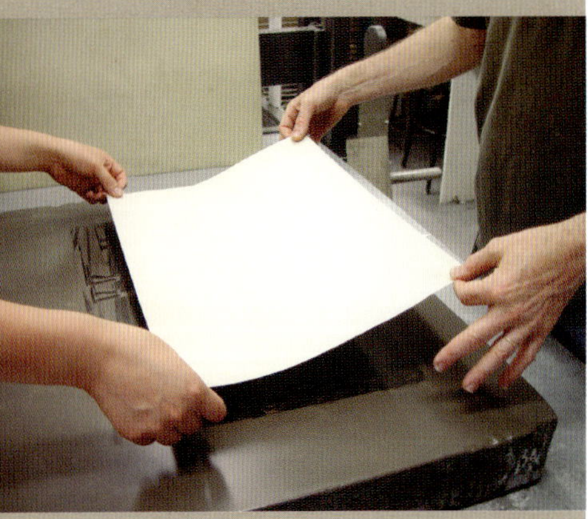
POSITION THE IMPRESSION PAPER ON THE STONE.

CUT CORNER MARKS INTO THE STONE FOR ACCU-
RATE POSITIONING OF THE IMPRESSION PAPER.

impression paper is the practical choice for lithography. See pages 85–87 for instructions on how to prepare prepasted impression sheets.

1. **MAKE ONE OR TWO DAMP PACKS**

In lithography, gum arabic is used to protect the non-image areas. Repeated wetting and drying of the gum film (which occurs during printing with dry paper) causes the film to weaken and break down. Printing lithographs chine collé with damp paper maintains the moisture on the surface and so preserves the gum film better than printing with dry paper. Be careful not to use too much moisture. Overdampening is problematic in lithography, as excessive moisture will cause wrinkles and can prevent the image from printing evenly. Excessive moisture in chine collé is the chief cause of adhesion failure.

Using damp packs will help you guard against excessive moisture. In working with damp packs, be sure to reclose them each time after opening. Make a damp pack for your prepasted impression paper by wrapping moist (not wet) blotters or newsprint sheets in plastic and leaving a weight on the package overnight. Do not put your impression paper in the pack until just prior to printing.

You will need to use damp support paper as well, especially if you are working with a large image. Make another damp pack following the instructions on pages 44–47 and put the support paper in it the night before you plan to print.

TIP *You can use the same pack for both impression and support papers, but you may find it easier to use two different packages. You don't need a blotter for every impression sheet—five or six sheets can be stacked together.*

2. **SET UP FOR PRINTING**

   Your image on the plate or stone should already be processed, washed out, and ready to roll up. Set your registration, with the stops marked, and ink and proof the image.
   Following this, sponge-gum it to keep it stable during the
   time it will take to redampen and cut the impression sheets
   to size.

3. **PUT ENOUGH PREPASTED IMPRESSION SHEETS FOR ONE
   PRINTING SESSION INTO THE DAMP PACK**

   Mist each sheet very lightly or brush the unpasted side with
   a little water. Allow it to relax and stretch out for a moment,
   then place it in the damp pack. Position a barely damp blotter or newsprint sheet between every few sheets and weight
   the top of the pack. Wait 10 or 15 minutes for the moisture to
   even out.

   *TIP If you did not prepare your pack in advance so that it is
   evenly damp, and/or if the impression paper stays in it too long,
   the paper may pick up too much moisture between the time you
   put it in and the time that you are ready to print. This will cause
   adhesion problems.*

4. **TRIM THE IMPRESSION SHEETS**

   After a few minutes, when the sheets are evenly moist, remove
   them from the damp pack and trim them to match your image.

   Use a very sharp blade for trimming the damp impression
   sheets to size. You can trim against a straightedge or use
   a metal or plastic template. I like to cut on a mat made of
   self-healing rubber or plastic available in art supply stores.
   You can trim several sheets at the same time. Return the
   sheets to the pack after trimming.

   If you later discover that the sheets have further expanded
   in the damp pack, you may need to make an additional trim
   just before printing.

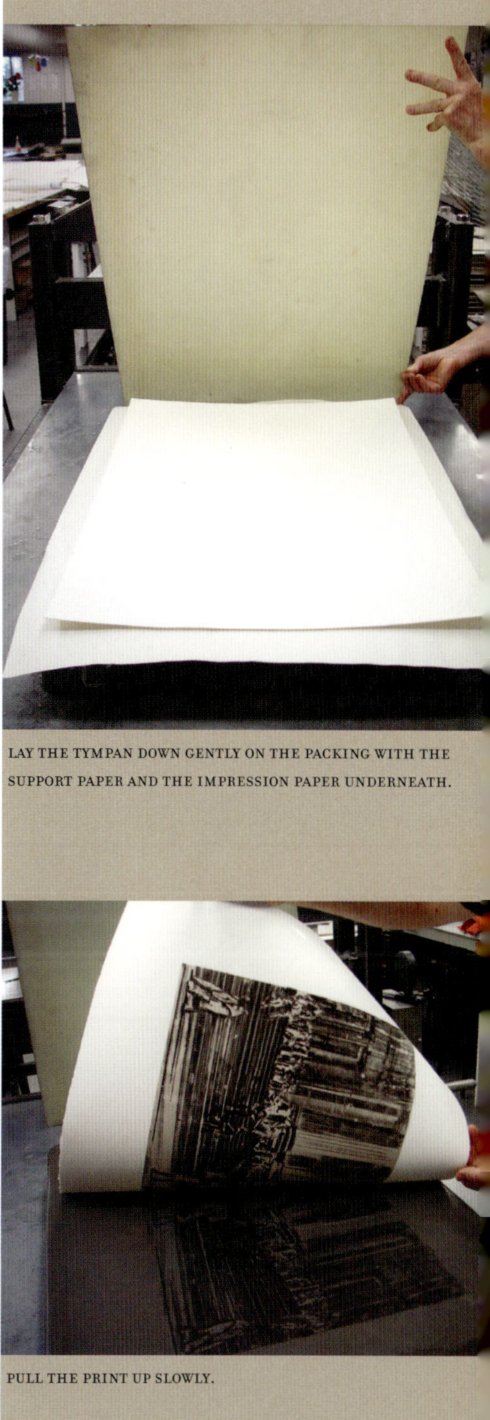

LAY THE TYMPAN DOWN GENTLY ON THE PACKING WITH THE
SUPPORT PAPER AND THE IMPRESSION PAPER UNDERNEATH.

PULL THE PRINT UP SLOWLY.

5. **POSITION THE IMPRESSION PAPER AND REGISTER THE SUPPORT SHEET**

   With the stone or plate fully inked and ready to print, re-move an impression sheet from the damp pack and posi-tion it paste side up on the image. For accurate positioning, cut corner guide marks into the stone or plate. Use a sharp blade and light pressure so that the cuts are very shallow— just enough be seen—and do not forget to desensitize them with a light etch before beginning to print. Register the sup-port paper on top of the impression sheet.

6. **PRINT**

   You may need to decrease the pressure slightly from the setting you used in proofing without the impression sheet. Lay the packing and tympan gently on top of the support sheet and run the stone or plate through the press.

   TIP *The damp paper will cause your newsprint and cover-stock packing sheets to become damp as you print. You may need to change them frequently to prevent wrinkles. I use a single sheet of newsprint for packing and replace it for each print. This way, the packing does not get very wet and can be reused after drying.*

7. **DRY THE PRINTS**

   Dry the prints between blotters (see page 155) or in a forced-air dryer in order to keep them from buckling due to the moisture (see pages 163–168).

8. **TROUBLESHOOT ANY PROBLEMS**

   If an impression sheet expanded too much and you realize after printing that it is too large, you can usually salvage the print by carefully trimming the excess with a very sharp blade against a straightedge laid on the margin. Cut only through the impression paper, then peel away the excess strip. Fibers on the support sheet will be pulled up, but these can be burnished back down with your fingernail or a bone paper-folder. In many nineteenth century lithographic chine collé prints, the impression paper is slightly larger—or smaller—than the image. It's up to you how closely you want your paper to fit the image.

If the impression paper did not adhere properly, or if you are having a problem achieving a clear impression, the image may have been improperly processed or incorrectly inked. If that is unlikely, there are several possibilities for error associated with the chine collé process. I describe these below, but remember that every image has a unique set of variables, and these can work together to cause failure in ways that can be difficult to pinpoint.

If the pressure is uneven (usually because of a damaged scraper bar or leather strap), or if the plate bed or stone is dished or uneven, it may be impossible to print well using the collé method, even if the image printed satisfactorily on a single sheet of paper. The additional layer of paper with its individual characteristics of expansion, moisture absorption, and ink-trapping properties, as well as the addition of a paste layer, can greatly decrease the tolerances within which one is used to operating. These problems increase geometrically as the image size increases.

Excess paste and too much—or, less likely, too little—moisture are the main sources of problems in getting the impression paper to adhere. All variables can—and usually do—affect one another.

The commonsense solutions to these problems are to adjust ink consistency, pressure, and moisture, and keep equipment in good condition. These solutions underscore the simplicity of the principles behind all printing processes.

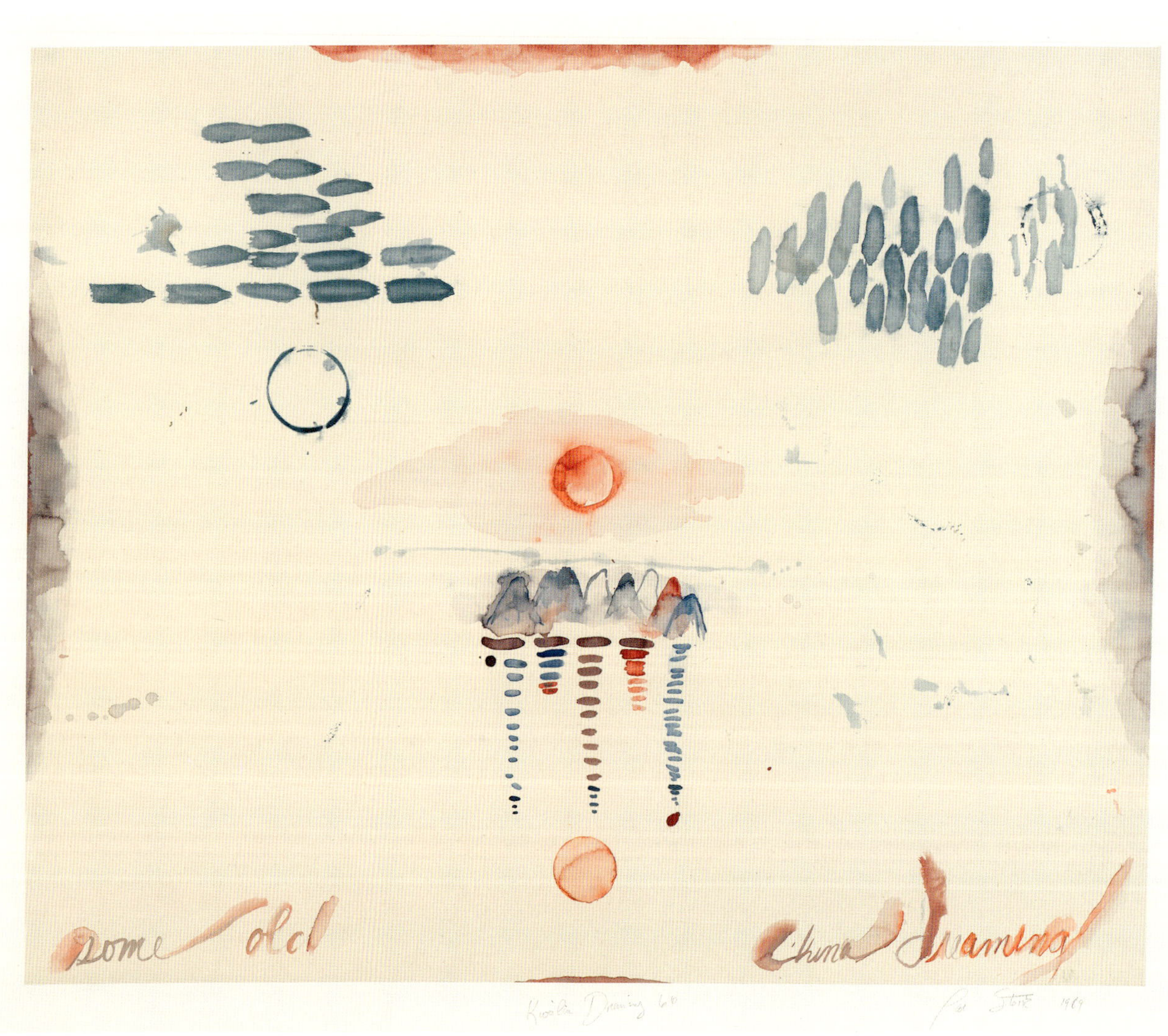
China Dreaming

# *Secret #4.* SIZING AND MOUNTING
## *Understand your materials.*

The secret to successful sizing and mounting is to understand your materials. As you work with each of the processes I describe in this section, you will learn to make adjustments that take into account your particular papers or fabrics and the way you are using them. Simply following instructions can lead to failure if you don't understand the reasons behind the instructions and how various procedures can affect your particular project. Materials vary: even machine-made papers developed to provide consistent quality can differ from batch to batch. Pay close attention to the way your materials respond to each step. For example, if the paper absorbs moisture too quickly when you dip it into a water bath, drain it very thoroughly before you lay it in the damp pack. Learn to judge moisture by comparing the weight of the paper stack before and after you have dipped the sheets, and by changes in the paper's flexibility.

Don't take anything for granted. As you work, observe your materials closely and learn to adjust your paste, sizing, moisture level, or ink consistency as needed. Expert printers and mounters don't just get it right as they begin and then sail through the work. They are constantly looking for signs of potential problems and making adjustments to keep the quality and the flow of the work consistent.

PLATE 22 (OPPOSITE)
Pat Steir, *Kweilin Dreaming, Part C, #60*, 1989.
Color woodcut printed on silk with hand painting by the artist, 26½ × 32¾ inches.

Sizing is a general term for a variety of glutinous or resinous substances used to fill the interstices in paper, fabric (such as silk for printing or canvas for painting), and other materials such as plaster, wood, and leather. The words *sizing* and *size* are interchangeable in this context. Without enough sizing, papers tend to absorb moisture too quickly and unevenly, but too much sizing can interfere with the proper trapping of the ink layer in printing. In the first part of this chapter, I make some general comments about sizing and illustrate them with work by Pat Steir done in Crown Point's China project. The step-by-step section gives specific instructions for sizing paper and fabric.

Mounting, the other subject of this chapter, differs from chine collé in that it involves pasting paper or another flat material onto a support sheet, without printing and usually without a press. Most of the woodcuts produced in China for Crown Point Press were printed on silk. To stabilize the silk before printing, the Chinese craftsmen almost always mounted it onto thin paper backing sheets. Then, in San Francisco, we mounted the prints with their backing sheets onto Western paper. I use work by Francesco Clemente and Robert Bechtle to illustrate some ways in which I learned about mounting. In the step-by-step section, you will find instructions for mounting silk to backing paper and for mounting paper or a silk-paper laminate to a support sheet. These are rudimentary mounting procedures, not as complex as scroll mounting.

Asian craftsmen have been mounting artwork on scrolls for centuries, and understanding something about scroll mounting is useful for understanding the chine collé process. In traditional Asian scrolls, several layers of paper are laminated using very thin paste mixtures. This technique provides the lasting flexibility that allows the artwork to be frequently rolled and unrolled without damage.

I had the opportunity to create etchings that were mounted as traditional scrolls by Japanese scroll mounter Shosaku Yoshimura. Later in this chapter, I discuss and illustrate that work and also speak briefly about the history of scroll mounting. Traditional scroll mounting procedures are so lengthy and subtle that it would take a separate book to detail them, but in the step-by-step section, I include a simplified introduction to mounting. The DVD accompanying this book has a compressed demonstration of the scroll mounting process by Master Yoshimura, with my explanatory comments. Watching it a few times will help you learn about handling paper and applying paste.

Pat Steir's works (pls. 22 and 23) are woodcuts printed on silk in China and hand worked after printing by the artist at Crown Point Press with watercolor, water soluble crayon, and anything else she felt like using. In some cases, as in plate 23, she also added small figures stamped from an old Tibetan woodblock.

Steir created eighty-nine unique prints in this series over nine years, and the project as a

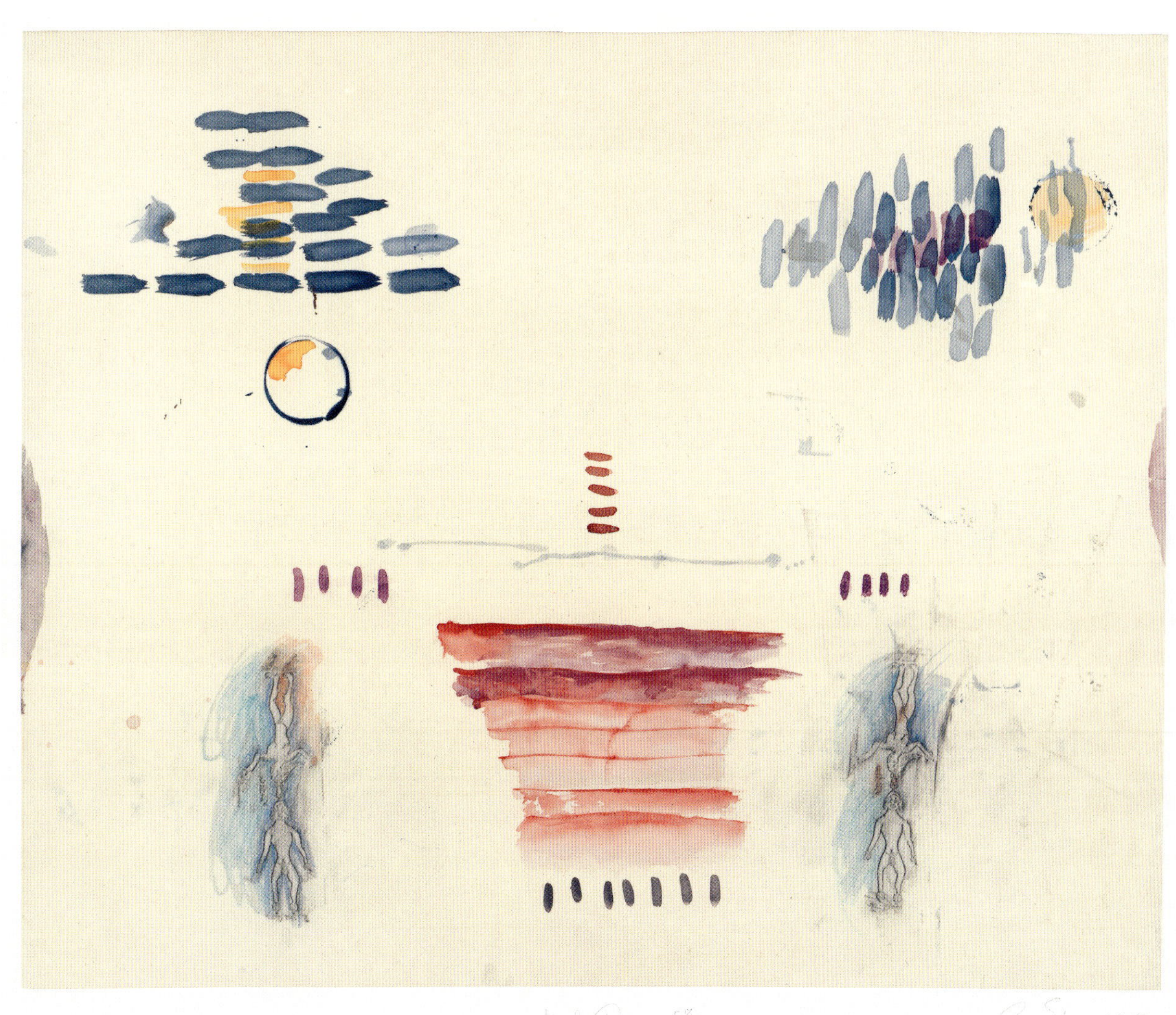



**PLATE 23**

Pat Steir, *Kweilin Dreaming, Part C, #58*, 1989.
Color woodcut printed on silk with handpainting
by the artist, $26^{1}/_{2} \times 32^{3}/_{4}$ inches.

whole records her responses to a single idea over an extended period of time. She titled the series *Kweilin Dreaming* after the picturesque karst formations at Kweilin in the Li River Valley where she traveled on her first trip to China to work on an earlier woodcut.

Steir started *Kweilin Dreaming* as a watercolor sketch that she intentionally left incomplete and mailed to the workshop. Carvers at Rongbaozhai, the woodblock studio in Beijing where Crown Point began its China project, carved pear wood blocks and hand-printed the image on silk with traditional Chinese mineral inks. They sized the silk and mounted it on a thin backing paper before printing. The materials they used were completely stable, and if Steir had not added handwork, additional sizing would have been unnecessary.

For the prints we received from the professional wood block printing studios we worked with in China, sizing was not necessary. However, an independent printer in China printed Tom Marioni's *Pi*, which I discussed in the preface to this book (see page 13 and pl. 3). It was printed in watercolor ink on unsized silk without a backing sheet. When we wet the silk to mount it, the color ran. Because the printer had not truly understood his materials, we had to size those prints after we received them in San Francisco.

Steir's *Kweilin Dreaming* was different. In most of the images, we added additional sizing only to prevent bleeding in some areas to which she had added drawing in unstable materials. It is best not to use more sizing than necessary, as a heavy layer can become brittle, attract microorganisms, and cause discoloration. Used judiciously, however, thin applications of sizing will remain undetectable over time.

Understanding materials is also important for understanding mounting principles. The first project Crown Point did in China was a small image titled *The Two Flames* (pl. 24) by Francesco Clemente. We sent the drawing to Rongbaozhai and expected to receive proofs for approval,

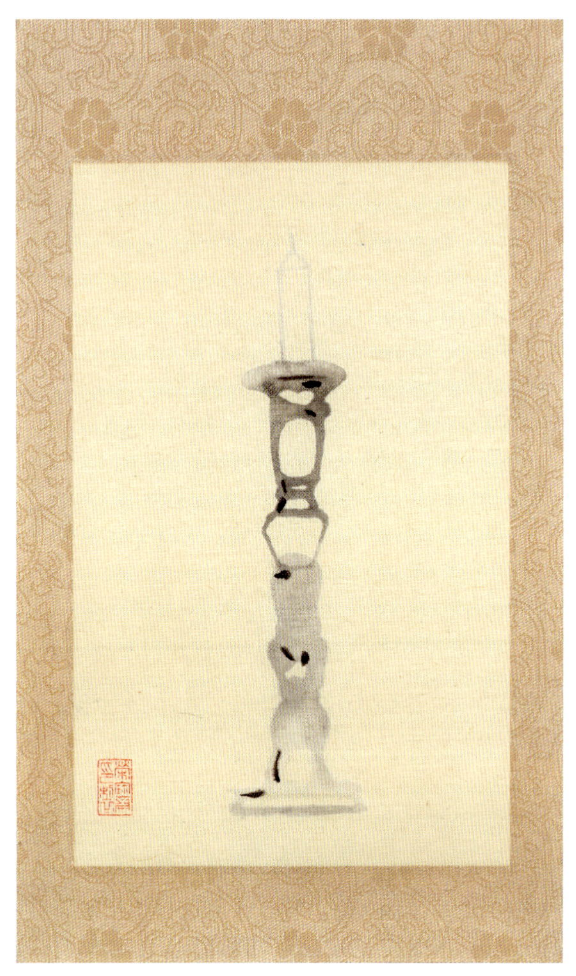

**PLATE 24**
Francesco Clemente, *The Two Flames*, 1987.
Woodcut printed on xuan zhi paper with silk
brocade border, 10¼ × 6 inches.

but instead the entire edition was printed and mounted in traditional album style with decorative silk borders. It was ready for Kathan Brown when she arrived in China in 1987 to talk about the project and negotiate bringing Clemente there to proof the work. As it turned out, Clemente loved the piece, especially the mounting, so Crown Point released it for sale in that format.

Subsequent artists in the project did travel to China for proofing. Robert Bechtle went there in 1989. Bechtle is best known for his oil painting, but he is a consummate watercolorist as well. He shows us what he sees with great economy. *Portrero Houses—Pennsylvania Avenue* (pl. 25), printed in watercolor ink from forty-two woodblocks at Rongbaozhai, shows one of his iconic street scenes as if through the windshield of a car. It is hard to believe that the fine detail in the print was carved in wood.

Bechtle did not want a brocade border on his print but at first agreed to a plain silk border all around, and the earliest proofs arrived that way. Then Bechtle realized that he preferred a mounting on Western paper, and we decided to mount all the China project prints in San Francisco on Western paper. I began by taking apart some of the prints to understand how the mounting was done. The printers at Rongbaozhai had mounted the silk on thin paper before printing, and then after printing had mounted the silk-paper laminate on more layers of the same thin backing paper and added the silk borders. I gained an appreciation of the way the materials were used in mounting, but I needed a better understanding of the process. After my trip to China in spring of 1989, I unmounted the entire Bechtle edition and remounted it on our standard Somerset paper.

On my 1989 trip, my primary goal was to learn from the scroll mounters how I could attach the woodblock prints they printed for Crown Point on extremely thin paper or silk to heavier Western papers for sale in the Western print market.

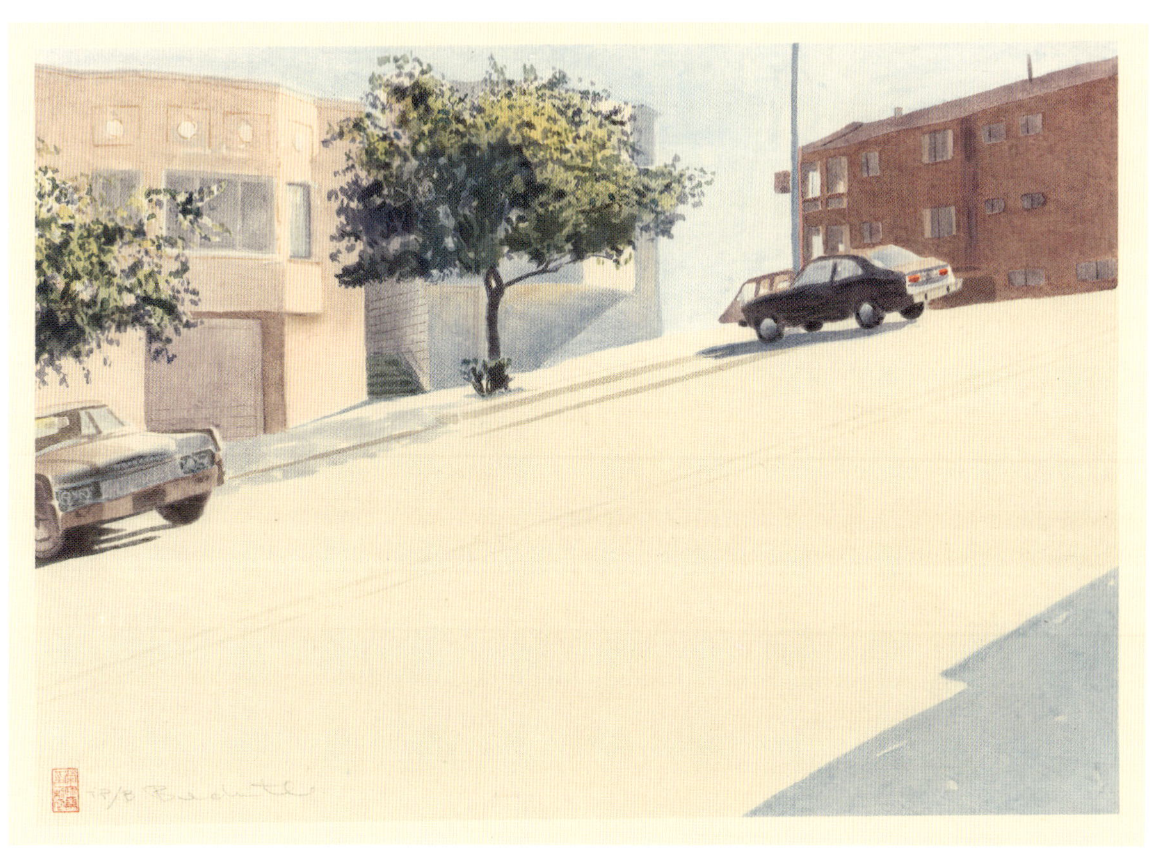



PLATE 25
Robert Bechtle, *Potrero Houses—Pennsylvania Avenue*, 1989.
Color woodcut printed on silk, 11 × 16 inches.

At the same time, however, I fell in love with the mounting process and with the aesthetic of the scroll.

The hand scroll was the original book format worldwide, and the hanging scroll, developed in eleventh century China as a means of displaying works on paper, is still widely used for that purpose in China, Korea, and Japan.

In Asia, the texts and accompanying imagery were generally printed on very thin papers. With the addition of rollers and ties, backing and fabric margins, and extra paper at the beginning and end (or top and bottom) for adding commentary and/or poetry, the printed materials became scrolls that could be easily rolled up for safe transport and storage.

The margins of a scroll are of greater thickness than the backing for the art, so the delicate surface of the artwork is suspended without touching the backing materials when the scroll is rolled. The final backing layer is lightly waxed and then burnished to flatten any loose fibers and minimize the possibility of friction. The scroll, wrapped in paper or fabric, is usually stored in two airtight boxes.

Scroll mountings can last for centuries  but are made with the premise that the work of art will be reconsolidated onto a new mounting from time to time. A minimal amount of reversible adhesive ensures that the art can be removed from the backing and safely remounted.

My direct involvement with scrolls began in the summer of 2000 at Tokugenji Press, an etching workshop and publisher in Nara, Japan, owned by Paul Mullowney, a Crown Point master printer in etching and an accomplished artist in etching and woodcut. Mullowney is now master printer and artistic director of HuiPress in Maui, Hawaii. His Tokugenji Press was located in a historic Buddhist temple in a small village that was also home to one of the best scroll mounters in Japan, Shosaku Yoshimura. When Mullowney invited me to make etchings with him, I inquired if it might be possible to present them in a scroll format. It turned out that Master Yoshimura was excited by the challenge of mounting etchings as traditional scrolls.

I began the project by making ink drawings at Ise Shrine, *Ise Jingu*, Japan's main pilgrimage site for indigenous rituals that mark nature's seasonal cycles and mankind's relationship to patterns of renewal. Then I worked at Tokugenji to re-create the drawings on etching plates.

*Naiku* (pl. 26) and *Geku* (pl. 27) are images of the Upper and Lower Shrines, dedicated to Amaturasu, the Sun Goddess, and associated with rituals for worshipping the sun and ensuring the rice harvest. The etchings are printed in silver and gold etching inks on dark aizomi gampi, a thin handmade paper dyed with natural indigo. The dye gives the paper a deep tonality, increases its strength, and imparts a crisp finish so that every nuance of the metallic inks transfers perfectly.

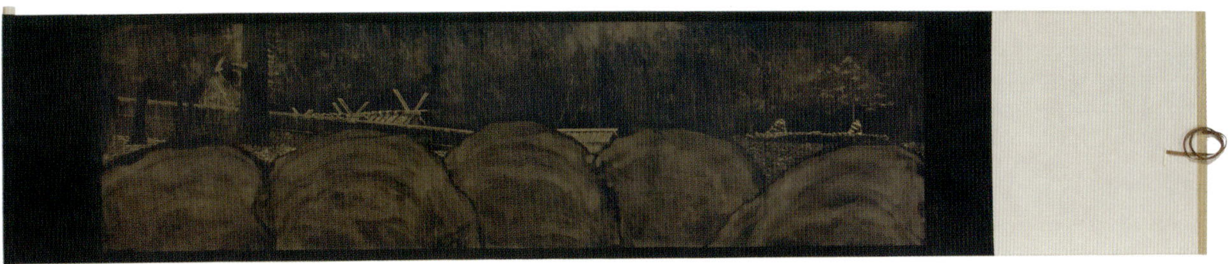

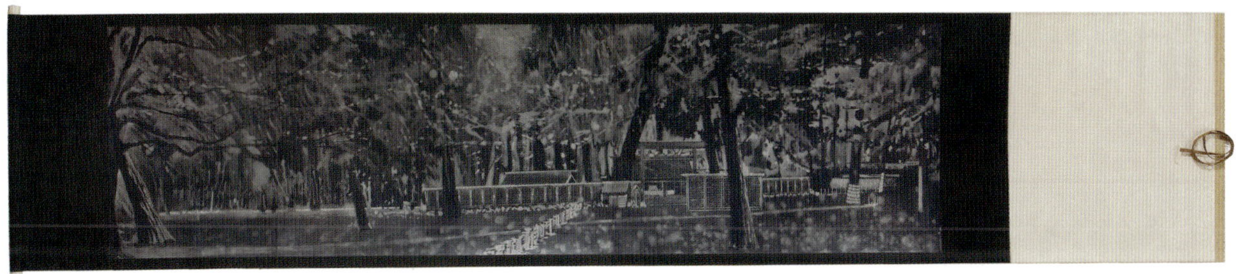

PLATE 26 (TOP)
Brian Shure, *Naiku*, 1989.
Drypoint with spit bite aquatint printed in gold on aizomi gampi paper chine
collé mounted on a handscroll, 18 × 68 inches. Published by Tokugenji Press.

PLATE 27 (BOTTOM)
Brian Shure, *Geku*, 1989.
Drypoint with spit bite aquatint printed in silver on aizomi gampi paper chine
collé mounted on a handscroll, 18 × 68 inches. Published by Tokugenji Press.

# Sizing Paper or Fabric Step-by-Step

Sizing can be made from animal- or vegetable-derived gelatins dissolved in water, and also from other materials such as emulsions—egg or milk, for example—or even solvent-based resin or varnish. Sizing is widely used to isolate paper or canvas from oil media, which are acidic and cause deterioration when in contact with cellulose fibers. Any medium that is sensitive to water, particularly watercolor and gouache, can be sized with gelatin with added alum (potassium aluminum sulphate). In Asia, the gelatin normally used for sizing is derived from the bladder of fish or from seaweed or other mucilaginous plants. I prefer rabbit skin glue because I am familiar with its characteristics from using it as sizing for canvas. Knox brand gelatin will work as well.

Sizing adds both strength and flexibility to paper, makes it more resistant to the absorption of moisture, and inhibits or prevents water-based media from spreading through the fibers. Western papers are usually sized during manufacture, normally by internal sizing, a process devised in the early nineteenth century. In internal sizing, the pulp is sized in the vat before the paper is formed. Surface sizing is added to paper by dipping sheets after they are formed and dried, then drying them again slowly under pressure. Papers termed *waterleaf* have no sizing, although they may contain almost undetectable levels of plant or animal gelatin added to the pulp to prevent clumping of the cellulose fibers and consequent uneven sheet formation. Asian papers are generally waterleaf papers, and printers using the watercolor woodblock process in Asia add sizing to the paper and in varying degrees to inks in order to prevent the colors from bleeding.

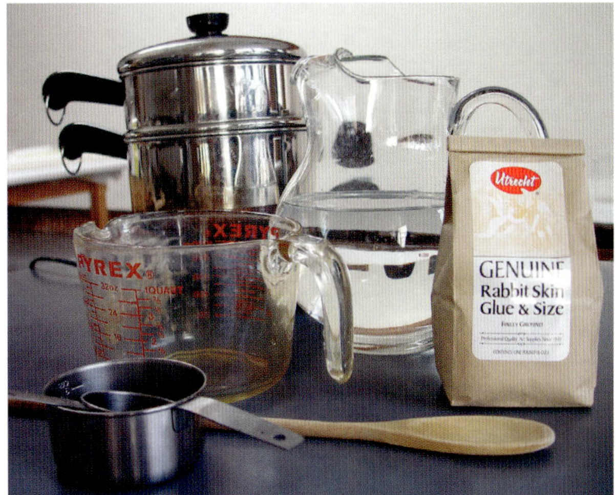

SIZING SETUP.

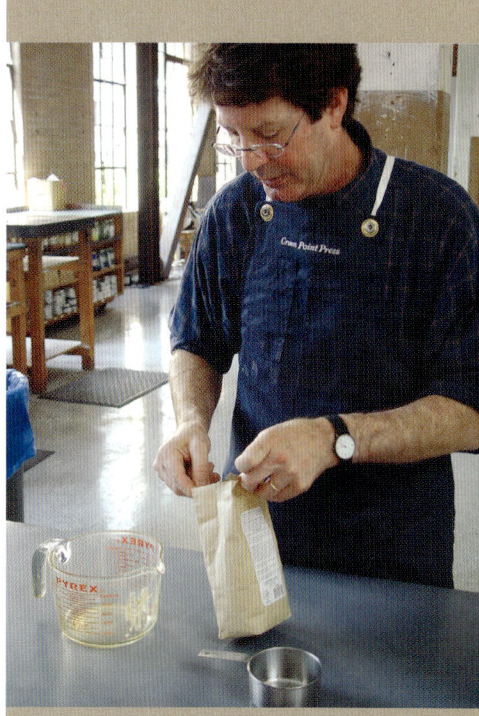

MEASURE THE GELATIN.

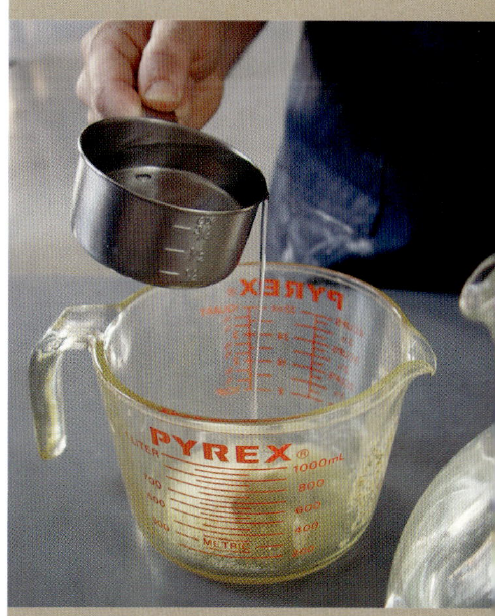

POUR WATER OVER THE GELATIN POWDER.

# Preparing Sizing for Paper or Fabric

1.  **ASSEMBLE THE MATERIALS**

    Rabbit skin glue or other gelatin powder

    Alum

    Cold water, purified if possible

    Double boiler, hotplate, and spoon for stirring

    Measuring spoon, cup, and pitcher

2.  **MIX THE GELATIN WITH WATER**

    In your measuring pitcher, stir together 1 part gelatin
    powder and about 16 parts cold water. You may need to make
    an adjustment in the formula, especially if you are not using
    rabbit skin glue. Err on the weak side if you are uncertain.

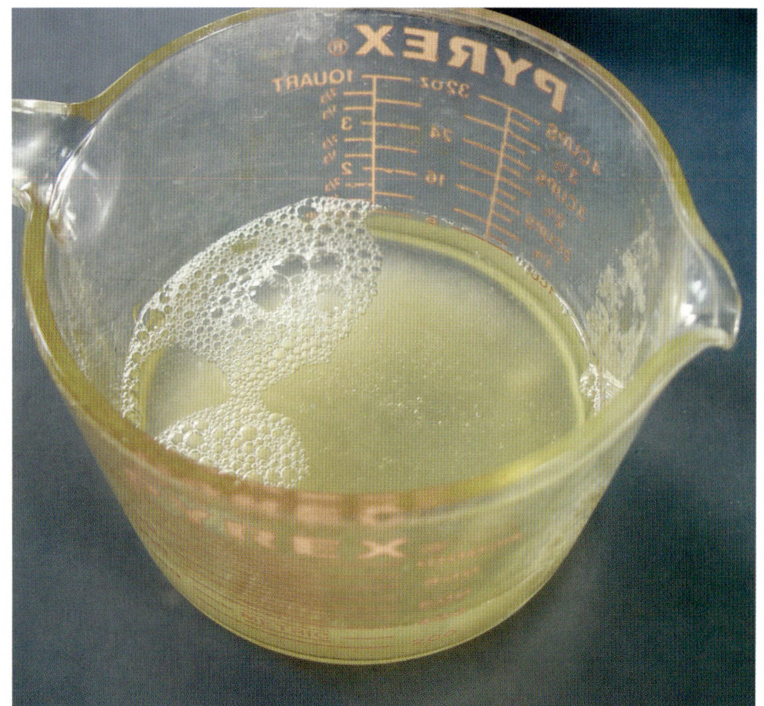



LET THE MIXTURE SIT.

USE A DOUBLE BOILER OVER LOW HEAT.

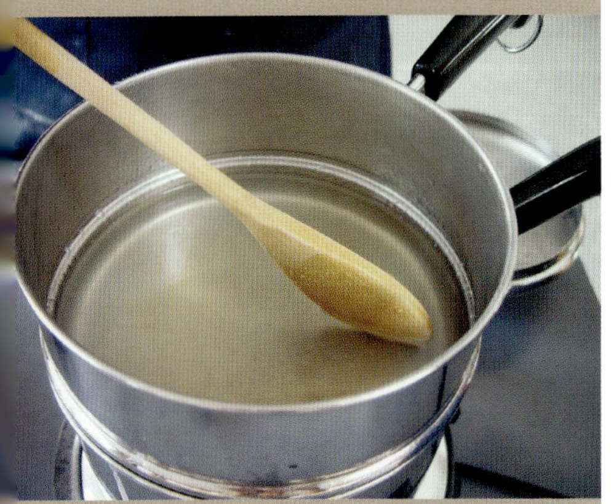

THE GELATIN LIQUEFIES AS IT WARMS.

3.  **LET THE MIXTURE SIT**

    The gelatin will not dissolve until it is heated but will swell noticeably. Let it sit at least 4 hours, or preferably overnight.

4.  **TRANSFER THE MIXTURE TO A DOUBLE BOILER**

    After the mixture has been sitting overnight, the gelatin will have swelled into a soft mass. Pour this and the water into the top of the double boiler.

5.  **HEAT SLOWLY AND STIR CONSTANTLY**

    Stir the gelatin constantly until warm and liquefied. It must never be allowed to boil.

6. **ADD THE ALUM**

   Return the liquefied gelatin to the pitcher and stir in a small quantity of alum, no more than 5 percent of the original amount of gelatin powder. If alum constitutes more than 5 percent of the gelatin, it may deteriorate the paper or fabric over time.

7. **COOL THE SIZING AT ROOM TEMPERATURE**

   The solution will turn into a soft gel but will be too weak to gel completely.

8. **STORE IN THE REFRIGERATOR**

   Prepared sizing will remain usable for weeks if you have a refrigerator that is free of mold. If mold appears, discard the sizing and prepare a fresh batch.

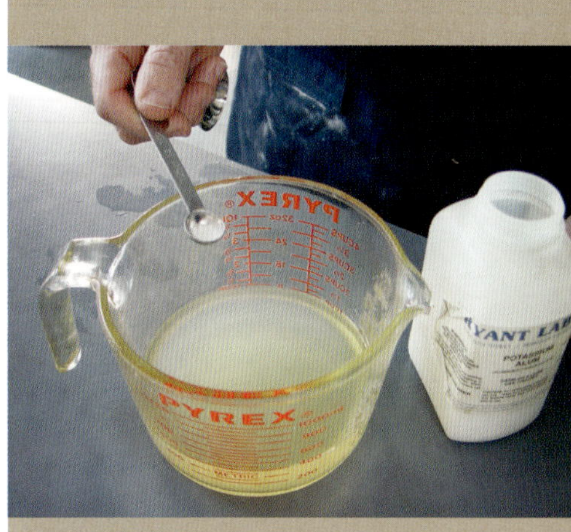

ADD ALUM TO THE LIQUEFIED GELATIN.

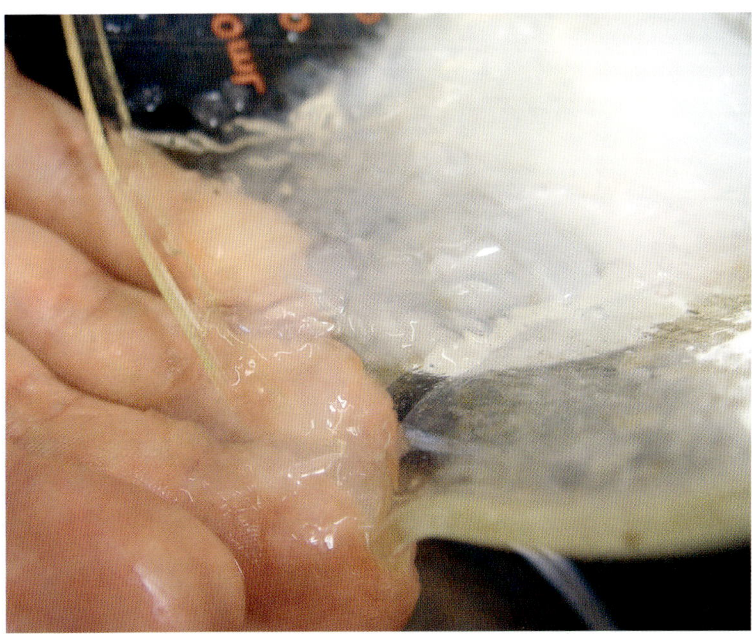

THE SIZING SHOULD ONLY PARTIALLY GEL.

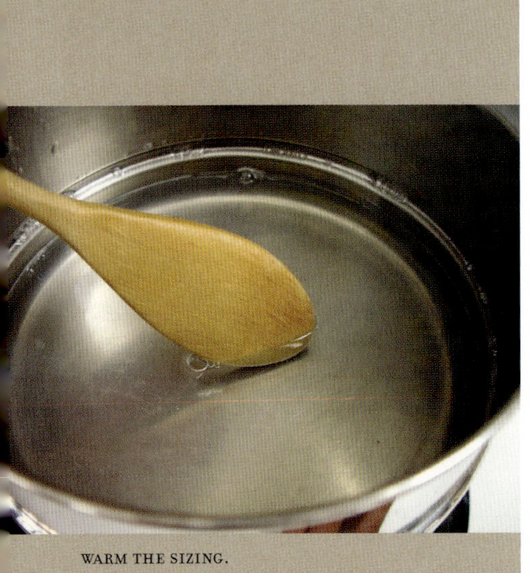

WARM THE SIZING.

A DRAWING READY TO BE SIZED.

# Applying Sizing to Paper or Fabric

1. **WARM THE SIZING**

   Using a double boiler, warm the sizing just enough to liquefy it.

2. **LAY OUT THE WORK TO BE SIZED**

   Spread tissue, unprinted newsprint, or other absorbent material down first. Place the work on top, face up.

3. **BRUSH ON A THIN LAYER OF SIZING**

   Start with an area not prominent in the work. Make long continuous brushstrokes and never stop on the image. Reload the brush with sizing each time you make a stroke. Let the sizing dry. If you see evidence of a distinct sheen on the surface, thin your sizing. Sizing should never be applied heavily enough to form a distinct layer.

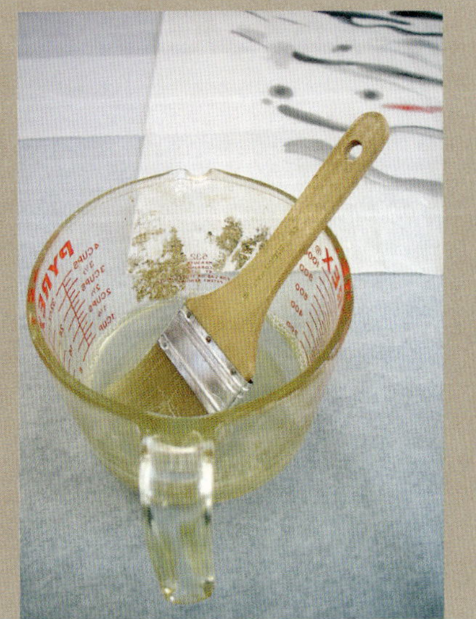

USE A CLEAN, SOFT BRUSH.

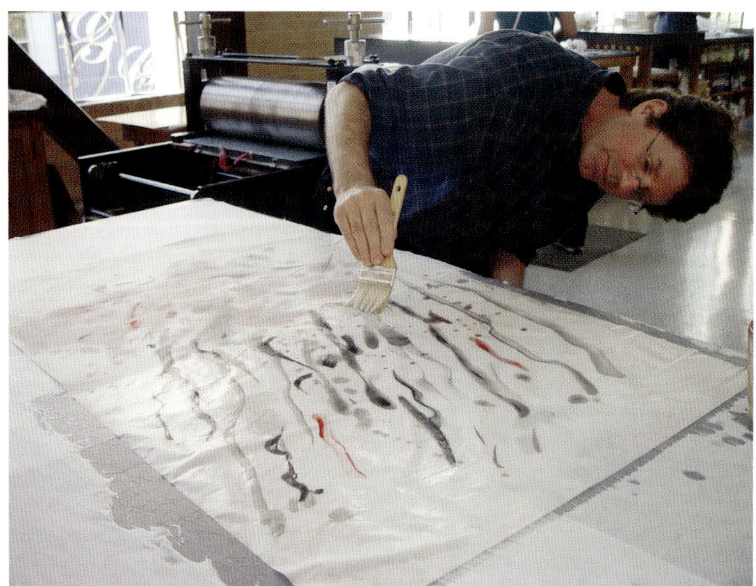

BRUSH ON THE SIZING SPARINGLY, A LAYER AT A TIME.

4.  ALLOW THE SIZING TO DRY

The sizing should be left to dry slowly.

5.  CONTINUE TO ADD THIN LAYERS OF SIZING

It is better to overlay several weak applications, allowing
complete drying in between, than to apply one thick coat. If
the work has isolated or dense areas of color, you may need
to brush additional layers over them. If the paper is already
sized but has been drawn on with unstable material, you
can brush the sizing only onto these image areas. Start
with an area you can read easily and watch for the rate of
absorption. After the first layer has dried, each subsequent
layer will be absorbed less quickly.

6.  TEST TO SEE IF YOU HAVE DONE ENOUGH

Sizing requires testing for each material used in the
artwork. Testing will help determine the strength of the
solution and how applications are needed. After one or
two applications have dried, carefully apply a drop of cold
water with the tip of a clean brush to the edge of an area of
ink or paint to determine if the color starts to bleed. Have
an absorbent towel ready to blot immediately. If the color
does not bleed, try dampening a larger area, proceeding
cautiously until you know you have used enough sizing
everywhere.

TIP *If your image is very scattered or large, it may be preferable
to spray on a fine mist of sizing instead of brushing. Use as little
as possible and always let each layer dry slowly and thoroughly
before proceeding.*

TIP *By carefully applying sizing to a charcoal or pastel drawing,
it is possible to fix the medium to the surface of the paper so it
will not dust off.*

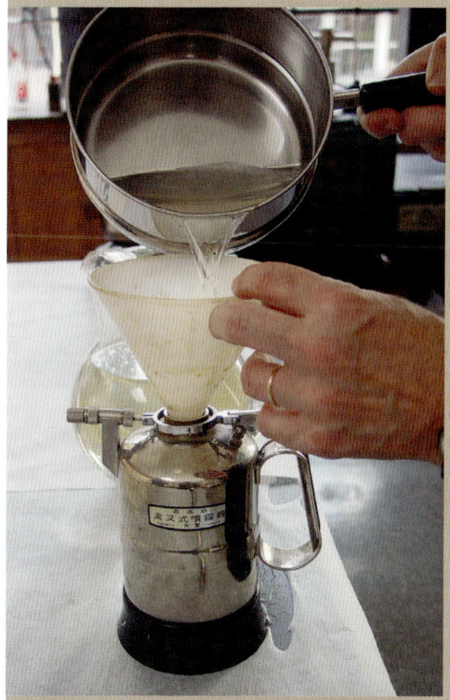

USE A PLANT SPRAYER TO MIST SIZING ONTO A LARGE
DRAWING.

# Mounting Paper or Fabric on Backing Paper Step-by-Step

Demonstrated here is the most common use of simple mounting procedures: mounting a print or drawing on a sheet of backing paper. At Crown Point Press we often mount woodcuts printed on thin paper to backing sheets, sometimes to provide margins or to facilitate display and handling. We also use this procedure to mount silk-paper laminates (on which many of our woodcuts from China were printed) on Western paper.

A layering approach is the best way to achieve dimensional stability when printing on fabric, and it also provides durability. The section concludes with notes on how to adapt the step-by-step mounting procedures to create a silk-paper laminate by mounting a piece of silk on a thin sheet of support paper. Silk-paper laminates are also available for purchase in Asian art supply houses. See www.magical-secrets.com for sources.

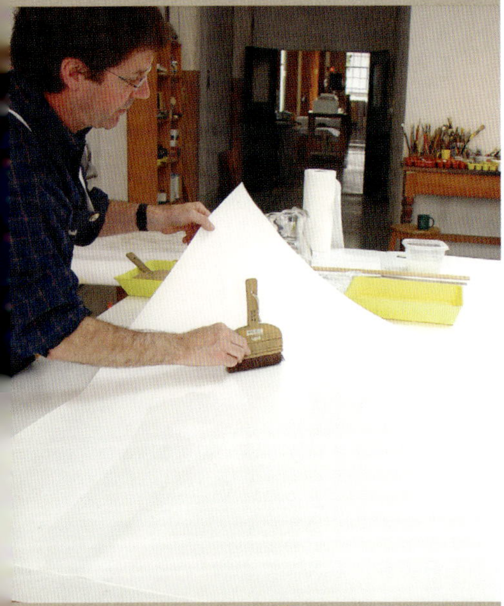

1. **DAMPEN YOUR SUPPORT PAPER**

   Best results will be had by dampening your paper a day in advance and putting it in a damp pack (see pages 44–47). Alternatively, you can brush the paper liberally with water, blot it, and wrap it in plastic until you are ready to use it.

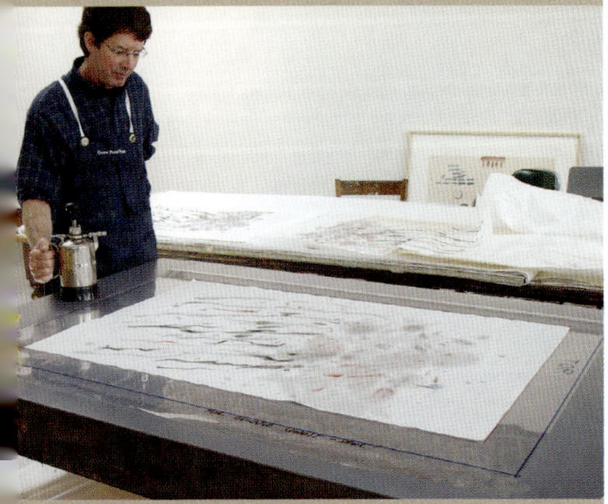

2. **MAKE A REGISTRATION TEMPLATE**

   Lay a sheet of clear Mylar on a smooth-topped table (Formica or something similar) and mark it with guidelines for placing the image sheet and the backing sheet so the margins of the mounted work will be correct. Turn the template over so the markings are against the table, and then place the art to be mounted face down on the template.

BRUSH WATER ON THE SUPPORT PAPER IF YOU HAVE NOT PREPARED A DAMP PACK.

MAKE A REGISTRATION TEMPLATE AND PLACE THE ART (IN THIS CASE A DRAWING BY PAT STEIR) ON IT FACE DOWN.

3.  SPRAY THE ART WITH A FINE WATER MIST

Spray evenly but do not soak the sheet. Wait a moment for
it to relax.

4.  APPLY A THIN LAYER OF PASTE

Brush outward from the center, gently pushing any large
wrinkles toward the edge.

5.  CLEAN THE EXPOSED MYLAR WITH A DAMP CLEAN CLOTH OR
SPONGE

It is important to completely remove all paste from the
template and the table.

6.  SET THE SUPPORT SHEET IN PLACE

Use your template as a guide. Gently smooth down the
support paper.

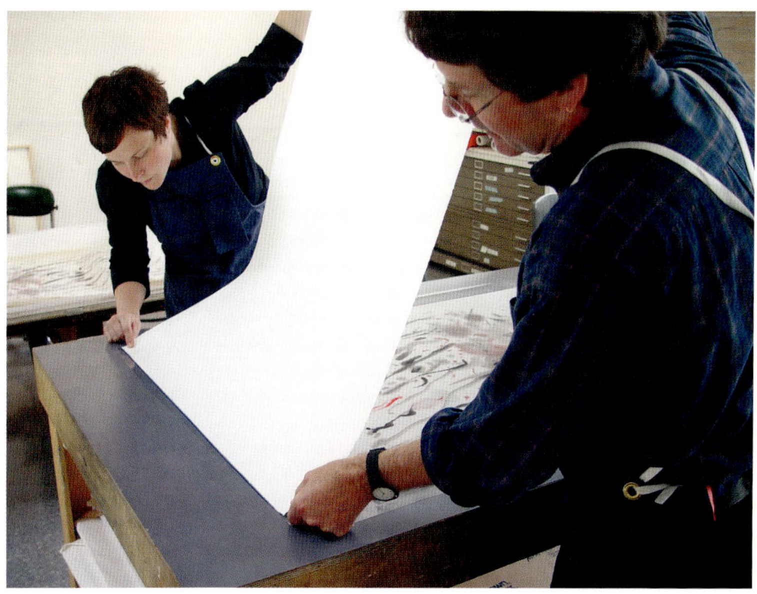

LINE UP THE SUPPORT PAPER TO THE EDGE OF THE MYLAR.

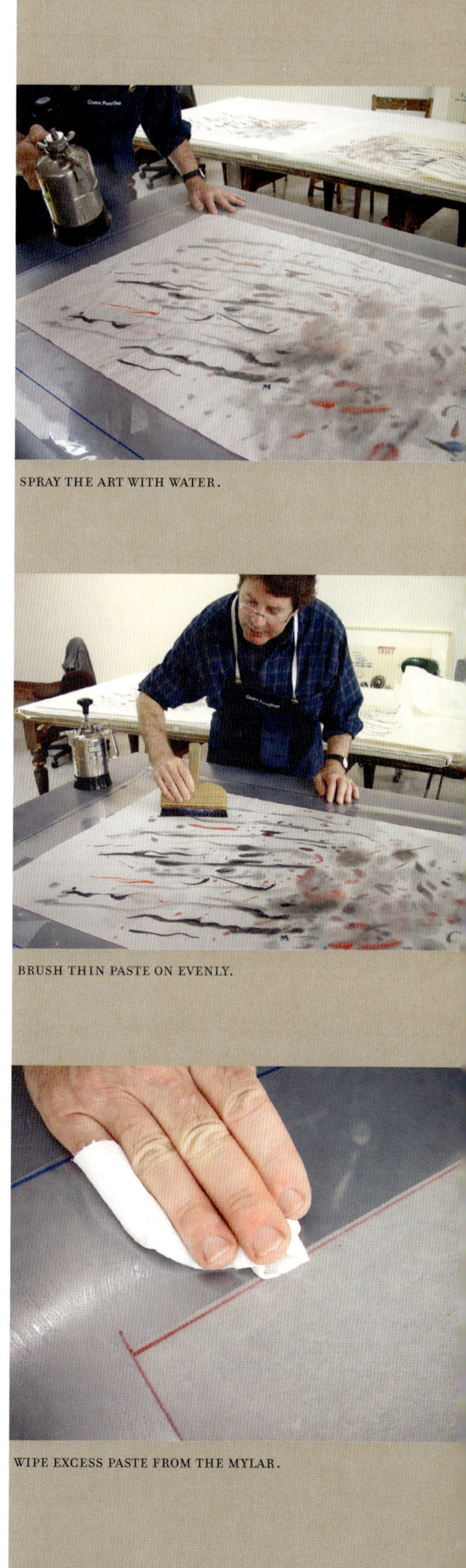

SPRAY THE ART WITH WATER.

BRUSH THIN PASTE ON EVENLY.

WIPE EXCESS PASTE FROM THE MYLAR.

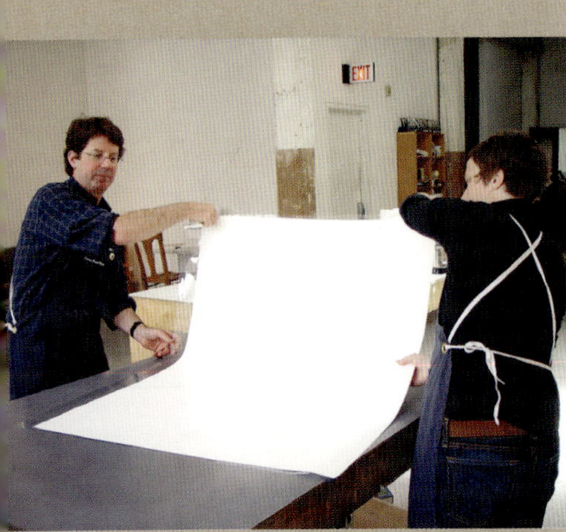

TURN THE SHEETS OVER.

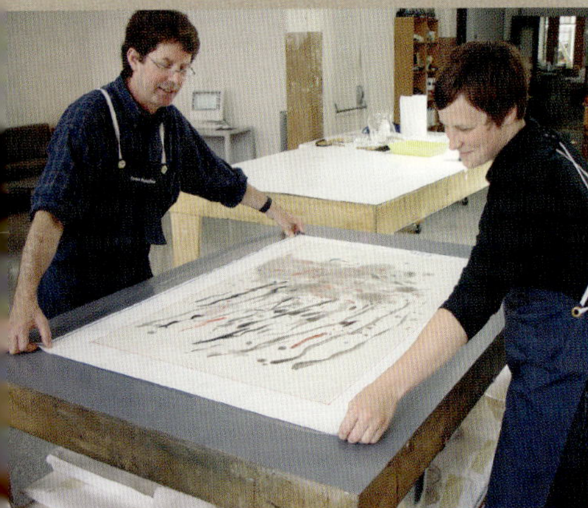

THE MYLAR IS NOW THE TOP LAYER.

7. **FLIP THE SHEETS SO THAT THE MYLAR IS ON TOP**
Start by reaching under to be sure the three sheets will come up together. The paste will not have much strength until it dries.

8. **MAKE SEVERAL PADS FOR APPLYING PRESSURE**
Fold sheets of tissue paper into themselves, similar to making a tarlatan pad for wiping etchings.

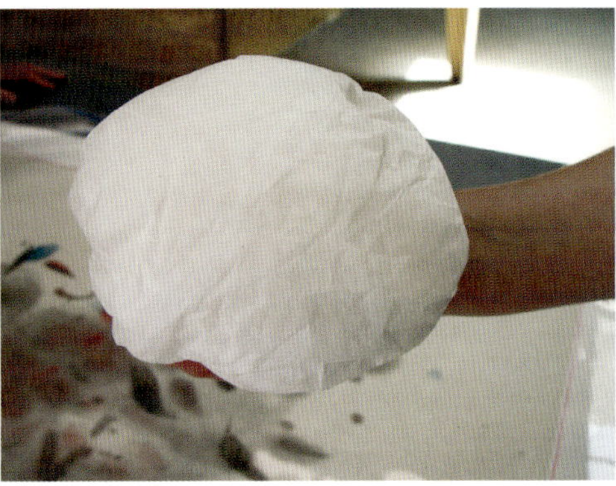

MAKE A PAD FROM TISSUE PAPER.

9. **WORK A PAD OVER THE SURFACE OF THE MYLAR, PRESSING OUT AIR**
If there are any bubbles, gently work them to the corners. You can lift a corner if necessary and press it back down.

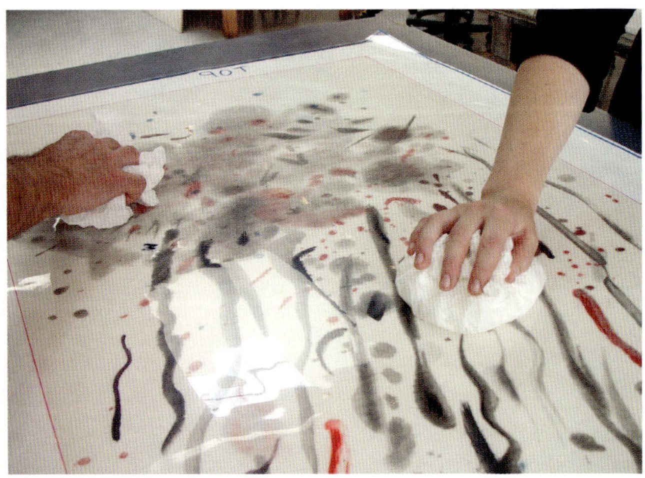

PRESS DOWN WITH TISSUE PADS ON TOP OF THE MYLAR.

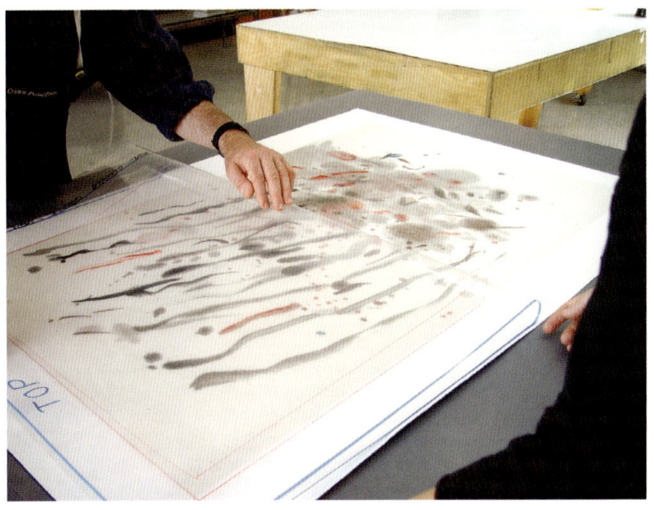

PEEL BACK THE MYLAR.

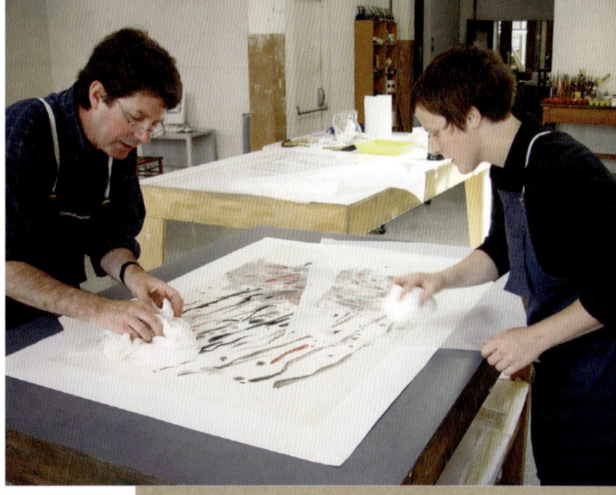

BLOT THE IMAGE WITH TISSUE PAPER.

### 10. REMOVE THE MYLAR

Peel it back slowly.

### 11. BLOT THE ART

Use flat sheets of tissue and continue applying pressure
with a tissue pad. Use a fresh pad if the one you are using
becomes wet.

TIP *If small wrinkles remain, gently press the air toward the*
*edges of the sheet.*

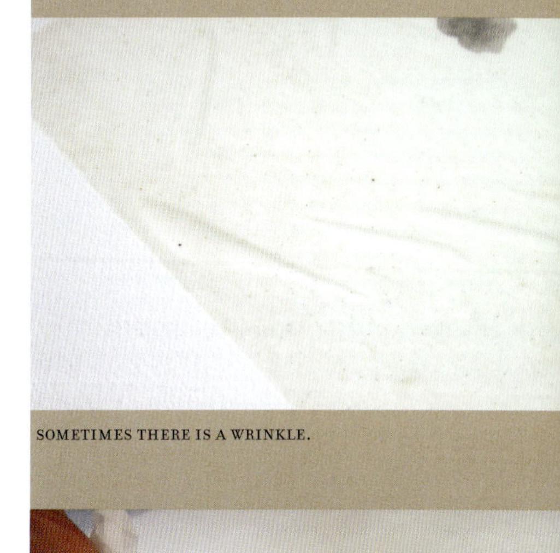

SOMETIMES THERE IS A WRINKLE.

NO MORE WRINKLE.

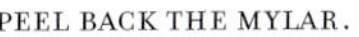

BLOT OUT THE WRINKLE BY PLACING A SHEET OF TISSUE
OVER IT AND PRESSING THE AIR TO THE EDGES.

12. **DRY THE MOUNTED ARTWORK**

Use one of the methods described in chapter 7.
A forced-air dryer is ideal.

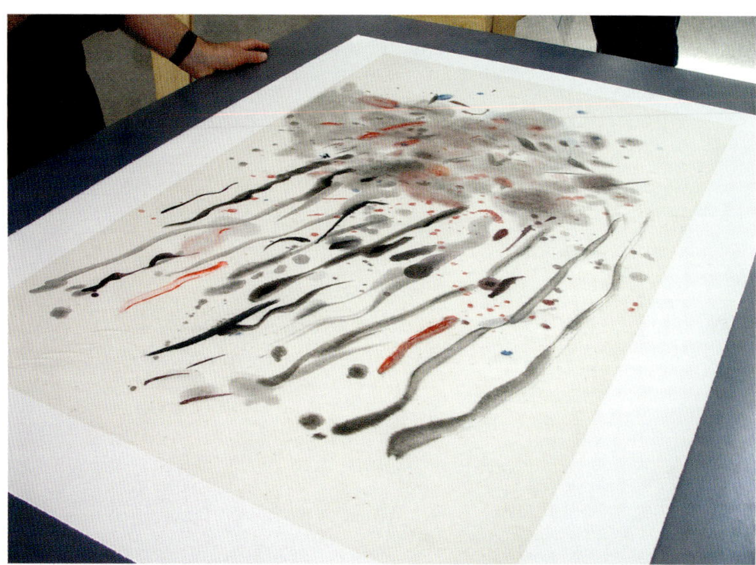

THE MOUNTED DRAWING, PAT STEIR'S WATERCOLOR ON CHINESE PAPER.

# Notes on Creating a Silk-Paper Laminate

You can adapt the procedure described above to mount a piece of silk or other fabric on a paper backing sheet. Thin Asian papers are preferred, and it is best to orient the grain of the paper and the fabric in opposite directions. When you wet the silk, completely saturate it and pull at the edges until it lies flat. Then adjust the warp and weft threads until they run straight in both directions.

After applying a very thin coat of paste, cut off any extraneous threads that pulled away from the edges.

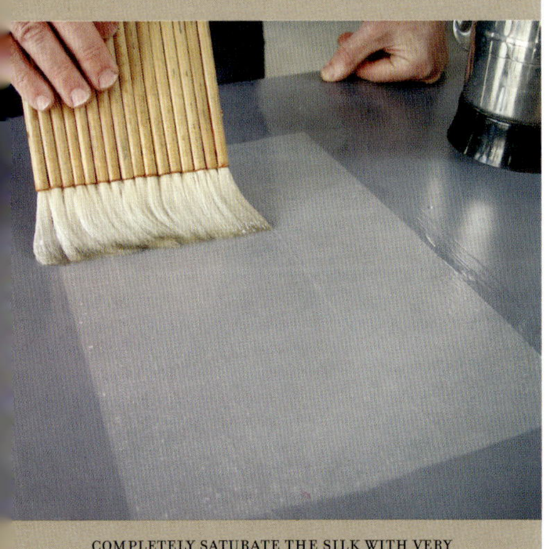

COMPLETELY SATURATE THE SILK WITH VERY THIN PASTE.

To position the backing paper on the silk, roll up a sheet of backing paper with the rough side facing out. This is the side that will be in contact with the silk. Place its leading edge (the beginning of your roll) on the work surface—aligning it with the silk but overhanging it to allow a margin all around. Then unroll the backing paper onto the pasted silk. At the same time, brush the paper down with a stiff brush. Unroll the paper evenly while brushing it so that it is in contact with the silk before it has had a chance to expand enough to wrinkle.

Brush the back of the paper gently but firmly in all directions until it becomes translucent and flat. After you have dried the paper, trim the edges of the silk and paper together cleanly with a sharp blade.

# A Simplified Introduction to Scroll Mounting

The process of mounting a print or a drawing on a scroll, though relatively simple and using only a few materials, involves hundreds of steps. The drying is traditionally done on boards that look simple but are complex devices for evening out moisture across the surface of the pasted material. Each board is a latticework of wood with a frame all around. The latticework is covered by seven separate layers, each made by overlapping small sheets of different papers. Care is taken to alternate the grain of the papers in the layers, and many of the small sheets overlap like roof tiles, with paste applied only to the edges.

Thicker and thinner pastes are used on the front and back edges of different layers of the boards. Before the final layers are applied, slits are made at the corners into the airspace between the lattices. This complex construction is calibrated to wick moisture into the airspace between the papers on the

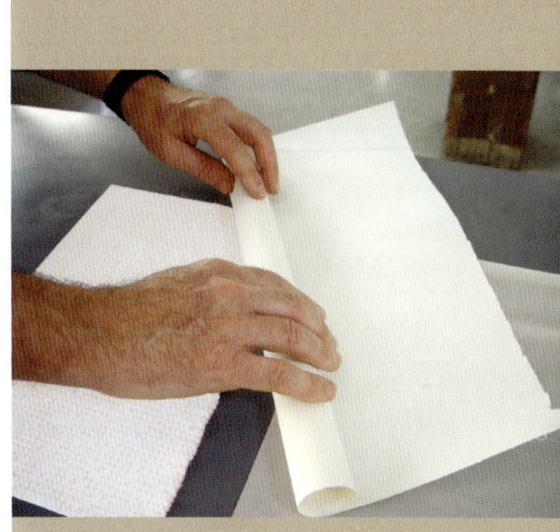

ROLL UP A SHEET OF BACKING PAPER.

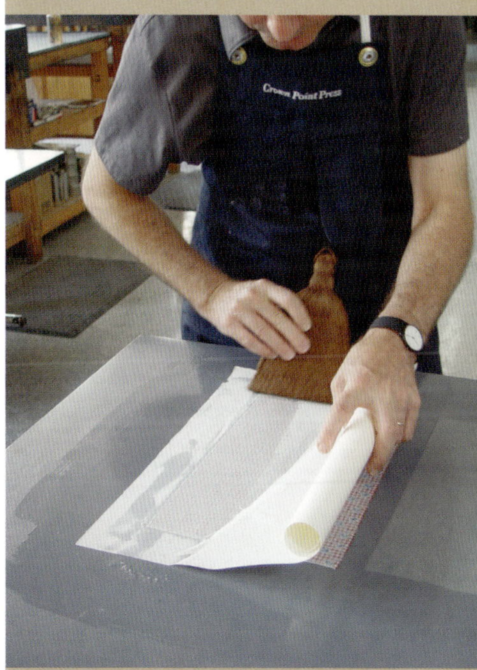

UNROLL THE PAPER AND BRUSH IT DOWN AT THE SAME TIME.

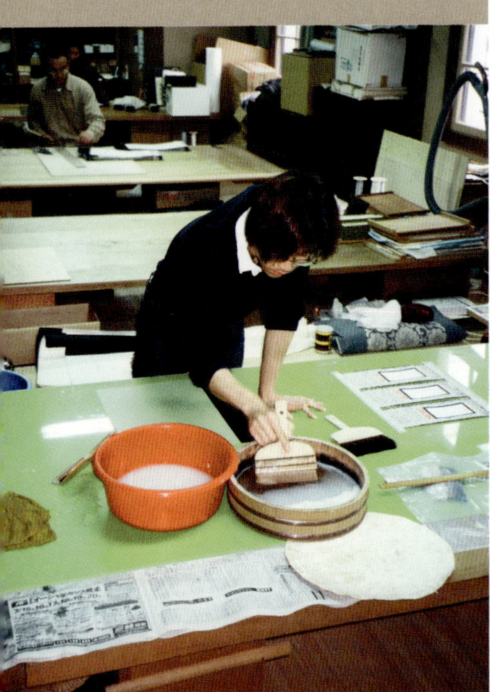

Scroll mounting studio, Kyoto.

front and back of a dryer board, and then to slowly and evenly release it back through the materials pasted down on the surface. Consequently, the tension between different materials making up the scroll releases slowly until the tension evens. Rapid drying would work against this principle. The boards are placed in close proximity to one another to trap the moisture between them and slow the drying process as much as possible.

Allowing for proper drying time for each pasting step necessarily extends the making of a scroll over several months. In traditional studios, no work is attempted during August, the hottest and most humid month, but in a studio with modern air-conditioning and dehumidifiers, drying periods are often shortened. Nevertheless, the backing of the completed scroll is usually left pasted to the drying board from three months to a year before finishing, which includes adding rollers, end knobs, straps for hanging and closure, and the label. The long drying period allows the scroll to go through many cycles of temperature and humidity changes during which it adjusts and evens out enough that it will not become buckled through decades or even centuries of storage, and through cycles of opening and closing with attendant periods of exposure to changes in humidity and temperature. Traditional scroll mounting procedures were developed with these long-term goals in mind.

For centuries, mounting facilities have existed in or near monasteries. The photograph on this page shows a mounting studio on the grounds of Higashi Honganji in Kyoto. It is still in use for mounting Buddhist images and prayers for the Jodo-Shinshu sect.

# Secret #5. UNUSUAL PROJECTS USING MOUNTING AND COLLÉ TECHNIQUES

*Take one step at a time.*

In this chapter, I describe unusual projects by Judy Pfaff and Richard Tuttle at Crown Point Press and Julie Mehretu at Highpoint Editions in Minneapolis, as well as two projects by Robert Kushner, one at HuiPress in Hawaii and the other at Brand X Editions in New York City. I also include a portfolio of young artists' work, from the Rhode Island School of Design where I teach. In the step-by-step section of this chapter, you will find guidelines for working with collage without a press and production illustrations of Mehretu's project and of dry mounting at Pace Editions showing the procedure used for Kushner's Brand X project. The art in this chapter moved into uncharted territories and was developed one step at a time.

One step at a time is the secret to successfully approaching nearly anything that is unknown or complex. Some of the projects in this chapter were extremely complicated, requiring innovation and careful planning. The printers respected the limitations of the materials they were using but didn't ignore the consequences of their actions. If you must get the print very wet at one stage, for example, it might become extremely weak and need to be handled on a sheet of Mylar or other backing material.

In 1987 Judy Pfaff did a project at Crown Point composed of six extremely large woodcuts, each with many individually pasted parts. The final assembly of each print took place over a period of weeks and seemed at times to be beyond control. Instead of being overwhelmed, however, we focused each moment on getting the part we were working on to function as perfectly as possible. In the end, each incremental step of the assembly was simple enough that the failure rate overall was very low. The key was careful planning of each step so it was simple enough to work reliably.

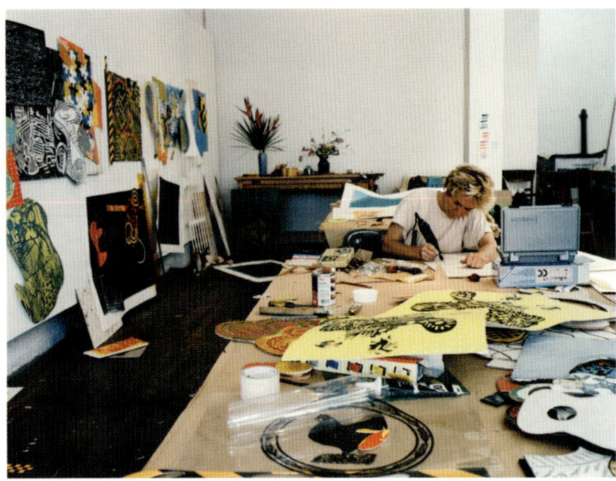

Without doubt, Judy Pfaff's way of making art is intensely physical, but it is important to understand that her approach is extremely thoughtful as well. The motions involved in drawing, carving, and building measure Pfaff's relation to the world around her. Whether she is working on delicate drypoints printed on feathery gampi paper, massive sculptural installations of glass, wood, and steel, or a series of composite woodblock prints, Pfaff is always working dynamically. Her finished pieces record her process of discovery and illustrate energy released by attending to the world.

In 1987 Pfaff transformed Crown Point's etching studio into a woodworking shop for nearly a month. Aided by master printer Larry Hamlin and three assistant printers (including myself), Pfaff carved and shaped hundreds of individual pieces. She had the printers proof them in a variety of colors and cut up the proofs so she could arrange and rearrange the elements on the studio floor and walls.

The elements eventually coalesced into the series of woodcuts titled *Six of One*. Because the images were composed of pieces on the wall, rather than on a block or plate, several ended up being larger than our largest press could accommodate. *Melone* (pl. 28) is printed from about sixty woodblocks, and the paper size is 55 by 63 inches. We printed *Melone* in two sections and pieced the sections together afterward with some additional shapes pasted onto the surface.

We premoistened the sections in the same damp pack so they would react evenly to the paste. Because it was nearly impossible to move the joined sections before the paste had set up, two of Crown Point's large forced-air dryers were positioned side by side, and the sections were aligned across the two dryers and pasted as they were loaded into them.

Richard Tuttle's *Naked IX* (pl.29), in contrast to Pfaff's print, is simple. It is a sublime example of this artist's delicate touch. Process and materials are clearly exposed: the bright

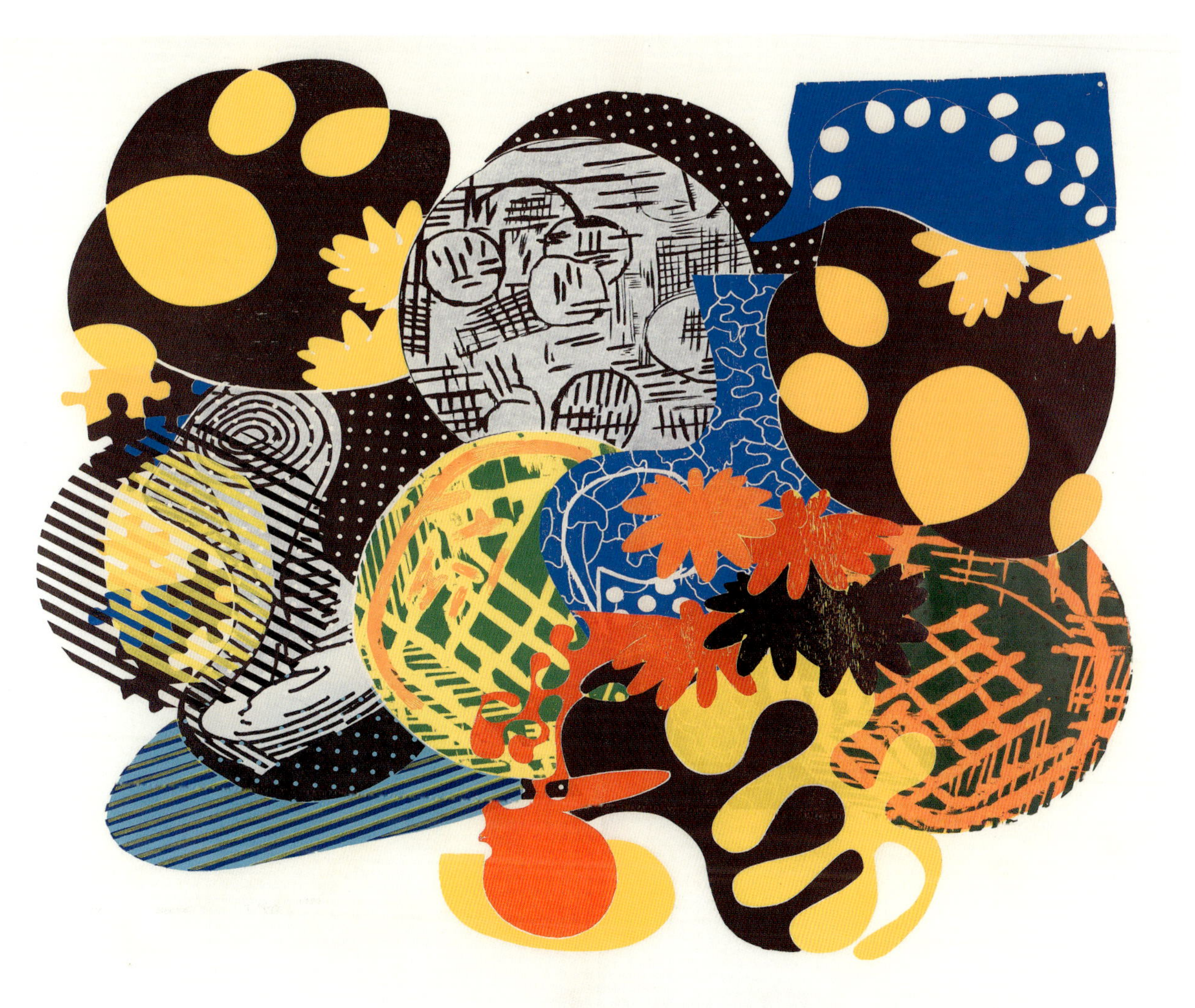



PLATE 28
Judy Pfaff, *Six of One—Melone*, 1987.
Color woodcut with collaged elements, 55 × 63 inches.

e/10
NAKED IX
RT 04

green gampi paper hangs loose, and the printed image is partly obscured. Rachel Fuller was the Crown Point master printer in charge of the 2004 project in which Tuttle created a group of ten *Naked* prints. Fuller told me that in printing *Naked IX*, the printers first folded the hosho support sheet in half horizontally and laid it on the press bed over the inked plate holding the crayonlike image. Then they applied wheat starch paste to a shaped piece of green gampi paper across its top and down the upper half of its straight side. They positioned it against the top and one side of the folded hosho paper—the gampi extended below the fold. They ran the papers and plate through the press, simultaneously printing the image and adhering the papers.

While the print was still folded and on the press, the printers applied black ink mixed with turpentine to the back using a nubbed hairbrush. This ink stained through to the front. In each of two applications, the black ink created a strong oval-shaped mark and a weaker one where the stain continued into the part of the sheet that was below the fold. The print was then unfolded and white acrylic gesso was applied with the hairbrush to the face of the print on the lower half of the gampi. Each step is distinctly recorded in the completed print, and each in some way heightens our awareness of the tactile qualities of the materials. The materials startle us in the clean, naked clarity of the presentation.

Over the past thirty-five years, Tuttle has steadily refined his vocabulary of materials defined by their lack of presence— by what they are not, how few of them there are, and the way they emphasize the space around them. His work is powerful, often to the point of making people quickly walk away, perhaps from fear of the emptiness conjured by the delicate works. Tuttle is telling us to pay attention to every simple thing around us—to its beauty and distinct qualities. This is the world he offers if we can take the time to share it with him.

PLATE 29 (OPPOSITE)
Richard Tuttle, *Naked IX*, 2004.
Color soft ground etching with hand staining on hosho paper with gampi paper chine collé,
27 × 20 inches.

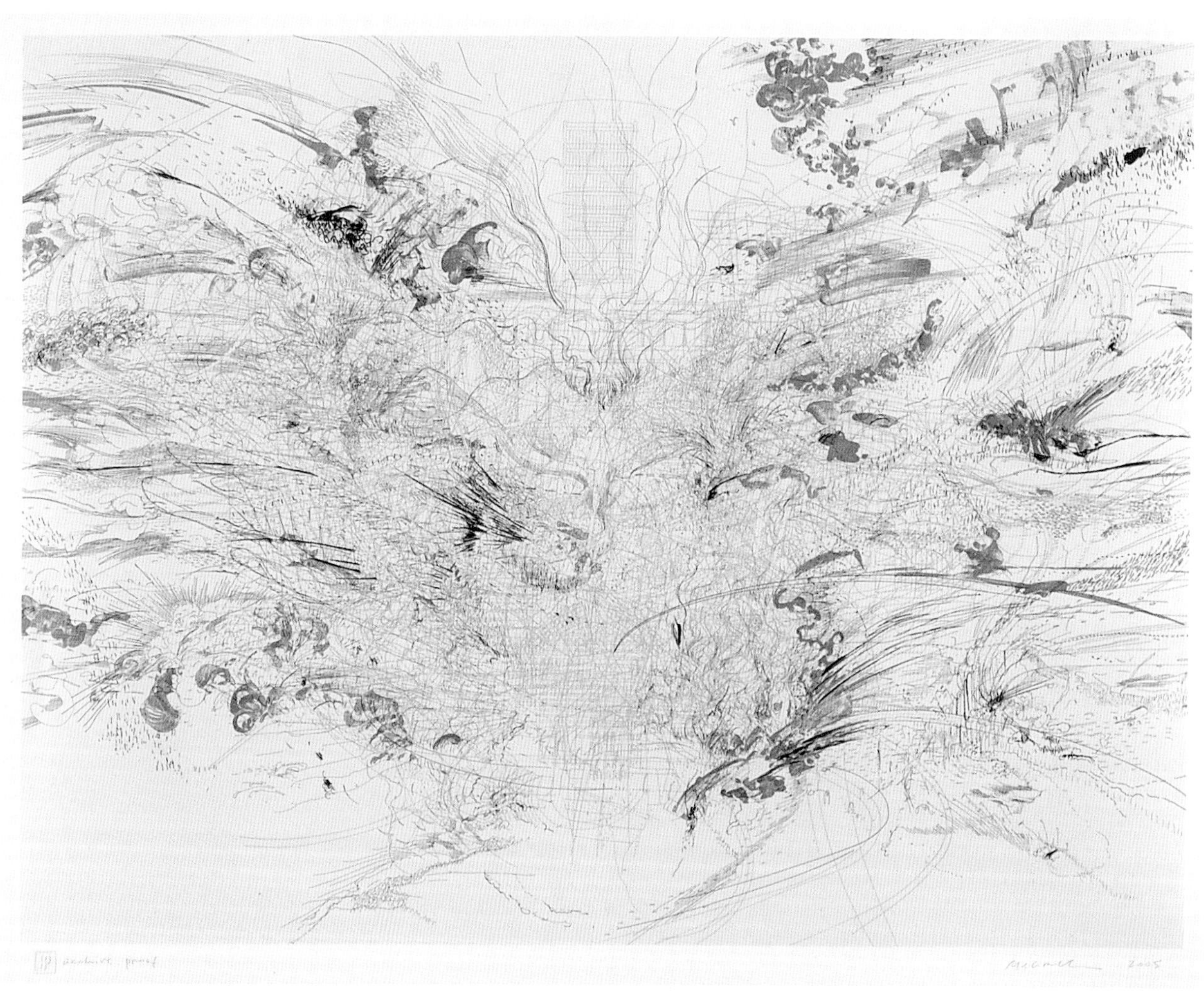



PLATE 30
Julie Mehretu, *Entropia: Construction*, 2005.
Lithograph printed on gampi paper chine collé, 29½ × 39¾ inches.
Published by Highpoint Editions.

Tuttle questions everything, including the steps of the printing process. In this case, we can see simple yet significant disruptions to conventional printing and collé processes and therefore understand more clearly not just this image, but the way all prints are made.

The pasting processes described throughout this book are generally derived from the scroll mounting process, but Julie Mehretu's *Entropia: Construction* (pl. 30), published in 2005 by Highpoint Editions in cooperation with the Walker Art Center, inventively adapts scroll mounting techniques to contemporary ends.

Mehretu creates her energetic large paintings with layers of marks. They are symbols for things in the world that matter to her: places she has been and ideas about the way people live and interact in space.  Her work sometimes includes diagrammatic marks that map specific cities, or refer to architectural plans for fortifications or large public spaces, but they are accompanied and overlaid by personal marks and do not read specifically.

During a 2003 residency at the Walker Art Center in Minneapolis, Mehretu worked with Highpoint Editions director and master printer Cole Rogers to create *Entropia (review)*, a large lithograph with silkscreen additions. Two years later, she returned to make *Entropia: Construction*, which involved printing four sheets of tissue-thin gampi, pasting the sheets one over the other, and mounting them on Somerset paper. Each of the first three sheets was printed from a plate used for the earlier work; the fourth was from a new plate. The result was a new and complex image. Details about assembling the print are in the step-by-step section.

Robert Kushner's *Night Blooming Cereus* (pls. 31 and 32) is a series of thirty-five unique prints all printed from a single plate on various combinations of antique kimono fabric. Kushner has been collecting kimonos for years, compiling a large library of patterns that he has used in several prints as well as in paintings and drawings. *Night Blooming Cereus* was done in Hawaii at HuiPress, located in the Hui No'eau Visual Arts Center in Maui.

Kushner was attracted to the night-blooming cereus found in profusion on the roads surrounding the center. The plant's large flowers open at dusk, each for only one night. If you sit quietly, you can see their movement. While driving home from dinner late one night, Kushner picked one of the notoriously delicate flowers and sketched it in the studio before it wilted. He drew his image as a sugar lift aquatint on a single plate.

The printers began the project by taking apart kimonos that Kushner had brought with him. For each printing, two different pieces, selected at random, were laid side by side on the inked plate and run through the press. The fabric was printed without a support sheet, so each press run yielded two separate printed pieces of fabric. This allowed a mix-and-match approach, and Kushner recombined the pieces, selecting pairs that would work well together.  Then the printers aligned the two parts of each pair, leaving about 1/8-inch overlap. The fabrics were joined with stiff starch paste, using the joining brush called the *Tsukemawashibake*, and left to dry naturally.

The joined swatches printed with Kushner's image were backed with two layers of support paper using mounting techniques that Paul Mullowney, director of HuiPress, learned from Shosaku Yoshimura in Ouda, Japan. The support paper is a thin kozo paper called hadaura, often used for mounting ink paintings on scrolls. The first layer was left to dry naturally, and the second was pasted down to drying boards to dry flat. When dry, the prints were removed from the boards and sent to Kushner to add gold and silver leaf.

Kushner used acrylic sizing on the areas that would carry the gold and silver leaf, and Mullowney told me that this caused wrinkling, so a third layer of support paper was added after Kushner returned the prints to the shop. The prints were again dried on boards. The printers then trimmed the edges and laid each edge flush with a table edge and brushed it with a bit of stiff starch paste to prevent the fabric from unraveling.

Robert Kushner made *Red Hibiscus* (pl. 33) with Brand X Editions in Manhattan. This screenprinting shop works with artists using traditional hand-drawn and hand-cut separations to prepare emulsion stencils on the screens. Kushner's edition of unique prints also incorporates two or more pieces of antique kimono silk behind the printed image.

Printer Steven Sangenario adhered the silk to the backing paper before printing, using a dry mounting procedure. He began by cutting the silk pieces slightly larger than needed and sandwiching them between sheets of silicon release paper with an adhesive film on the back. He then melted the film onto the fabric in a dry mounting press.

After the adhesive film had cooled and resolidified, Sangenario cut the excess film away and neatly trimmed the edges. Backing paper adhered with film like the one used in this project has a tendency to curl because the film is

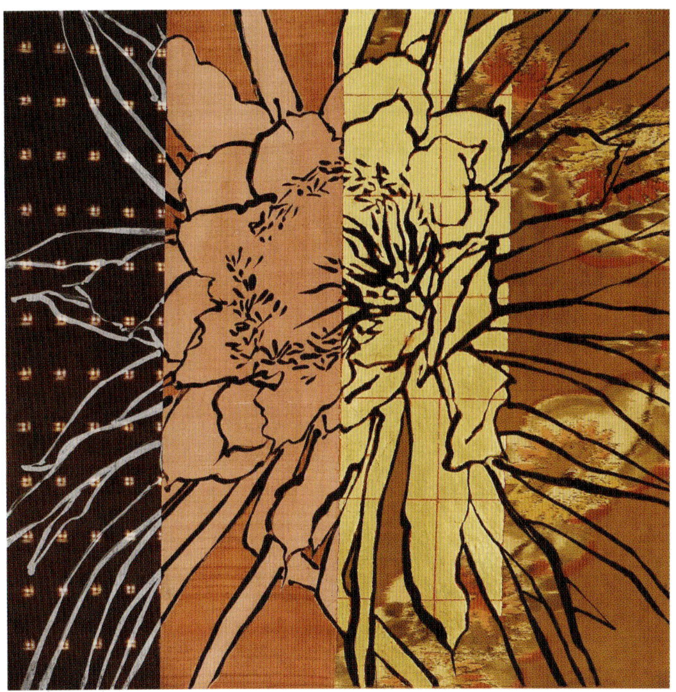

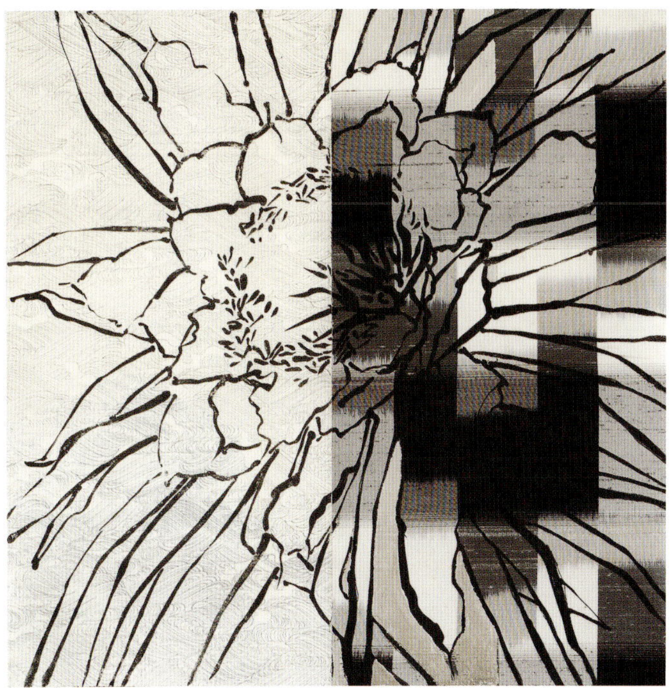


Robert Kushner, *Night Blooming Cereus XXIV*, 2006.
Sugar lift aquatint printed on antique kimono silk
with gold leafing, 24 × 24 inches. Published by
HuiPress.


Robert Kushner, *Night Blooming Cereus IV*, 2006.
Sugar lift aquatint printed on antique kimono silk
with palladium leafing, 24 × 24 inches. Published
by HuiPress.

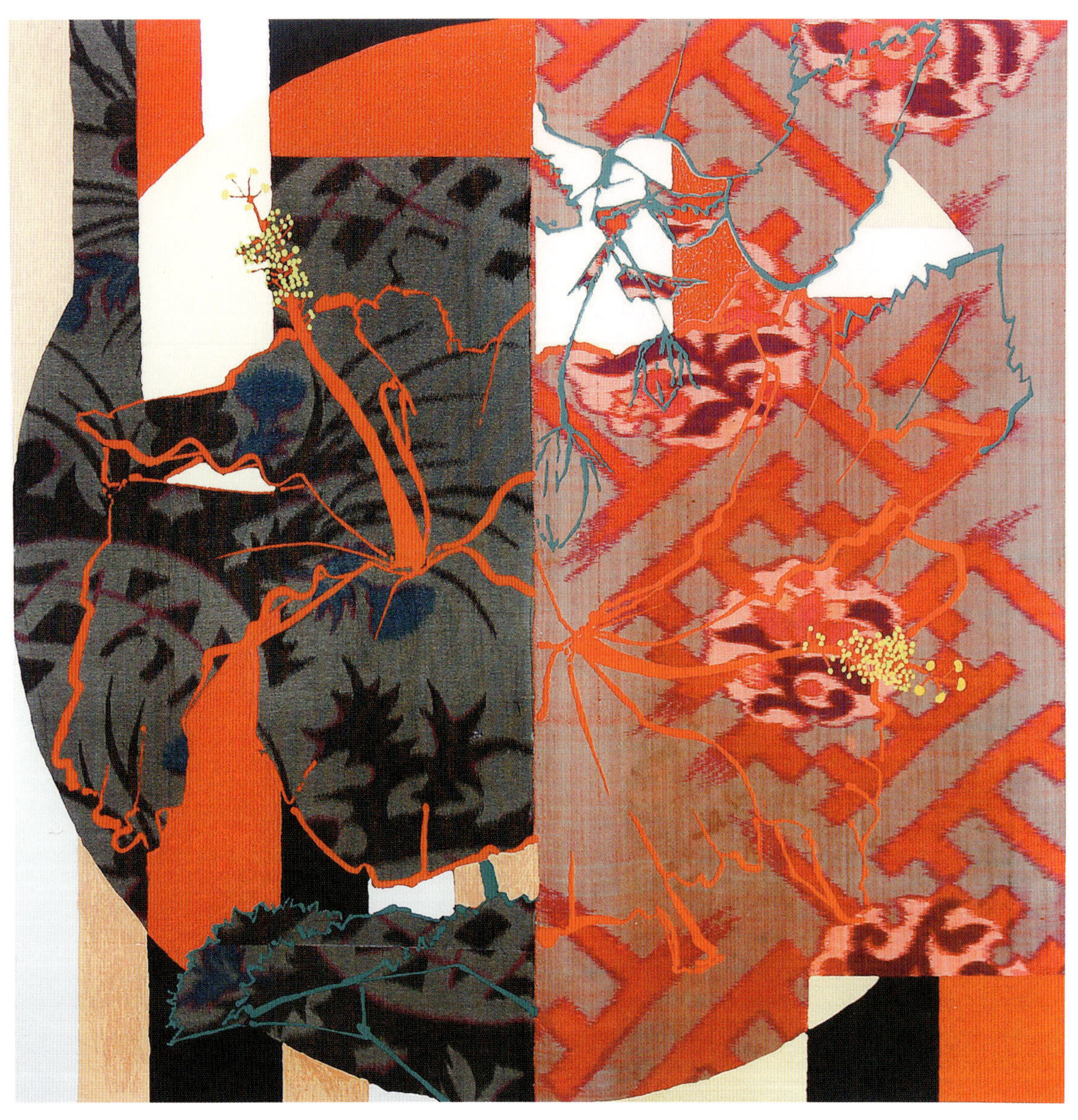

PLATE 33
Robert Kushner, *Red Hibiscus XXVII*, 2007.
Screenprint on antique Japanese fabric, 28 × 28 inches.
Published by the artist.

impervious to moisture. Once the fabric is adhered, tension
is set up between it and the backing, and every change in
humidity alters that tension and consequently can cause
curl. For this reason, Sangenario chose a heavy paper for the
backing. In the step-by-step section, you will find photographs
of this dry mounting process along with a detailed description.

To conclude this chapter, I present a portfolio of five works
by young artists who worked with chine collé techniques as
students at the Rhode Island School of Design and extended
the techniques in ambitious and inventive ways.

# Portfolio

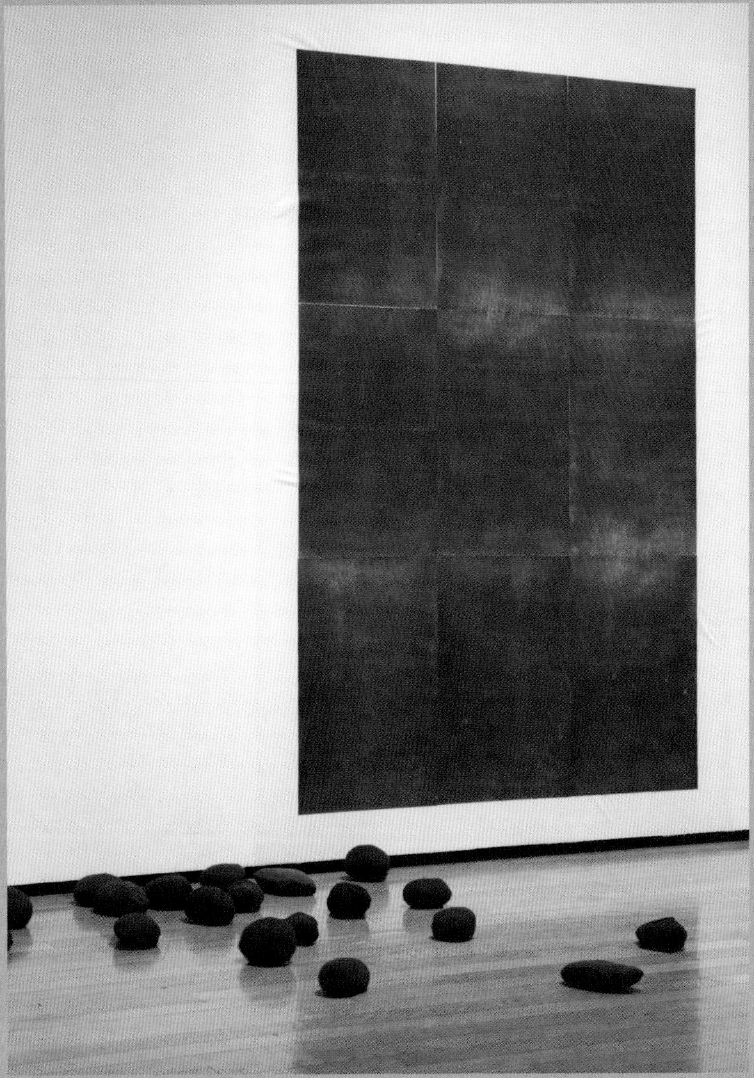



Agata Michalowska's installation (pl. 34) is a meditation on mortality and time. Michalowska made the impression paper, indigo dye, and indigo natural pigment etching ink used for the work. She first etched nine aquatint plates and printed them on handmade paper. She sealed the prints with wheat starch paste to keep the pigment from smudging, and then mounted them on mulberry support paper. She adhered the support paper sheets to the wall by applying thin starch paste to the back around each outside edge. She misted the back of each sheet with water, lifted it, laid it against the wall, and brushed it out flat. The paper shrank slightly as it dried, pulling tightly to the wall. The river stones on the floor are sewn into indigo-dyed felted silk and wool blend casings.

Meg Turner, *Bricks*, 2007.
Installation consisting of twelve hard ground
etchings with aquatint and drypoint on Rives
Lightweight and mounted on the wall,
98 × 76 inches.

Meg Turner's *Bricks* (pl. 35) is composed of twelve states of the same intaglio image printed to the edges of separate sheets of Somerset paper. Turner drew the detailed image of a brick in hard and soft grounds and also used soap ground aquatint, lithographic tusche, and spit bite aquatint. After the ink on the prints was thoroughly dry, Turner redampened the prints, applied paste to the backs, and let them dry. For installation, she lightly dampened the prints in a damp pack, applied paste to the wall, and brushed the prints in place against the wall. For removal, she misted the prints and covered them with a plastic sheet until the moisture penetrated the paper and softened the paste, allowing her to gently peel them away. She removed the residual paste on the wall with a soft sponge and warm water.

# Portfolio

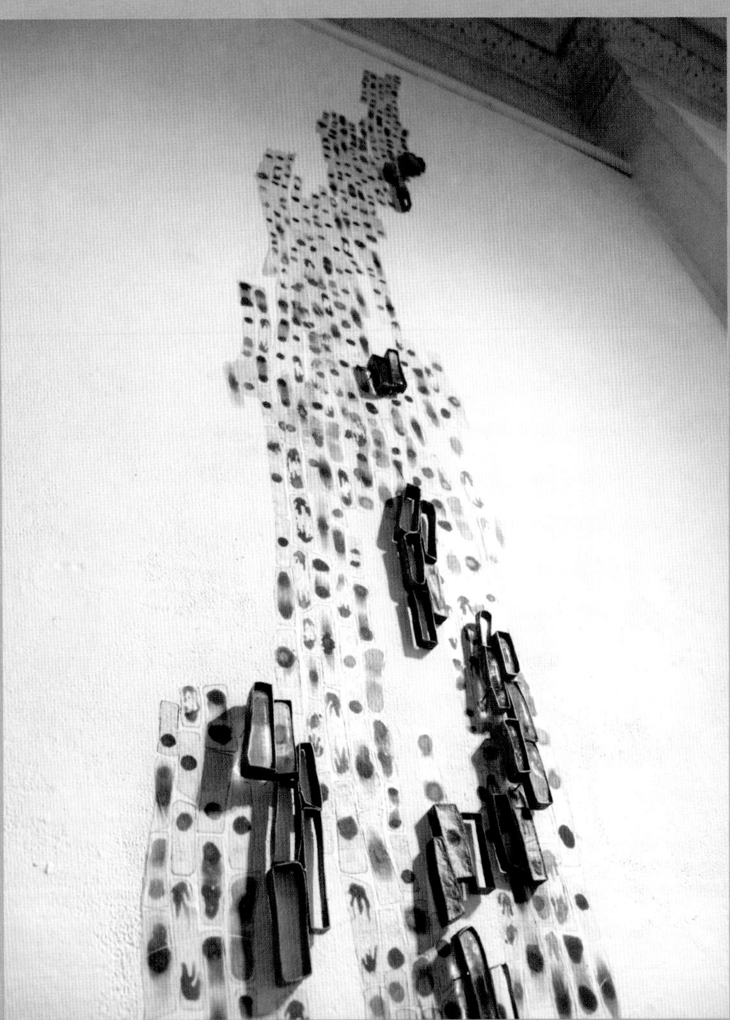



Francesca Lohmann's *Mitosis* (pl. 36) is made up of nearly sixty small spit bite aquatint cells printed on gampi and installed on a wall along with three-dimensional cells hung on pins. The three-dimensional elements are made of copper, beeswax, hand-blown glass, and/or print fragments. The entire installation is removable and can be reinstalled in other venues. To install the printed cells, Lohmann laid them on Plexiglas sheets, misted them until they stretched out flat, then applied thin wheat starch paste to the backs and left them to dry completely. At that stage, the gampi cells were easily stored flat. To install them, Lohmann sprayed the wall and simply placed each cell against the moist wall, where capillary action pulled it tight. At the close of the exhibition, the gampi cells were misted, gently lifted from the wall, and set on Plexiglas sheets to dry.

Solange Roberdeau's *Albion Faun* (pl. 37) is a hard ground etching printed chine collé on raw Indian silk in contrast to the fine, evenly grained silk fabric normally used for fine-line and photographic work. In spite of the variations in the color, surface texture, thread width, and thickness of the fabric, the delicate image printed evenly and clearly. The coarse colléd material is an important element of the composition. Almost all fabrics will print chine collé beautifully. To achieve the best possible impression, the challenge is learning to accommodate the fabric's particular characteristics of absorption and stretch by controlling moisture as you work.

Juan Garcia's *Wall Street* (pl. 38) is a traditional mezzotint with gold leafing. Mezzotint is extremely time-consuming, and Garcia said that "it forced me to spend time looking at the composition, and allowed me the time to consider why I was doing what I was doing."

Garcia's leafing process was as follows: He printed the mezzotint image and let the ink dry. He then applied a water-based, pressure-sensitive adhesive sizing called Old World Art Gold Leafing Medium to the white areas of the image and let it dry for about 30 minutes. Then he placed sheets of gold leaf carefully on the adhesive areas and ran the prints through an etching press to thoroughly adhere the leaf. With a stencil brush, he removed the excess gold leaf from the surface of the print. To increase the sheen and richness of the gold, he added a second layer, following the same process of sizing, leafing, and then applying pressure with the press to ensure adhesion. Once the leafing process was complete, Garcia applied a satin sealer from the same manufacturer to protect the surface of the leaf. "The end result," Garcia says, "is a high gloss gold-leafed area set against the velveteen surface of mezzotint."

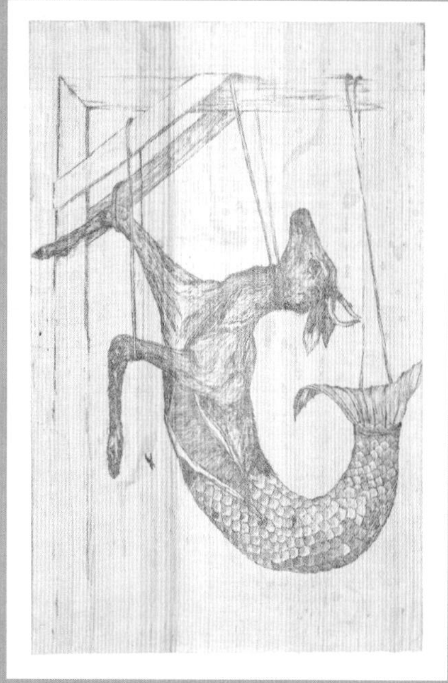

PLATE 37
Solange Roberdeau, *Albion Faun*, 2005.
Color hard ground etching with aquatint and spit bite aquatint printed on silk chine collé,
12 × 17½ inches.

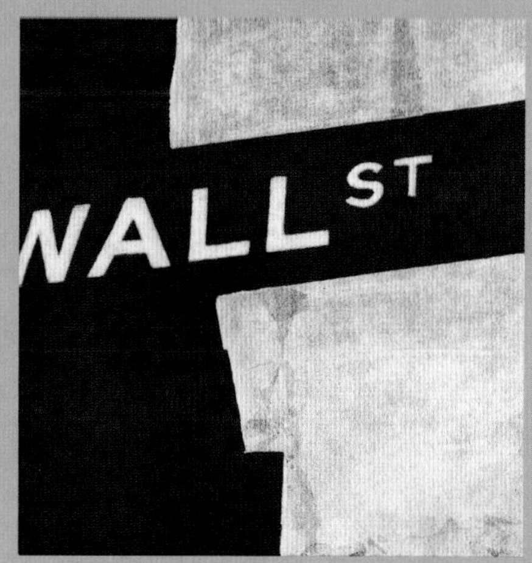


PLATE 38
Juan Garcia, *Wall Street*, 2007.
Mezzotint with gold leaf, 11 × 11 inches.

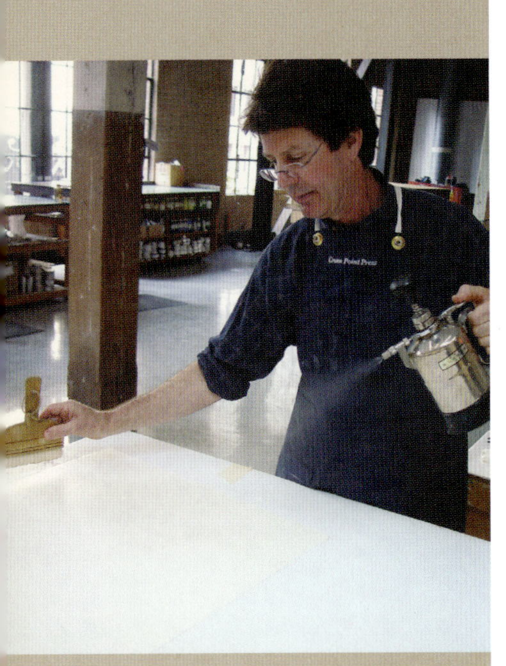
DAMPEN THE SUPPORT PAPER.

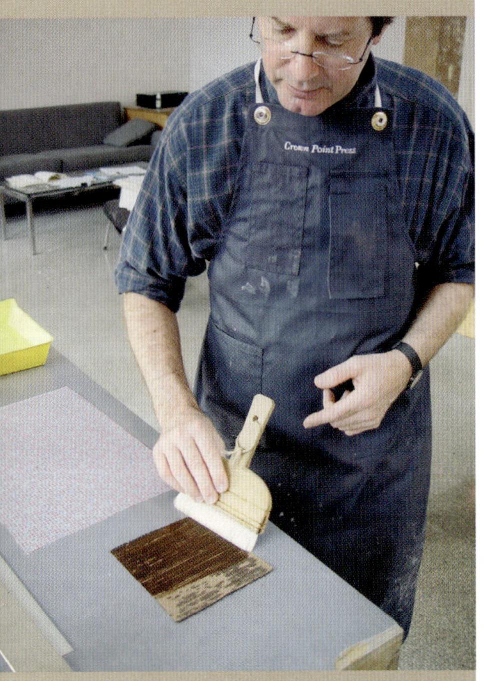
MOISTEN THE COLLAGE ELEMENTS.

# *Working with Collage Step-by-Step*

The best way to keep collage material from buckling as the work dries is to apply paste to already damp material. If any of the material might bleed or run, first apply sizing (see pages 108–9) and allow it to dry. Then, if possible, place both the backing paper and the collage elements in a damp pack (see pages 44–47) until they have relaxed and softened.

You can apply collage materials to paper with or without a press. If you use a press, follow the instructions in chapter 3. I recommend you prepaste the collage fragments if you are using a press.

The following instructions are for pasting a collage on backing paper without a press.

1. **DAMPEN THE PAPER**

   If your support paper is not already in a damp pack, dampen it by misting it. Then wrap it in plastic until it has relaxed. Blot it well before using it.

2. **DAMPEN THE COLLAGE ELEMENTS**

   Moisten your collage elements with water on a brush if they are not already in a damp pack. Let them relax. Blot them well.

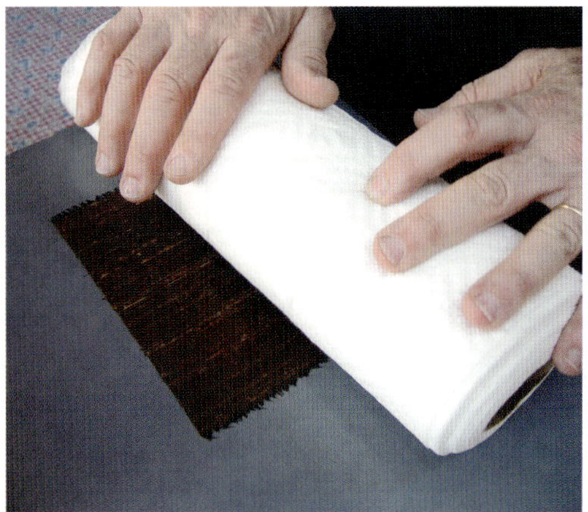
BLOT THE MOISTENED ELEMENTS.

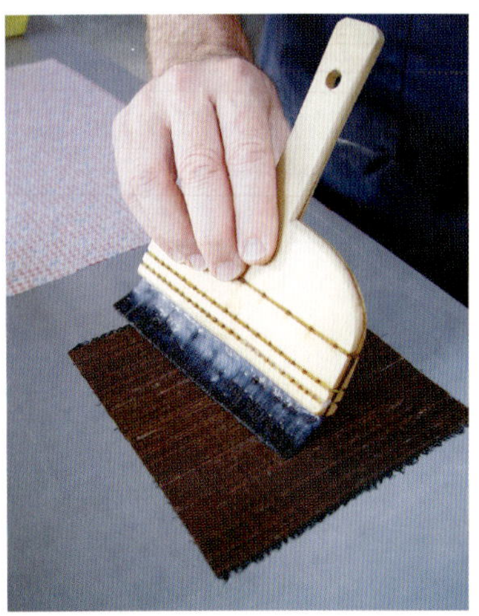

BRUSH ON PASTE.

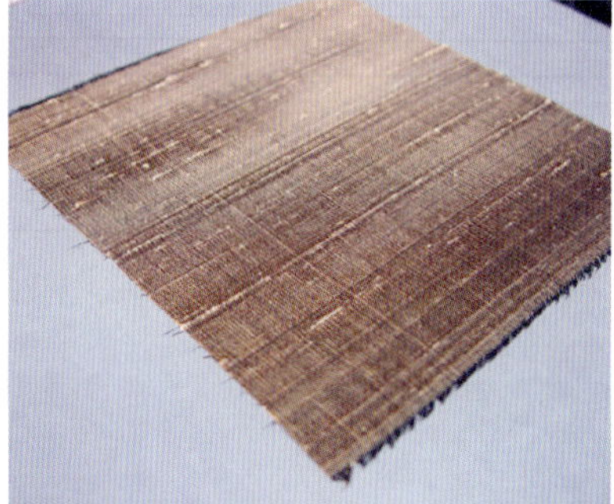

DRY THE PASTE UNTIL IT IS SEMI-OPAQUE.

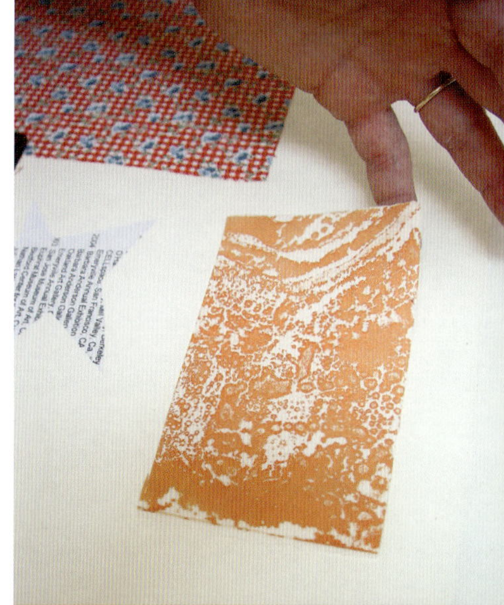

LAY THE COLLAGE ELEMENTS ONTO THE DAMP SUPPORT SHEET.

3.  **PASTE THE COLLAGE ELEMENTS**

    Brush on a thin layer of paste. Let the paste dry until it is
    semi-opaque. You can use a hair dryer, but the bond will be
    stronger if the paste dries slowly. For fabric that is thick,
    add a second layer of paste after the first has dried. Then
    dry the paste again.

4.  **CREATE THE COLLAGE**

    Arrange your collage elements on the damp backing sheet.

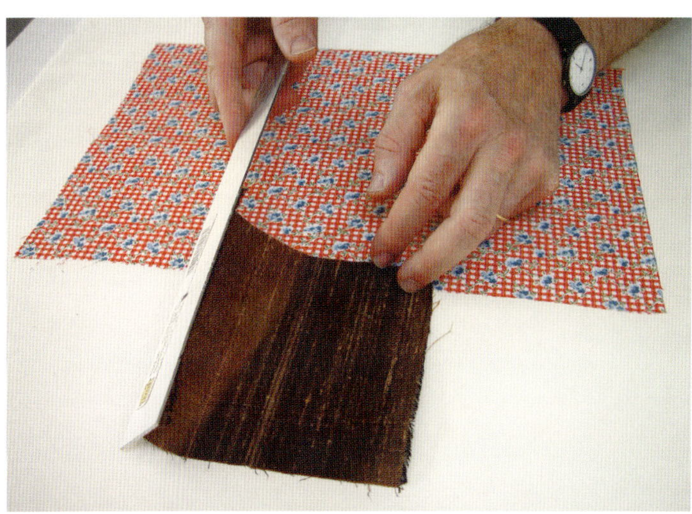

ARRANGE YOUR COLLAGE.

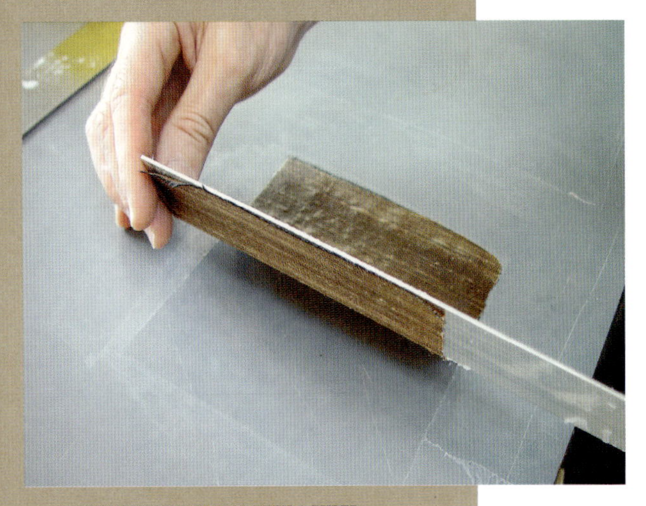

LIFT THE PASTED FABRIC WITH A RULER.

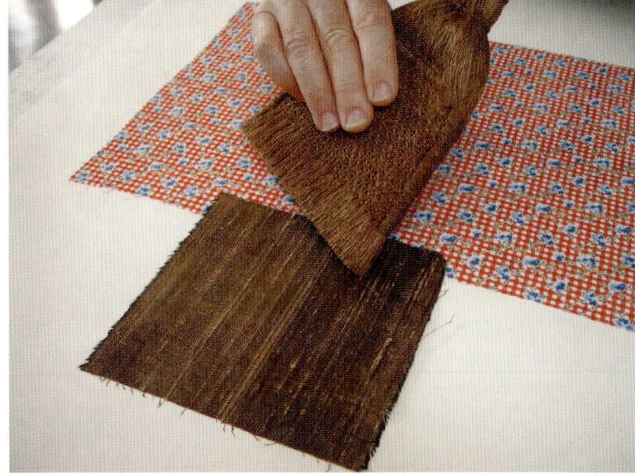

TAMP DOWN THE ELEMENTS WITH A STIFF BRUSH.

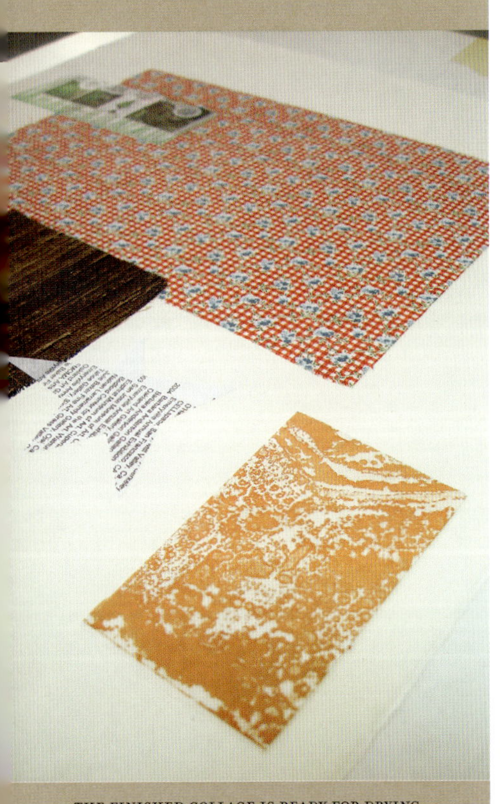

THE FINISHED COLLAGE IS READY FOR DRYING.

*TIP It is easy to lift and position a pasted piece of fabric or flexible paper by pressing a ruler against the paste along one side of the material. When you lift the ruler, the fabric will come with it.*

5. **ADHERE THE COLLAGE**

   Tamp down each piece of pasted material with a stiff brush.

6. **DRY THE COLLAGE**

   Dry the collage using one of the procedures described in chapter 7.

# Pasting Layers Using Scroll Mounting Techniques Step-by-Step

Julie Mehretu's lithograph *Entropia: Construction* (page 122, pl. 30) evolved from a thirty-two color litho/screenprint titled *Entropia (review)* that she created with Cole Rogers at Highpoint Editions in Minneapolis after finishing a residency at the Walker Art Center in 2003. The print began as a working drawing on Mehretu's computer. From this image she created stencils for screenprinting layers. To these were added four lithographic layers printed from photo plates exposed to drawings Mehretu made on translucent drafting vellum. Mehretu liked the way the drawings looked on the vellum when the sheets were stacked together. The look was similar to the translucency she builds up on the surface of her paintings.

After completing *Entropia (review)*, Rogers pulled a proof of the same image on gampi, then cut it into four pieces  and pasted them together to produce a translucency similar to that of the drawings on vellum. Mehretu chose three of the four plates for *Entropia: Construction* and added a new drawing.

The litho plates were printed separately on four sheets of gampi that were then layered on a sheet of Somerset support paper with wheat starch paste. The scale of this work made prepasting—a necessity in lithographic printing—impractical because the tissue-thin gampi would dry, shrink, and curl too much for proper registration and adhesion. The elegant and consistent process Rogers worked out to register and paste the edition parallels the scroll mounting process, which was developed to adhere similarly gossamer materials. I am grateful to Cole Rogers for providing the photos in this section.

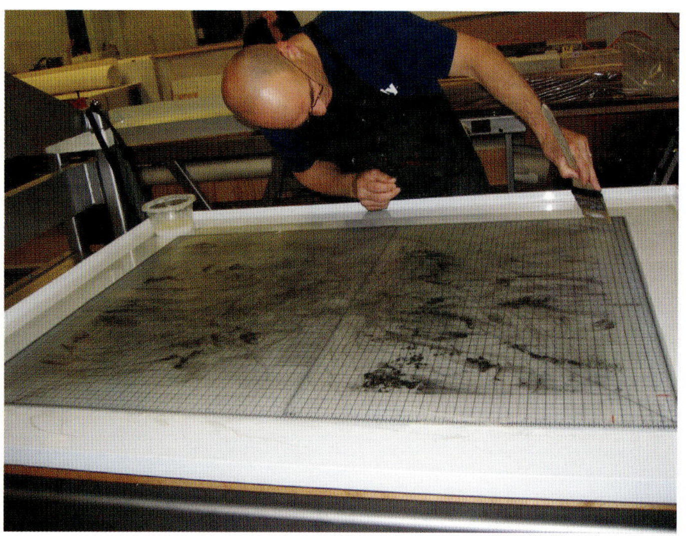



## ENTROPIA: CONSTRUCTION

1. **SET UP THE MATERIALS**

   First the backing sheets were dampened and placed in a damp pack so that they would dry in concert with the four sheets of gampi, minimizing the tension between paper layers. Very thin paste was prepared. The setup included a table with a mat of self-healing plastic, Mylar sheets for transporting the pasted gampi, a sprayer for misting, sharp single-edge razor blades, a straightedge, a fan with a heater, squeegees, and brayers.

2. **REGISTER THE FIRST SHEET AND APPLY PASTE**

   Each sheet of gampi was misted prior to laying it on a Mylar sheet. Additional misting was necessary to accurately register the gampi to guides marked on the Mylar and also to brush out wrinkles that occured while pasting. The first sheet of gampi was registered with its image side directly on the self-healing plastic and was pasted in that position. Cole Rogers applied a very thin layer of paste. The face of this sheet, the side against the Mylar, became the top surface of the print.

COLE ROGERS BRUSHES THE PASTE ONTO THE GAMPI PAPER.

3. **POSITION AND PASTE SUBSEQUENT SHEETS**

The second sheet of moistened gampi was transported clinging face down to a Mylar backing sheet. The printers used pinhole registration to position it on the previously pasted gampi sheet, then lifted away the Mylar. Paste for the next sheet was applied, and the remaining two sheets were similarly moistened and transferred. After the fourth sheet of gampi had been transferred, excess moisture was squeegeed out from under the Mylar backing sheet before it was removed.

4. **TRIM THE STACK**

The stack of four pasted images was trimmed to the final size by following a guide marked on the self-healing plastic mat.

5. **BRING THE STACK TO THE CORRECT MOISTURE LEVEL**

Rogers checked the tackiness of the paste as he finished bringing the stack of pasted gampi sheets to the correct moisture level, using a fan with a heater

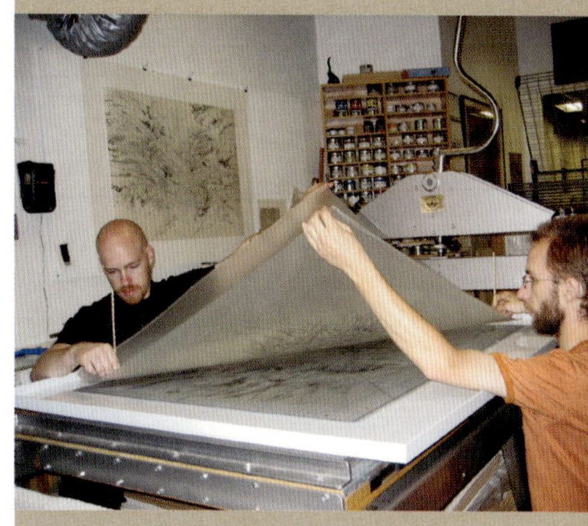

JUSTIN STROM AND ADAMS REGISTER A SHEET OF PASTED GAMPI TO THE PREVIOUSLY PASTED-DOWN GAMPI SHEET.

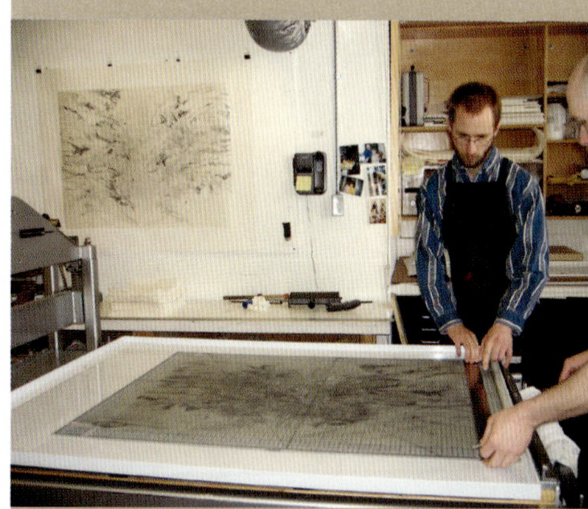

THE PRINTERS TRIM THE FOUR SHEETS OF PASTED GAMPI.

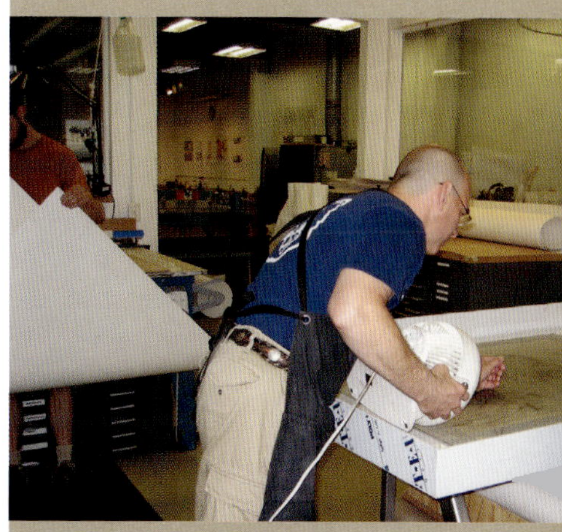

ROGERS USES A FAN TO BRING THE STACK TO THE CORRECT MOISTURE LEVEL.

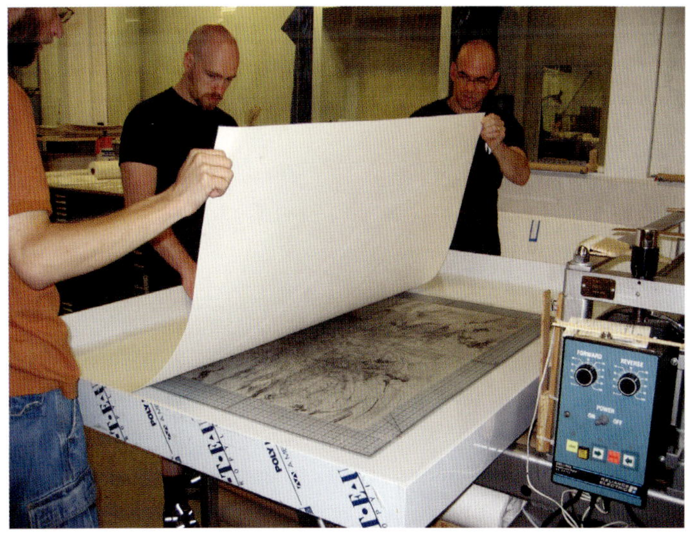

THE PRINTERS POSITION THE SUPPORT PAPER .

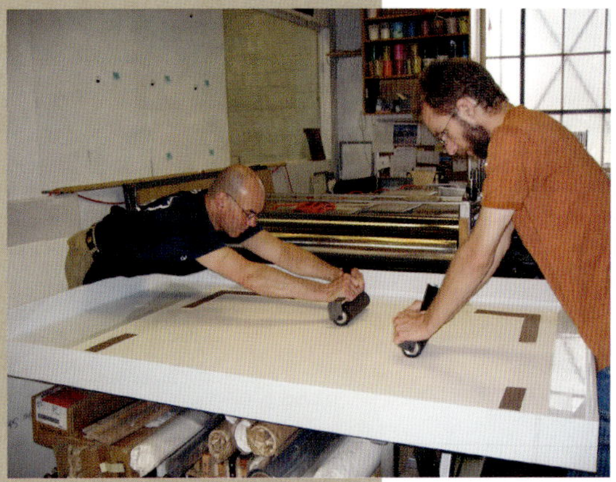

ROGERS AND ADAMS ROLL BRAYERS OVER THE MYLAR COVERED BY A
SHEET OF MAT BOARD TO ENSURE ADHESION OF THE PRINT TO THE
SUPPORT PAPER.

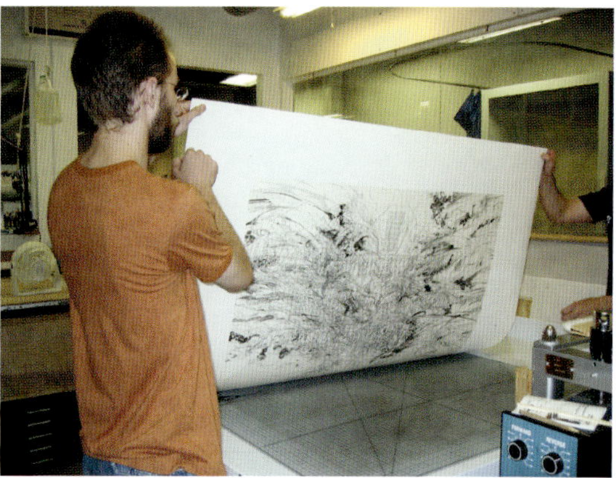

THE PRINT IS PULLED AWAY.

6. **ADHERE THE SHEETS**

   The Somerset backing sheet was covered with Mylar. A sheet
   of mat board protected the backing sheet from damage while
   brayers were used to ensure thorough and even adhesion.

7. **COMPLETE THE PROCESS**

   The mounted print was pulled away from the self-healing
   plastic mat. The print was then dried.

## *Dry Mounting as an Alternative to Chine Collé Step-by-Step*

Master printer Steven Sangenario of Brand X Editions in New
York City graciously provided a demonstration of the process
he used in dry mounting Robert Kushner's *Red Hibiscus* and
allowed Sasha Baguskas of Crown Point to photograph it. The
dry mounting press shown is at Pace Editions, New York City.

The fabric Robert Kushner chose was adhered to a backing sheet in the mounting press. The print was completed at
Brand X Editions by printing silkscreens in eighteen runs on
the mounted fabric using solvent-based inks.

## RED HIBISCUS

1. **SET UP THE MATERIALS**

   The setup included a handheld temperature-controlled
   tacking iron, Fusion 4000 adhesive film, silicon release
   paper, a needle in a pin-vise for lifting the adhesive, and a
   dry mounting press.

2. **POSITION THE FABRIC ELEMENTS**

   The silk strips were cut slightly larger than needed and
   were laid on silicon release paper. Then the strips were
   covered by a sheet of adhesive film and another sheet of
   silicon release paper.

3. **MELT THE ADHESIVE FILM INTO THE FABRIC**

   The paper-fabric-film-paper sandwich was inserted into
   the dry mounting press, which melted the film into the
   fabric. The press had been brought up to temperature
   (180° to 200° F) before mounting began.

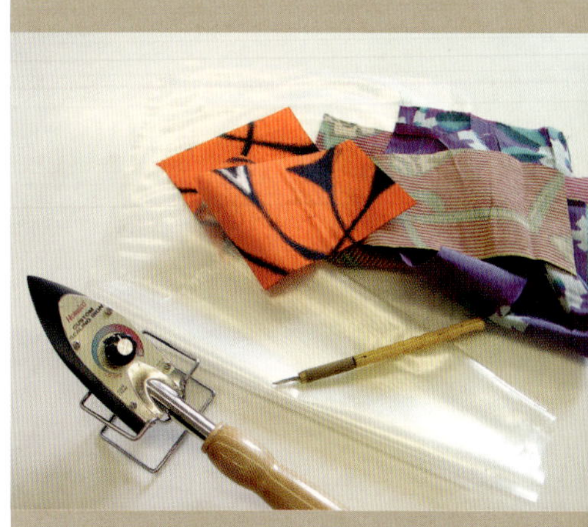

DRY MOUNTING SETUP: FABRIC, ADHESIVE, HANDHELD
IRON, AND A NEEDLE IN A PIN-VISE. NOT SHOWN: SILI-
CON RELEASE PAPER.

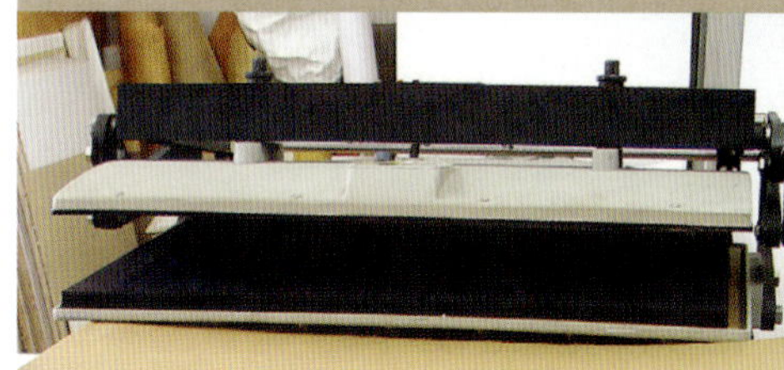

BIENFANG SEAL MASTERPIECE 250 DRY MOUNTING PRESS.

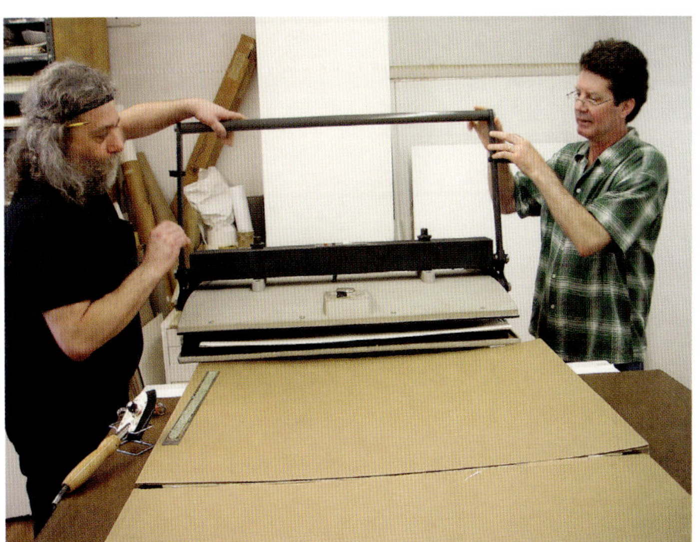

STEVEN SANGENARIO AND BRIAN SHURE USE THE DRY MOUNTING PRESS. THE FABRIC IS
COVERED BY ADHESIVE FILM AND SANDWICHED BETWEEN SHEETS OF SILICON RELEASE
PAPER, WHICH SHOWS WHITE IN THE PHOTOGRAPH.

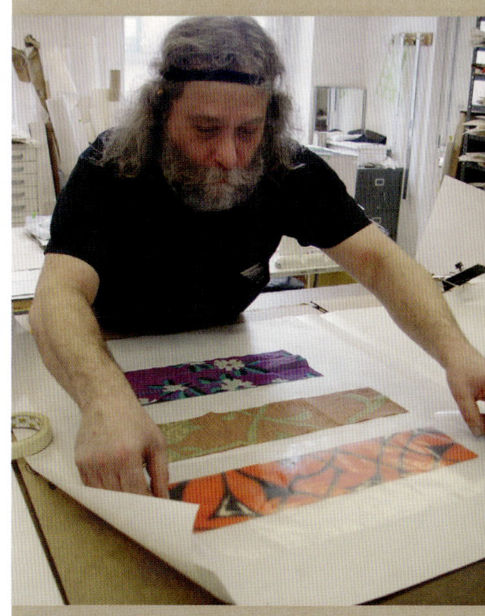

SANGENARIO LAYS ADHESIVE FILM OVER THE SILK,
WHICH LIES ON THE SILICON RELEASE PAPER .

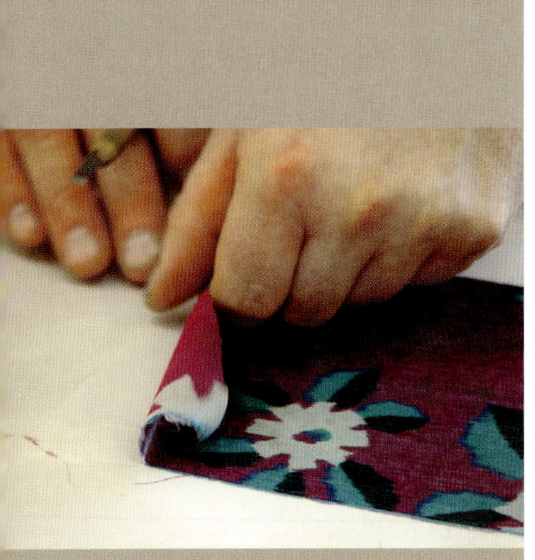

THE FABRIC IS PEELED BACK FROM THE SILICON
RELEASE PAPER.

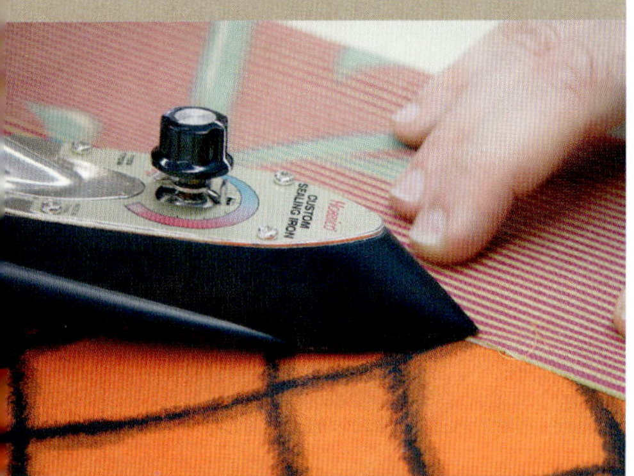

USING A TACKING IRON TO ATTACH THE ADHESIVE-
BACKED FABRIC ONTO THE BACKING PAPER.

4. **PREPARE FOR MOUNTING**

After the adhesive film melted and was cooled to resolidify
it, the fabric was peeled away and the edges were trimmed.
The film is visible on the fabric as the shiny side. Because
the film is impervious to moisture, future changes in humidity may cause the backing paper to curl. Consequently,
a heavy backing paper—Saunders Waterford Hot Press,
410 grams per square meter—was chosen. Sangenario
placed the fabrics on the backing paper with a slight overlap and lightly touched the fabric pieces with the hot tacking iron at their corners. This kept the fabric from moving
while he placed it in the press.

5. **MOUNT THE FABRIC**

The backing sheet with the fabric in position was placed
in the press, positioned with the backing sheet facing the
heating element. This ensured that the film melted into the
backing paper rather than into the fabric, where it could
disrupt the soft, reflective quality of the silk. Heat was
applied for approximately 2 minutes. The 3-millimeter-
thick layer of acid-free adhesive film melts at 180° F. Care
was taken to monitor the thermostat to make certain it did
not rise above 200° F, which would cause the adhesive to
flow excessively.

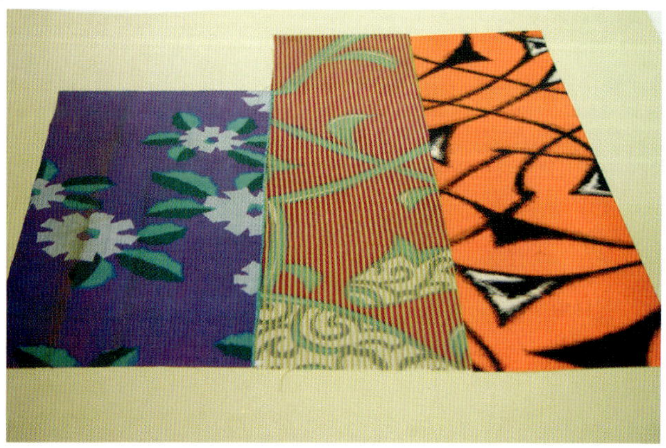

THE FABRIC MOUNTED TO THE BACKING PAPER.

*Secret #6.* LEAFING WITH GOLD AND OTHER METALS
*Allow plenty of time.*

When I started working at Crown Point, several large projects
were backlogged for editioning.  Master printer Nancy Anello,
who had worked at the press a decade earlier, had returned for
a few months to help us out. Because we were trying to catch
up, there was a natural tendency to see if we could save some
time by cutting a few corners. Nancy noticed this and told us
that when she started working at Crown Point, an old piece
of paper was taped to the aquatint box—no one remembered
who had put it there—that said, "There is never enough time to
do it right, but there is always enough time to do it over." The
secret in this chapter, like the other secrets in this book, is
universally applicable. But this one is particularly appropriate
for gold leafing, where temperature and humidity can cause
the useful working times of the adhesive size to vary by hours
or even days. Leafing is simple if you set aside enough time for
each step. Failure to pay attention to proper set times will lead
to waste, frustration, and the need to start over.

I begin this chapter with background on traditional gold
leafing materials. Then, to acquaint you with a reliable method,
I describe working processes developed over the past twenty-
five years by Robert Kushner in his extensive use of leaf,
powdered mica, glitter, and other reflective and interference
powders. *Hand-Painted Daphne I, #46* (pl.39) started as a
watercolor woodcut that Kushner created with master printer
Tadashi Toda in 1985 in Crown Point's woodcut project in Kyoto.
Six years later, in 1991, Kushner added hand painting, glitter,
and/or gold or silver leafing to a few impressions, making

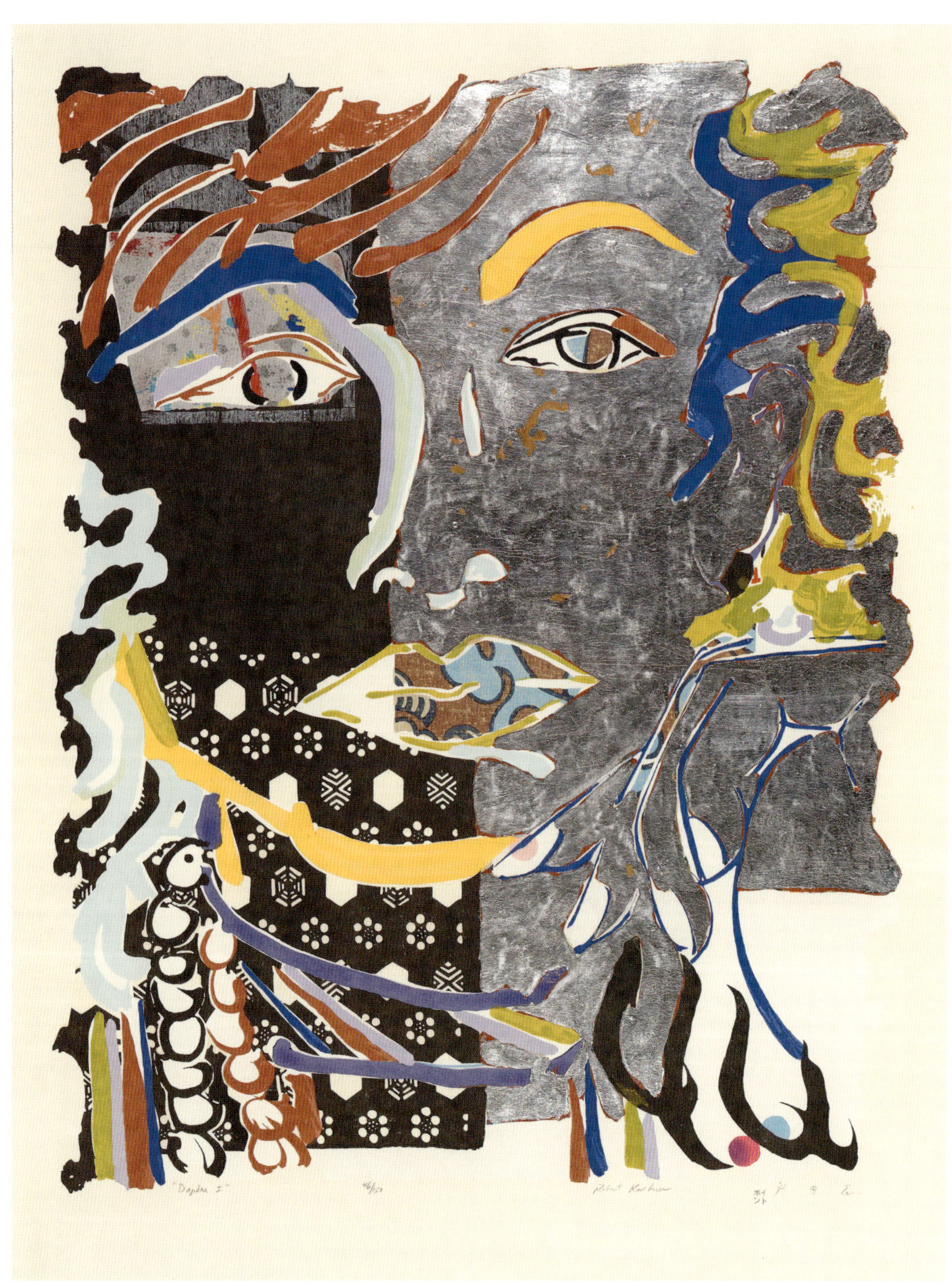
"Daphne I"
46/50
Robert Kushner

each one unique. Kushner works with acrylic size and acrylic undercoating, which is traditionally called bole. For another approach, see page 131, pl. 38, a work by young printmaker Juan Garcia. Garcia used water-based pressure-sensitive size and effectively combined brilliant gold leaf with the rich, soft black possible only through the laborious mezzotint process.

Gold is not in any way a neutral material. It is implicitly luxurious, flashy, and decorative. Its use goes back millennia, and it is still employed in many different types of artistic practice. Although it is one of our most precious substances, gold is so malleable that it can be worked into thin sheets that are affordable for extensive application.

Gold has an advantage over other metals used for leafing in that it is completely inert. Unlike silver leaf and the many metallic leaf products made with less expensive metals, gold does not tarnish and does not need to be sealed. Quality sealers are available to prevent oxidation of silver and other metallic leaf, but there is also a long tradition of using silver, copper, bronze, and other metallic leaf without sealer to encourage oxidation. In some cases, craftsmen even add a chemical patina to darken or mottle the surface with various oxides.

PLATE 39 (OPPOSITE)
Robert Kushner, *Hand-Painted Daphne I, #46*, 1985–91.
Color woodcut with hand painting and silver leaf, 22½ × 19 inches.

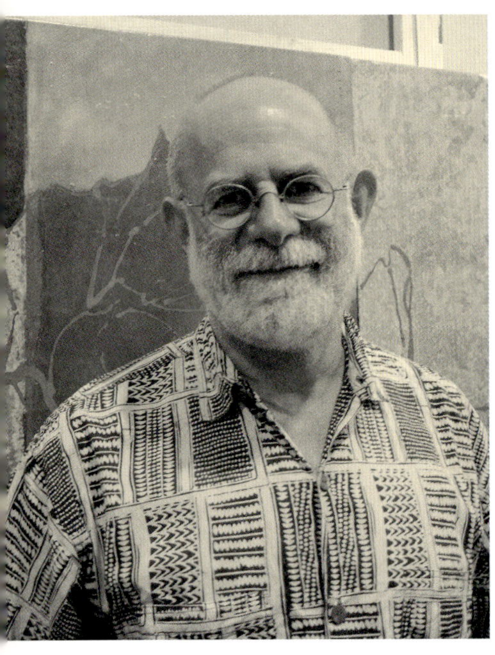

Leaf gold is prepared by rolling gold under immense pressure and then beating it—more than a hundred sheets at a time are layered between goldbeater's skins (the outer membrane of calf's intestine)—until the gold averages three- to five-millionths of an inch in thickness. At three-millionths thickness, 1 ounce of gold makes two thousand $3^3/_8$-inch square sheets. These sheets, or leaves, are usually supplied in books of twenty-five sheets each. Leaf gold is sold in $23^1/_2$-karat deep rich gold, $18^1/_2$-karat lemon gold, and 16-karat pale gold. The leaves are customarily applied in a grid over a reddish-toned bole, traditionally made of iron oxide clay mixed with gelatin or glue.

Traditional sizing used to adhere leaf gold for illumination is a mixture of several ingredients, each of which imparts specific desirable qualities to the solution. A weak adhesive, such as gum arabic or glair, is necessary. Glair is egg white that has been whipped until it is like snow. After sufficient beating, it should not move even if the bowl containing it is inverted. The whipping fundamentally changes the character of the emulsion and removes the stringiness. The glair combines readily with water or other materials, and it becomes thin and free-flowing after it has been left for a while and the air has escaped. Many old recipes call for a good quantity of "fig milk" mixed with glair. "Fig milk," a sap similar in consistency to latex, adds flexibility. Another common adhesive was garlic juice.

A colorant, usually ocher or red oxide, in the bole makes adhesive sizing visible. Chalk or clay in the bole adds bulk so

the gold is raised above the surface and looks thick. A
hygroscopic substance, usually honey or sal ammoniac
(ammonium chloride), added to the sizing extends its
working time. This is necessary because the leaf must be
applied while the sizing remains tacky.

One of the most influential living artists using
metallic leaf in his work is Robert Kushner. Kushner
has consistently explored pattern and decoration
since the early 1970s. He has traveled extensively to
research decoration. On a trip to the Middle East in
1974, he found that little distinction was made between
decorative and fine art, an attitude that he productively
incorporated into his work. Throughout his career, he
has studied nature, often working from fresh flowers in
his studio and frequently traveling to gardens to draw
directly from growing plants. Water lilies in bloom in
Hawaii and in their winter skeletal phase in Hangzhou,
China; spring lilacs in Massachusetts; and night-
blooming cereus on Maui are just a few of the plants that
have provided inspiration.

Like many artists who traveled to Japan in the 1980s
for the Crown Point Press woodcut program, Kushner
feels that the trip had positive repercussions on his work
that continue to this day. He was particularly inspired
by the vigor of the decorated screens in many of Kyoto's
temples. The temples, like most traditional Japanese
buildings, have heavy roofs that overhang beyond the
surrounding verandas, keeping the interiors cool and

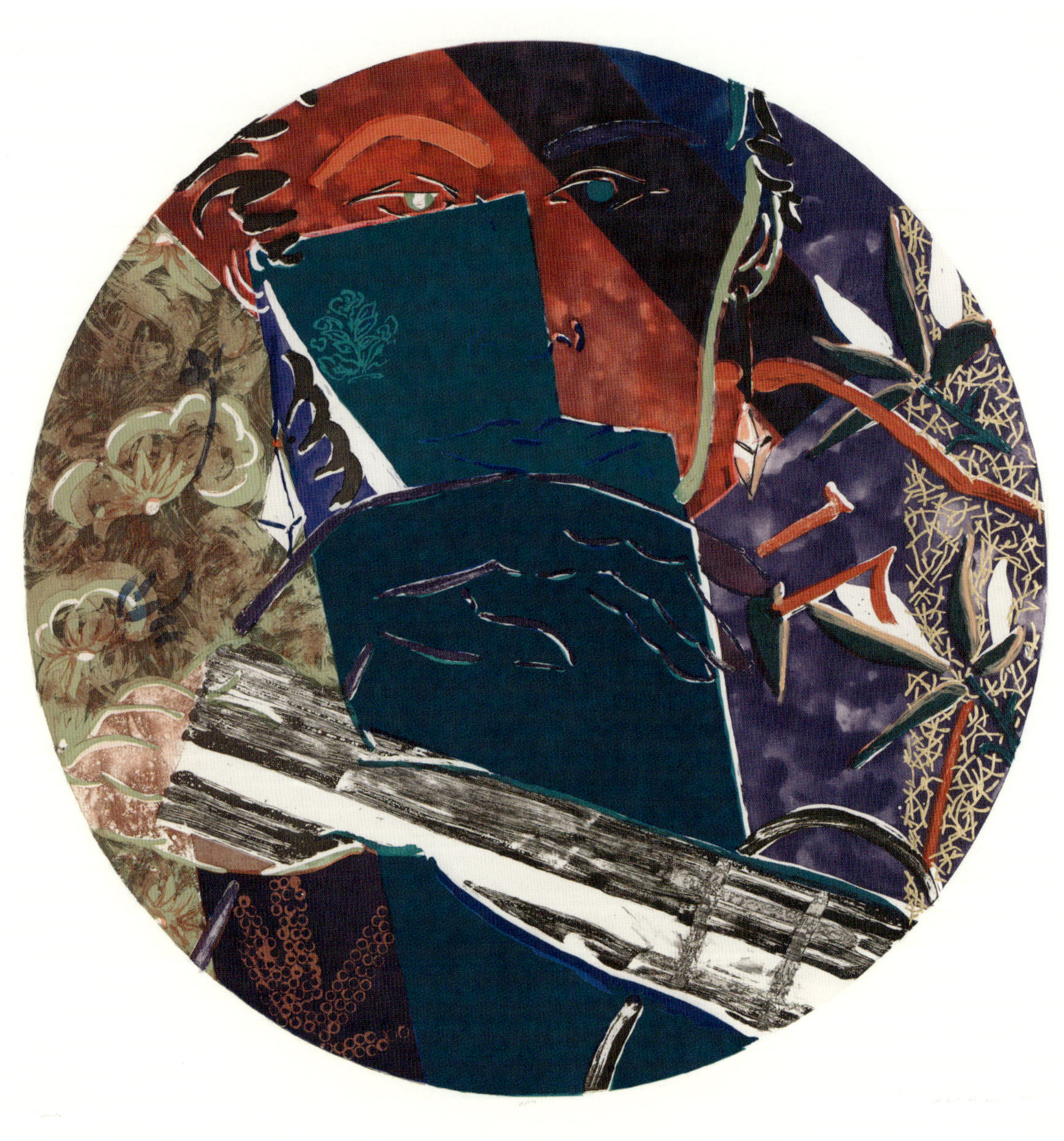

PLATE 40
Robert Kushner, *Tondo*, 1987.
Color aquatint,drypoint, and sugar lift,
spit bite and soap ground aquatints,
with gold leaf, 36 × 36 inches.

dark. The extensive use of metallic leaf on decorative screens is particularly effective in this low light.

Since the mid-1980s, the shimmering reflectivity of metallic leaf and the distinctive grid of the applied leaves have become prominent elements in Kushner's prints and paintings. Even his large public commissions, such as mosaic decorations for the New York City Public Transit Authority, glitter with gold tiles. As Kushner continues to explore the seemingly inexhaustible heritage of decorative art in his distinctive floral imagery, he mentors a young group of artists in Brooklyn who draw inspiration from his work and from concepts underlying the use of pattern and decoration.

In Kushner's large etching *Tondo* (pl.40) from 1987, a drawing of a woman resting her chin on the back of her hand is interwoven into patterns from Japanese and Indian fabrics. Kushner combines lush colors and rich marks with sugar lift, spit bite, and soap ground aquatints, and with drypoint. Drypoint marks on the right side of the print were covered with gold leaf after the edition was printed.

Adding metallic leaf to paper and fabric has a rich tradition. The step-by-step instructions in this chapter should help you to gain an understanding of how to combine these materials. As with all the other processes described in this book, once you have learned to respect the properties and limitations of the materials you are working with, you will find it easy to have a high rate of success. Within what may at first seem to be narrow parameters, you will find endless possibilities for experimentation and innovation, as Kushner has done with leafing. Just take your time.

# Gold Leafing Step-by-Step

Unlike chine collé, gold leafing cannot be done directly during printing in any medium. You can silkscreen leafing size onto paper and subsequently, once the size has set up, add gold leaf. Or you can roll size onto a relief matrix, print it, and then, after it has dried the correct length of time, adhere the leaf.  Pochoir, where size could be brushed through a stencil, might work well. I have not tried these procedures, however. I believe you would need to size the paper first with hide glue or gelatin (see pages 108–9), and you might need to modify the consistency of the leafing size so that it prints and sets up without soaking into the paper so much that it loses its effectiveness.

Most gold leafing applications do not depend on printing. Size normally is painted by hand with a brush, then the leaf is applied during what is called the "tack" or "open" time, the time for that particular size during which leaf can be successfully adhered. The same techniques can be used for any type of metal leafing.

Gold leaf can be purchased in rolls or ribbons but is most commonly supplied in books of leaves $3^3/_8$ inches square. A full pack contains five hundred leaves in twenty books. The twenty-five leaves in each book are between tissue pages. A full pack covers $39^1/_2$ square feet if you apply it without waste or overlap. Loose leaves are applied by lifting them with a flat brush made of natural hair called a gilder's tip and floating the fragile leaves onto the sized surface. Application with a gilder's tip is tricky, but if the surface you are leafing is uneven or curved, it may be your best choice.

Patent leaf, also called transfer leaf, is gold leaf that is supplied lain down onto (rather than interleaved with) tissue paper. You apply it by pressing the back of the tissue onto the sized area of your work. It is easier to control than loose leaves.

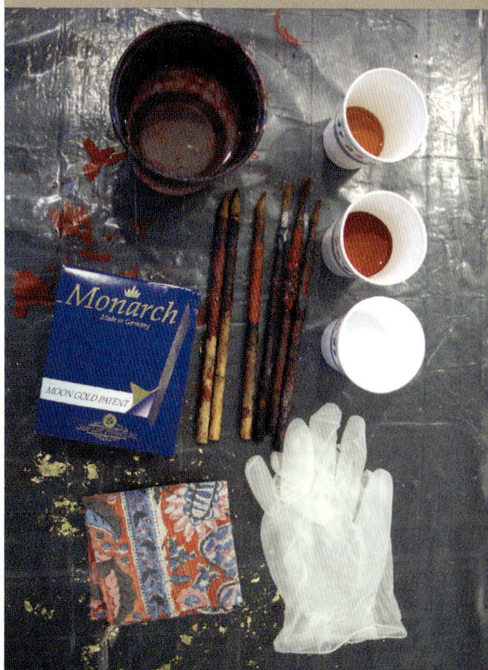

METALLIC LEAF, SOFT BRUSHES, SOLVENT-BASED SIZE,
FLUID ACRYLIC OXIDE PAINT, GLOSS ACRYLIC MEDIUM,
GLOVES, AND A SOFT CLOTH. (VAPOR MASK NOT SHOWN.)

TIP *Store patent leaf, wrapped in tissue, in a slightly damp environment. If the leaves become dry, they can loosen from their backing sheets. If that happens, place the book of leaves under pressure in a humid spot and the leaves will remount.*

A variety of leafing systems are on the market, and suppliers offer instruction sheets on how to use their products. Working times, both the time it takes the sizing to set up (the time needed to "come to tack") and the tack time, vary enormously. Some systems are water based, and others—like the one developed by Robert Kushner and demonstrated here—are solvent based. A third option, called water gilding, uses rabbit skin glue as size. This method requires the greatest skill. To locate recommended distributors of products for gold leafing, check www.magical-secrets.com.

Robert Kushner's leafing process is a hybrid method that combines traditional leafing techniques with innovations he has found particularly suitable for leafing paper and fabric already containing printed and/or painted areas. He enjoys creating brilliant gold surfaces and no longer uses water-based size because, in his experience, it has produced finished work that appears dull.

1.  ASSEMBLE THE MATERIALS

    Metallic leaf. Kushner prefers patent leaf because it is less troublesome than loose leaves and has less waste.

    Soft brushes.

    Gloss acrylic medium for sealing the paper before beginning the leafing process. Less porous materials do not need sealing, but work on paper does.

    Tinted medium such as fluid acrylic red oxide paint sold in jars. This substitutes for the bole, traditionally made of hide glue and mineral pigment. The acrylic paint is very stable and has none of the adhesion or chipping problems that sometimes occur with traditional bole.

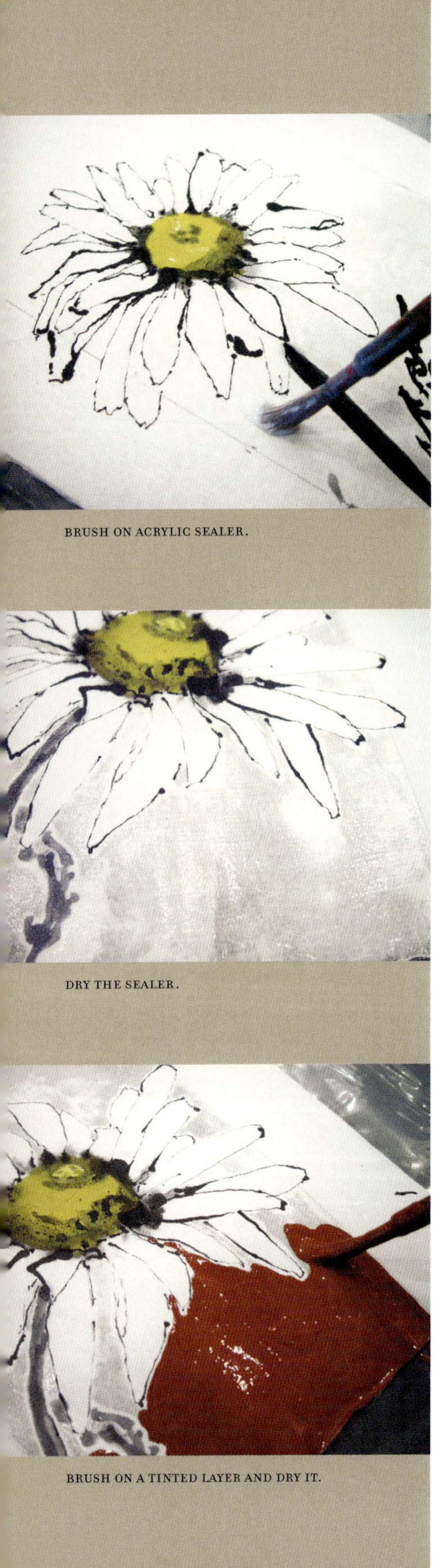

BRUSH ON ACRYLIC SEALER.

DRY THE SEALER.

BRUSH ON A TINTED LAYER AND DRY IT.

Solvent-based size. Kushner uses Charbonnel/LeFranc lead-free size, which is supplied in formulations that allow 3 or 12 hours before it comes to tack. He prefers the longer setting time, as it results in more beautiful surfaces.

Piece of soft cloth for finishing the application.

Gloves to protect your hands from the sizing.

Vapor mask for use during application of the sizing.

2.  **SEAL THE SURFACE**
    Brush the gloss acrylic medium, slightly thinned with water, onto the areas that will be leafed. This will seal the paper and prevent the size from soaking in and losing its tack. Kushner appreciates a bit of texture, which scatters reflections from the leaf. You can brush the medium out thinly if you prefer a smooth underlying surface.

3.  **DRY THE SEALER**
    Drying may take a couple of hours, a day, or anything in between, depending on thickness of application, humidity, and absorbency of the underlying paper. Kushner recommends drying at room temperature.

4.  **APPLY A RED OXIDE LAYER AND DRY IT**
    Brush a slightly thinned layer of fluid acrylic red oxide directly on top of the sealed areas. This acrylic paint is thinned with water and adheres well to paper, cloth, ink, and paint. It also forms an ideal base for the sizing that will be applied over it.

    TIP *The liquid version of acrylic red oxide comes in a bottle or jar rather than a tube. Golden and Liquitex both make red oxide in this consistency.*

    The drying time for a fluid acrylic red oxide layer varies, but Kushner estimates it at 1 to 3 hours. He advises not to speed drying with a fan or hair dryer, because size applied over an acrylic layer that was rapidly dried tends to bead up.

5. **APPLY THE SIZE**

Wear a vapor mask and gloves. Solvent-based size is a varnish and has strong fumes. If you can, work in raking light to best see what you are doing. The size is transparent and shiny, and it must be applied with care. Using a soft brush, apply a thin, even coating to the entire tinted layer. Be careful not to puddle the size, or it will not dry properly and the leaf will lift off. If the sizing layer is too thin, it will dry too quickly and lose tack before you apply the leaf.

Care must be taken to keep size off the unsealed paper, where it will quickly soak in and spread. Stains will appear about six months later.

TIP *Don't use old size because it won't set up properly. When beginning work, take a small amount of size out of the can and quickly reseal it. Never leave the can open so its solvent evaporates. When you get down to the last 25 percent in the can, dispose of it.*

6. **LET THE SIZE DRY UNTIL IT HAS COME TO TACK**

The minimum interval of drying or setup time before a size coating reaches its open or tack time is indicated on the instructions for the particular size you are using. Kushner's size does not reach its tack time sooner than 12 hours after application, and he usually waits 48 hours before applying the leaf. He believes that the longer you can wait, the more brilliant the leaf will be in the finished work.

After the minimum setup time has passed, begin testing for tack at regular intervals. Gently touch the size with a finger. It should not be at all sticky. It should feel like suede or chamois. It should be "beyond tacky," Kushner says. Once you have reached the open or tack state, you can maintain it for as long as 3 or 4 days, until it begins to feel dry. Although it is possible to wait too long, Kushner believes that most beginners start leafing too soon.

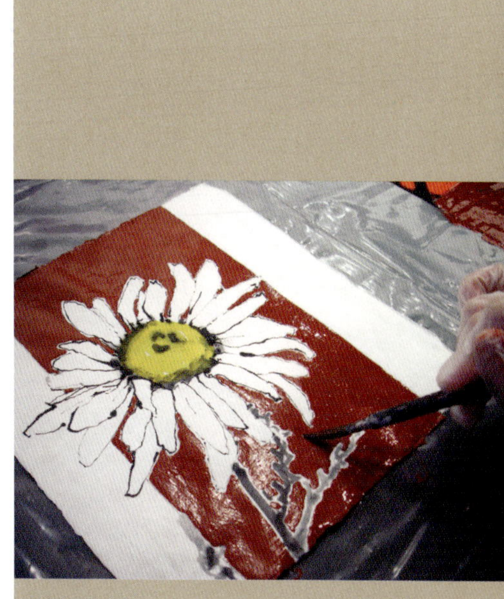

APPLY THE SIZE.

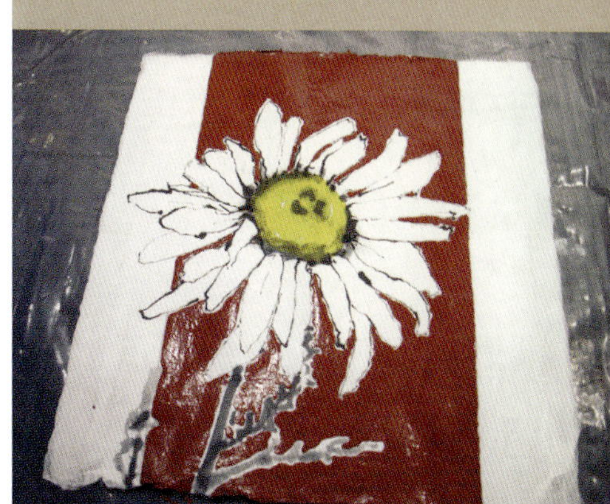

DRY THE SIZE UNTIL IT IS NOT STICKY.

SELECT A PATENT GOLD LEAF SHEET ON ITS
BACKING TISSUE.

POSITION THE LEAF AND PRESS IT DOWN.

LIFT THE TISSUE, LEAVING THE GOLD IN PLACE
WHEREVER SIZING WAS APPLIED..

7. **APPLY THE LEAF**

Select a sheet of patent gold leaf on its backing tissue. It
can be handled with relative ease. Be careful not to touch
the metallic leaf itself—it might stick to your finger. Place
the gold side down on the sized surface. You can take your
time to position it. When it is in place, rub the back gently.
Lift the tissue away carefully, and the leaf will stay stuck to
the size. Areas of leaf that did not touch the size will stay on
the tissue and can be placed elsewhere.

TIP *If patent leaf is difficult to separate from the paper, it is too
moist and warm. Chill it briefly in the refrigerator.*

If the leaf failed to stick to pinholes or other areas of
sizing, you can press on more leaf in a second application.
To finish the application and remove excess leaf from
nonsized areas, rub the leaf gently with your fingers or a
soft brush. Polish with a soft cloth.

TIP *On very smooth surfaces, you can increase the brilliance
of the leaf by smoothing it with a burnisher of agate or other
smooth material.*

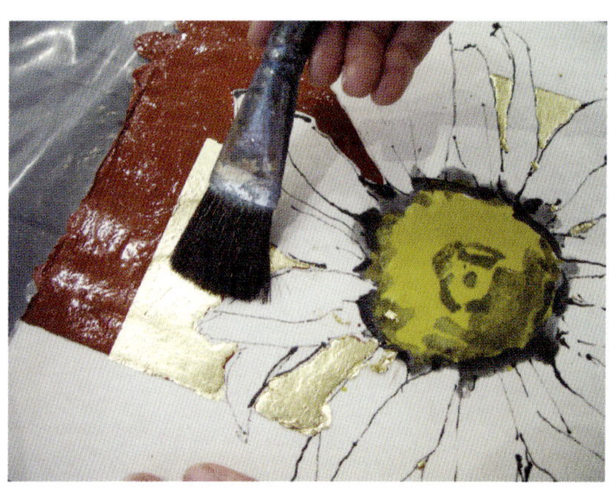

BRUSH AWAY EXCESS GOLD.

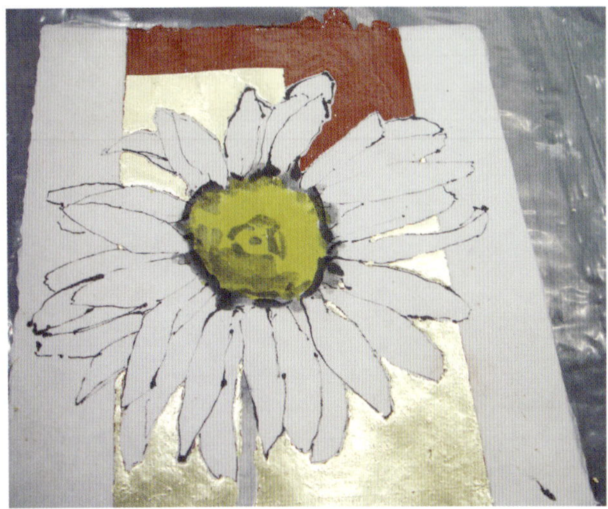

THE GOLD LEAF IS IN PLACE.

# Guidelines for Applying Mica and Other Particulates

You can apply mica, interference powders, glitter, and other particulate material using the same techniques as for gold leafing.

Always wear a particle mask. Even nonpoisonous powders like gold will cause silicosis if you breathe them into your lungs. There is no danger as long as you wear a mask during application and thoroughly clean up all residual powder afterward with a cloth and water before you remove the mask.

Apply the sealer, tinted acrylic, and size just as for leafing. After the size has come to tack, apply what seems like an excessive amount of powder or particles to the surface with a soft brush and thoroughly work the material into the size. Brush away the excess. Use a clean soft cloth to remove any powder not firmly adhered.

A traditional Japanese leafing technique (demonstrated on the DVD included with this book) employs small pieces of leaf, either scraps collected from other projects or little shapes cut from metallic leaves, scattered across the size and then brushed down firmly.

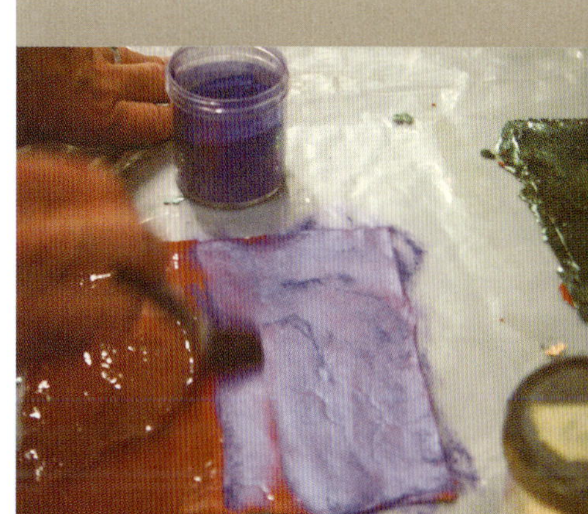

AFTER PREPARING THE PAPER, BRUSH ON THE PIGMENT WITH QUICK STROKES.

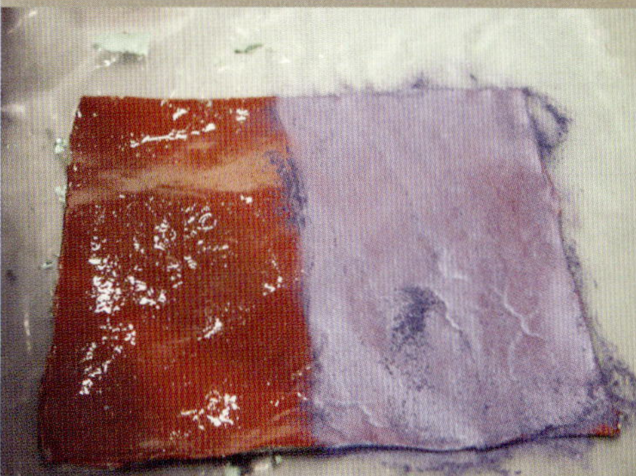

THE PIGMENT IS IN PLACE.

# *Secret #7.* DRYING THE FINISHED PRINTS
*Drive out all the moisture.*

The chine collé process uses dampened paper, as does all intaglio printing, and you must dry your finished prints under restraint if they are to dry flat and remain that way. The prints are likely to stay flat only if their moisture level is lowered to the lowest humidity level in the environment where they will be kept. For example, if you have dried a print just enough for it to remain flat on a rainy day when the ambient humidity is 70 percent, it will remain flat only until the sun comes out and the humidity drops to 40 percent. Then the print will resume drying and begin to curl. It is best to drive all the moisture out of the paper while you are drying it under restraint.

> TIP *Even a thoroughly dried print in a damp environment will take on moisture over time, and if the environment changes and the print begins to dry, it might ripple or curl. That is the nature of paper. Often it will flatten again on its own.  If you are bothered by curling or ripples, you can redampen the work. Mist or sponge the back, wait until the paper relaxes, and dry and flatten it again under restraint using one of the methods in this chapter.*

This chapter details three methods of drying works on paper: between blotters, on boards or a wall, and with a forced-air dryer.

Before using any of these methods, be sure the prints are evenly damp. The system at Crown Point, which uses a forced-air dryer, is to have the paper in a damp pack (see page 44) prior to printing, and to return the paper to the same damp pack, or another, after printing and hold it until all the day's work can be dried at the same time.

Drying on boards generally causes an intaglio plate mark nearly to disappear because the paper shrinks as it dries and on boards is pulled tightly. If you are drying on boards and want to retain clear evidence of a plate mark, let the print dry thoroughly in a drying rack, or stacked between tissue or newsprint, before you flatten it. Then follow dampening instructions on page 156.

If for any reason your prints have dried without restraint and are not flat, you must dampen them again by soaking, misting, or sponging before proceeding with the drying procedure of your choice.

# Guidelines for Drying Prints Using Blotters

This is the most common method for drying prints, and also the slowest, most labor-intensive, and riskiest. It is risky because if you do not change the blotters frequently, mold may grow on your damp prints and they will be ruined.

Lay out a piece of greenhouse plastic sheeting and put a dry blotter on top, then a damp print. If ink on the image area is still wet, cover it with tissue paper. Then put another blotter on top, then another print, and so on, until all the prints you are drying are stacked. It is necessary to use the plastic in order to keep the paper edges from drying first and wrinkling the prints. Fold the plastic sheeting over the stack to make a loose package and cover it with a weight. One or several etching plates, a piece of plywood, books, or any other flat weights will do.

Exchange the moist blotters for dry ones at intervals of several hours, or at least once a day, over a period of at least two days, until the prints are completely flat and dry. Test by pressing your cheek against a print. If it feels cool, it is not yet dry.

TIP *Moist blotters that you have removed from a damp pack should be dried by letting them sit on flat surfaces until they are dry to the touch. If you dry them rapidly, they will curl excessively. Almost all blotters, even those that seem dry, contain some moisture from the air, however. If you drive out residual moisture by heating blotters slightly before using them, you can speed the print drying process somewhat. Use a hair dryer or let them sit on a clean hot plate used for melting ground or for inking intaglio plates, or near a heater with a fan. Let them cool for a few minutes before placing them between the prints.*

# Drying on Boards Step-by-Step

This is the method used in Asia and in a simpler form in many art schools and universities in the United States. In Asia, the traditional drying board is a wooden stretcher covered with several layers of paper, the grain direction alternating in each layer. This provides a surface that is absorbent and dimensionally stable. Sometimes the paper is sized with persimmon juice, which makes the fibers waterproof though still able to wick water out of the prints as they air-dry. The prints are pasted to the boards using a thin layer of paste around the edges. At the end of this section, I show how to adapt the Asian approach to drying an artwork on a wall and removing it intact.

In the West, smooth sheets of plywood or hollow-core doors are used as drying boards, to which a print is taped rather than pasted. If you use unpainted wood, first paste down acid-free paper as a barrier to keep the chemicals in the wood from staining the damp paper.

You can dry your work face in or face out on the board. The step-by-step illustrations show a collage being dried face in, but a freshly pulled print, with wet ink, normally would be dried face out. If you apply tape to the front of the paper, your print should have extra margins all around so that you can cut or tear the edges inside the taped border.

> TIP *If you are working with a print on which you want to retain a strong intaglio plate mark, the print should be dry when you begin. Lightly mist it on the back and, before it has had much time to absorb moisture and expand, tape it face down with tissue between it and the board. After the print is taped, mist it a bit more to allow it to stretch further. Because it was taped before it was thoroughly moistened, it will retain a strong impression of the plate mark.*

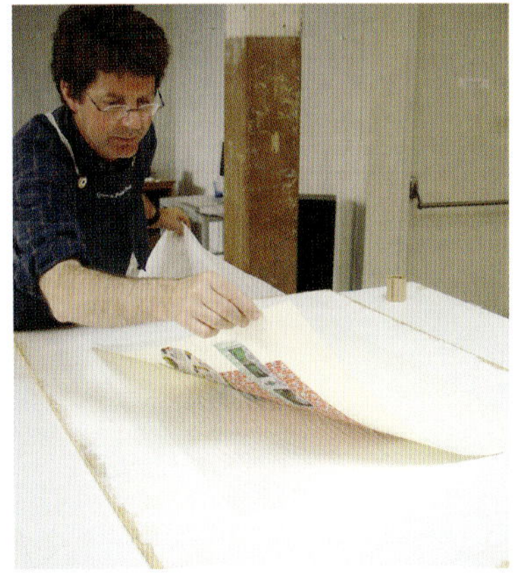

POSITION THE DAMPENED ART ON THE BOARD.

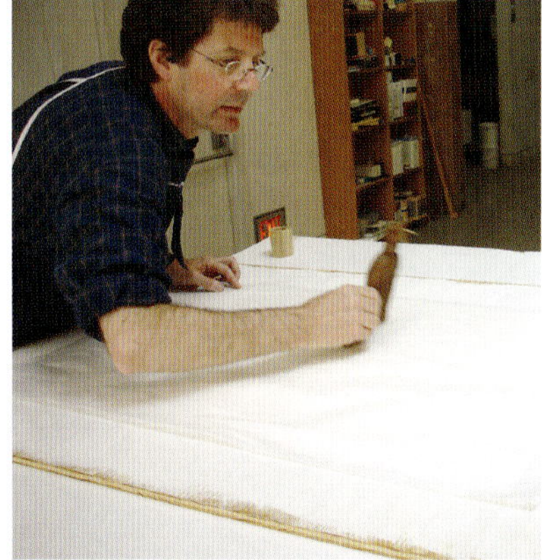

SMOOTH OUT THE RIPPLES.

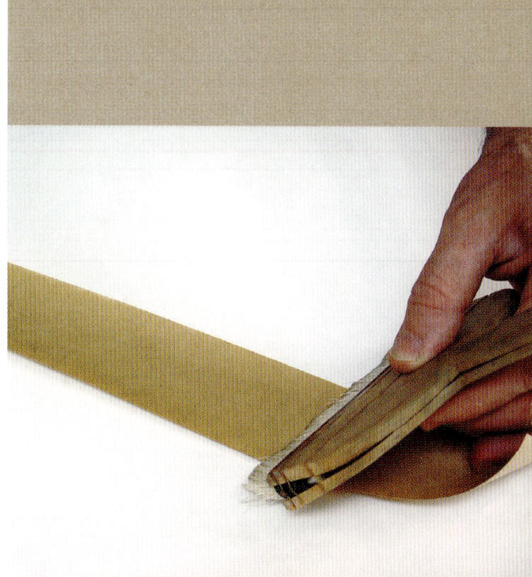

WET THE TAPE.

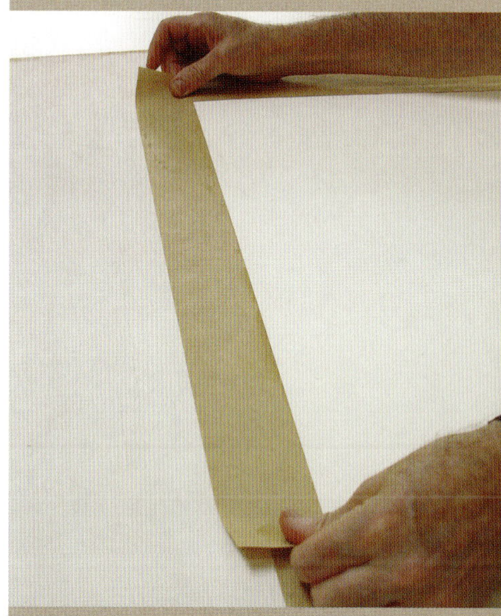

TAPE THE EDGES.

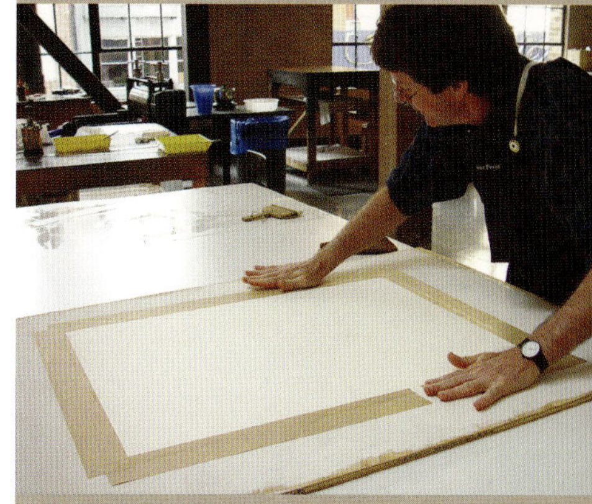

THE GAP ABOVE THE FINGERS OF SHURE'S LEFT HAND WAS LEFT INTENTIONALLY.

1. **LAY THE DAMP ARTWORK ON THE BOARD**

   If you are drying several works side by side, leave at least an inch of room between them to facilitate removal. If a work is face in, you may want to insert a piece of tissue between it and the board.

2. **SMOOTH OUT RIPPLES**

   Use a brush, a folded rag, or your hand to smooth the ripples from the artwork.

3. **APPLY TAPE**

   Cut strips of paper tape to the length of each side. On one side, use two strips with a gap between them. Moisten each strip and firmly tape the artwork to the board. Leaving a gap between pieces of tape along one edge makes later removal of the tape easy.

LEAVE THE ART TAPED OVERNIGHT OR UNTIL DRY.
NOTICE THE GAP AT THE SIDE.

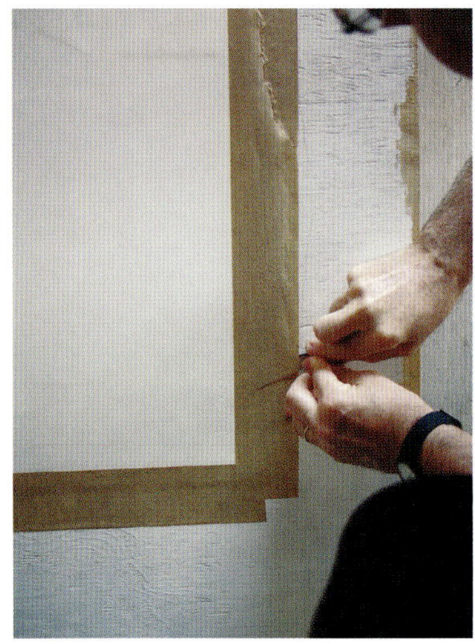

WORK A KNIFE DOWNWARD BETWEEN THE TAPE
AND THE BOARD, STARTING AT THE GAP.

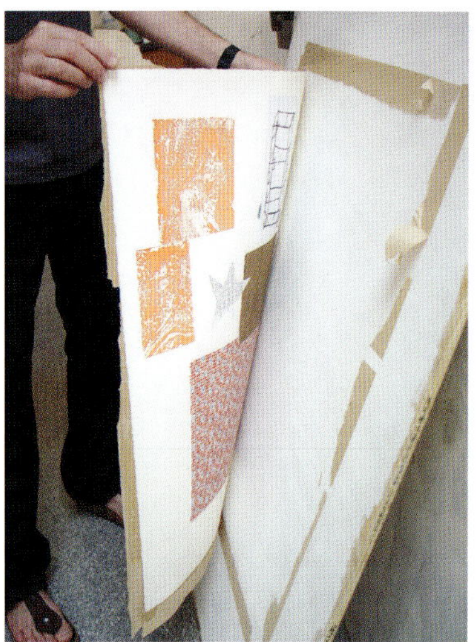

PULL AWAY THE ART.

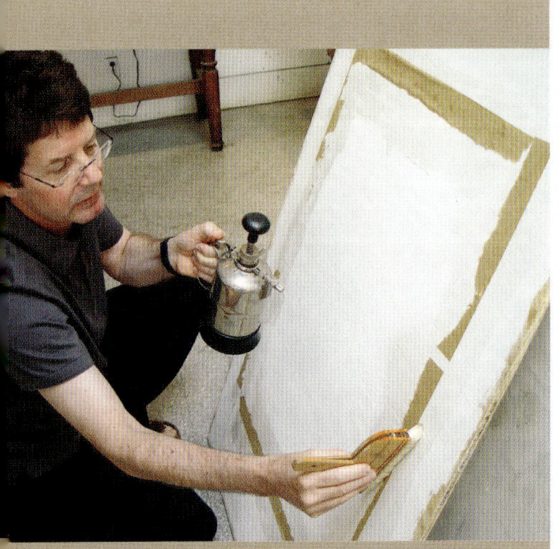

CLEAN THE REMAINING TAPE OFF THE BOARD.

4.  **LEAVE THE WORK OVERNIGHT TO DRY THOROUGHLY**

    If the weather is humid, leave the art taped longer. It
    should be completely dry and warm to the touch before
    you remove it. You can speed drying with a hair dryer or a
    heater with a fan.

5.  **REMOVE THE ARTWORK AFTER IT IS DRY.**

    Gently slip a knife or spatula underneath the paper at the
    space between the two pieces of tape, and slowly work the
    knife along, pushing against the tape with the blade held at
    an oblique angle. You want to tear rather than cut the tape,
    and with some practice you will be able to lift most of the
    tape cleanly away from the board by working up one edge
    with the knife and then lifting that edge.

6.  **CLEAN THE REMAINING TAPE FROM THE BOARD OR WALL**

    Brush or mist the tape with clean water and leave it for a few
    minutes until the paste has softened. Then peel it away and
    clean off any residue with a moist clean sponge or cloth.

7.  **IF THE ARTWORK WAS PASTED FACE IN, RETAIN ITS ORIGINAL EDGES**

    If the work was face in and you wish to retain the original edges, you can simply peel the paper tape away from the back of the work, then burnish the edges with a paper burnisher or similar tool.

8.  **IF THE ARTWORK WAS PASTED FACE OUT, TRIM IT INSIDE THE TAPED EDGES**

    Use a sharp mat knife to cut as close to the tape as possible. You can also remove the art as shown in step 7, then in a separate step, tear or cut the edges inside the attached tape.

    TIP *After you have cut the print away from the board, you can create a torn edge that simulates a deckle. Measure your margins accurately out from the plate mark on all four sides and mark them with pinholes. Turn the print over and tear it from the back against a beveled straightedge. After tearing, run your fingernail or a burnisher lightly around the edge of the paper to flatten it.*

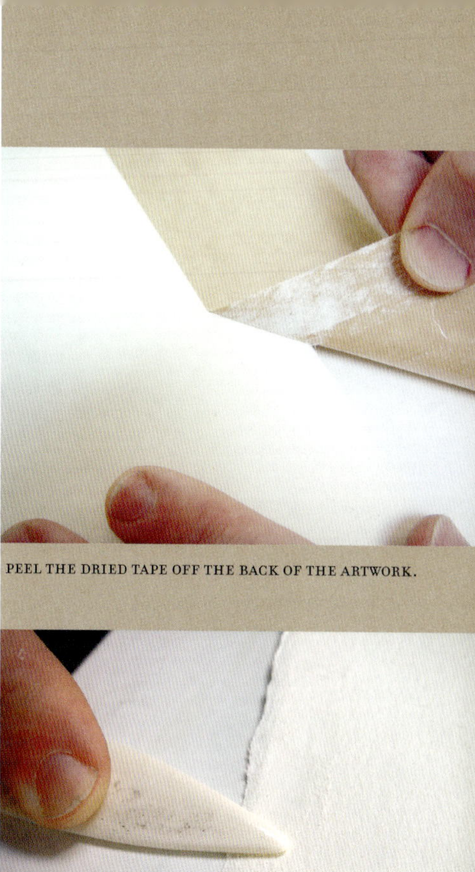

PEEL THE DRIED TAPE OFF THE BACK OF THE ARTWORK.

BURNISH THE AREA PREVIOUSLY COVERED BY THE TAPE.

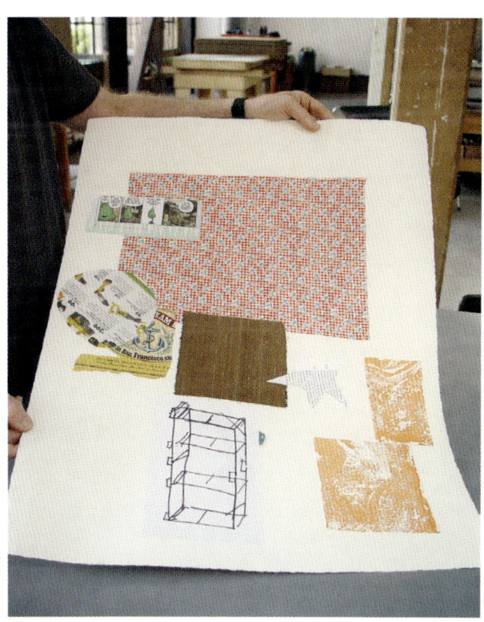

FLATTENED COLLAGE.

# Drying on a Wall and Removing the Work Intact Step-by-Step

This system, a modification of techniques used in drying prints on boards, can be employed to exhibit frail works on paper without frames or glass. After the exhibition, the works can be removed and stored rolled. They can be remounted at any future time.

1. **APPLY THIN WHEAT STARCH PASTE**

   You can apply it to the entire back of the artwork or to the edges only.

2. **ATTACH A TAB**

   With the artwork still flat on the table, paste a paper tab to the top edge at right angles to the sheet.

3. **POSITION THE ARTWORK**

   You can use a ruler pressed into the paste at the top edge of the work to help carry it to the wall and position it.

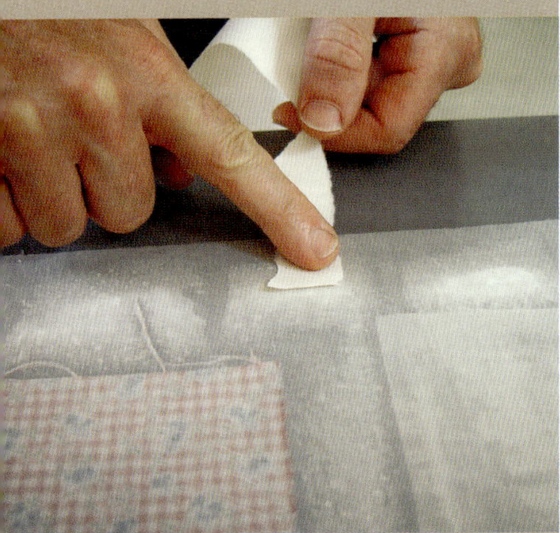

PASTE THE EDGES OR THE FULL SHEET.

PLACE A TAB ON ONE EDGE.

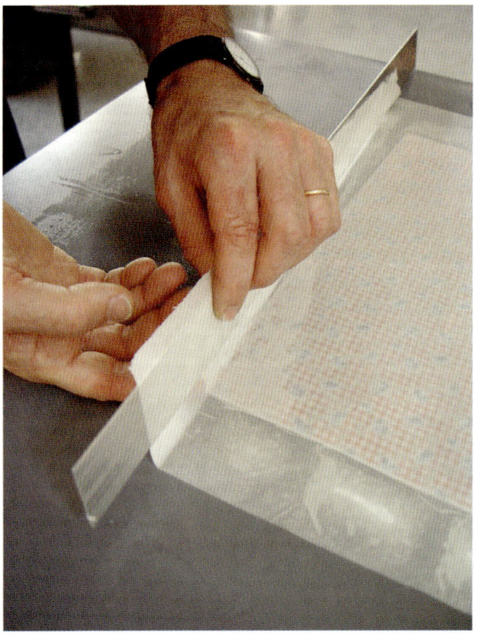

LIFT WITH A RULER.

4.  **ADHERE THE ARTWORK TO THE WALL**
Brush the edges and/or the face of the work against the
wall. Use tissue between the brush and the art if necessary.

5.  **DRY THE ARTWORK**
Leave the work at least overnight, or leave it in place for
exhibition if desired.

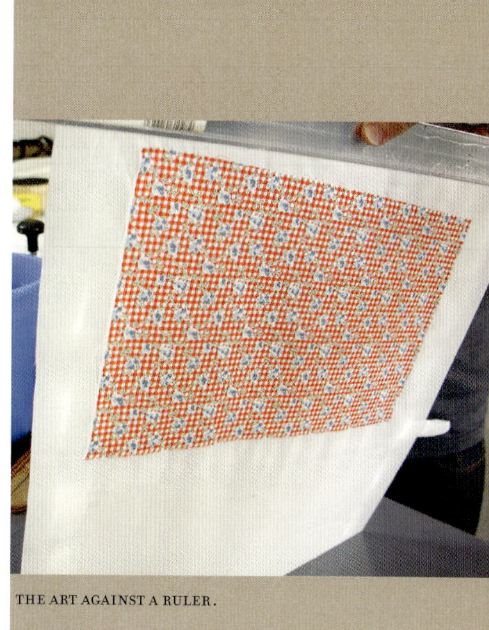

THE ART AGAINST A RULER.

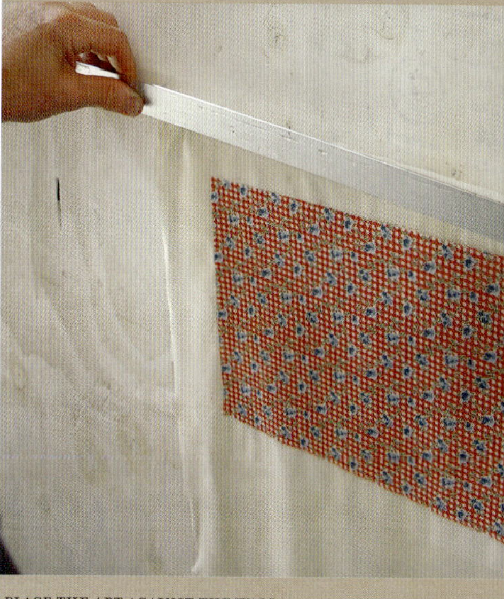

PLACE THE ART AGAINST THE WALL.

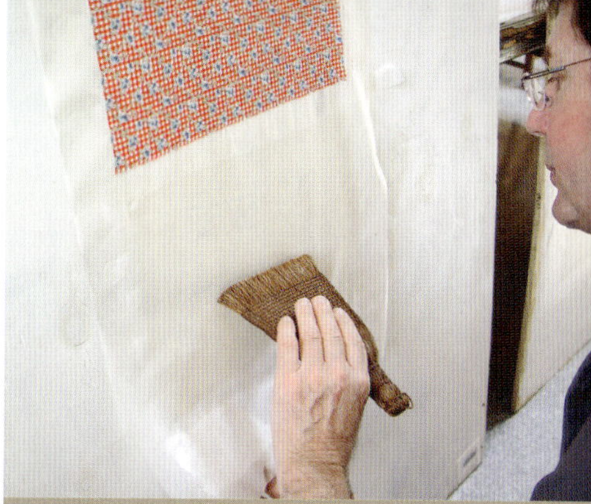

BRUSH DOWN TO ADHERE.

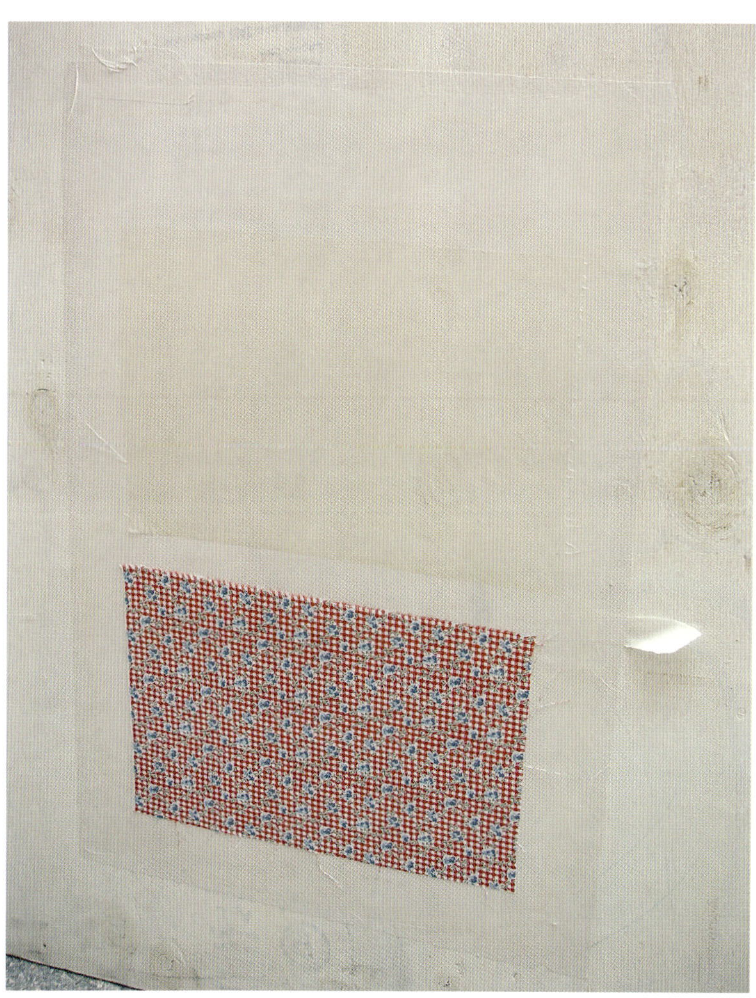

DRY THE WORK. THE TAB REMAINS.

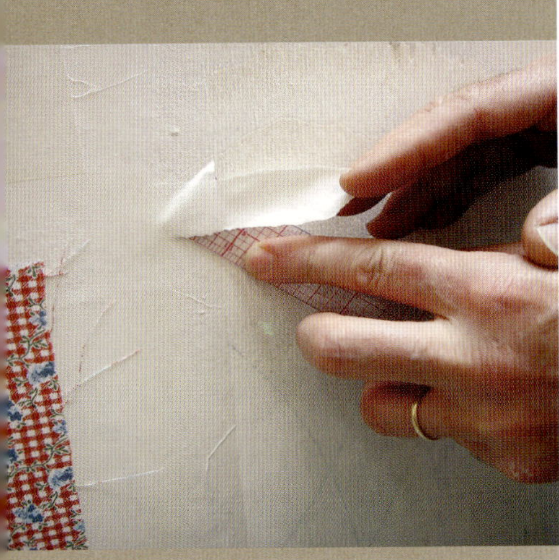

START LOOSENING AT THE TAB.

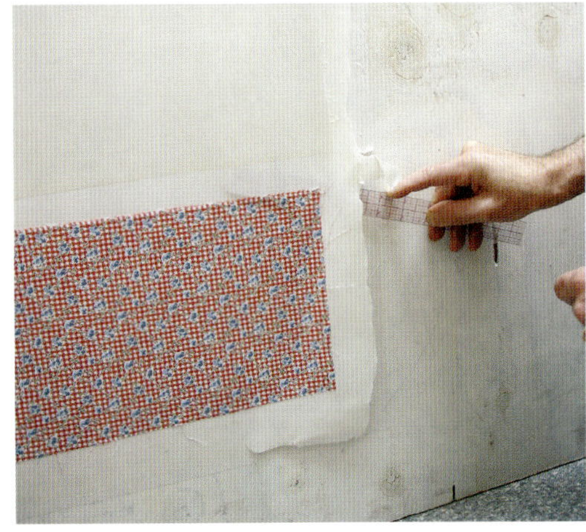

CONTINUE ALONG THE EDGES.

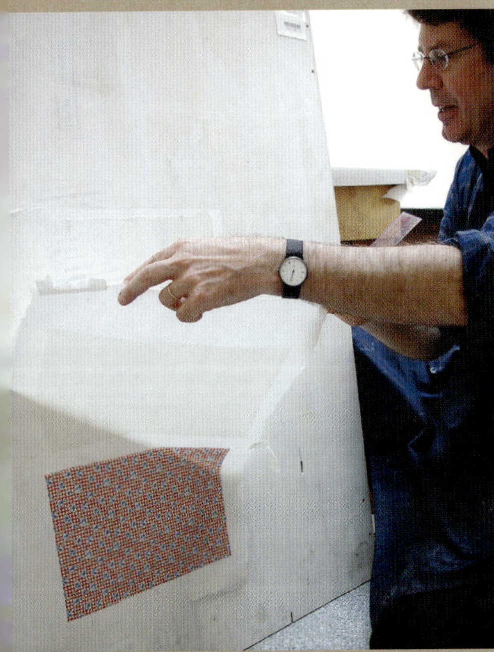

PULL OFF.

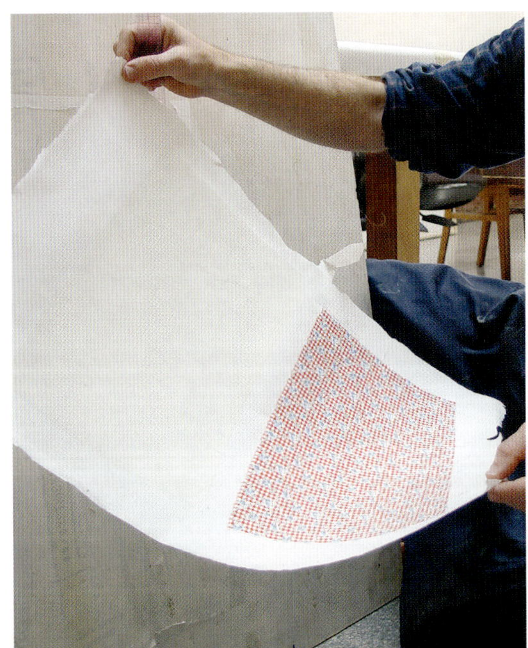

THE WORK IS INTACT.

6. **REMOVE THE WORK FROM THE WALL**
   Insert a thin plastic ruler or dull knife under the tab and slide the instrument along the edges between the wall and the paper.

7. **GENTLY PULL THE ARTWORK FROM THE WALL.**
   Store it until it is needed again.

# Using a Forced-Air Dryer Step-by-Step

A fast and efficient method of drying prints was developed at Crown Point Press in the mid-1970s and since then has been in continuous use there and at many other print workshops and paper conservation labs. For precise instructions for building a Crown Point dryer, visit www.magical-secrets.com. The dryer uses corrugated cardboard stacked alternately with sheets of dense smooth cardboard to hold the damp prints. The whole stack is then put under pressure, and hot air is forced through the corrugations to dry the prints.

The dryer has these essential parts: two same-size tables, larger than your largest prints; two types of cardboard sheets the size of the tables—double-walled corrugated cardboard and Upson Board (available from building supply outlets) or matboard; a squirrel cage blower; a small nontip electric heater with an internal fan; and a funnel-shaped bag, the small end sized to fit over the mouth of the blower and the large end sized to fit over the stack of cardboard.

The dryer setup is completed by applying pressure to the stack. The Crown Point dryer has slotted braces fitted with universal thread stock and nuts that are tightened with a wrench. If your prints are small and your stack short, you might get by with a sheet of plywood and some etching plates weighting the top.

At Crown Point, we are not concerned that acid from the drying boards might contaminate the prints. We have been using Upson Board for more than thirty years without any

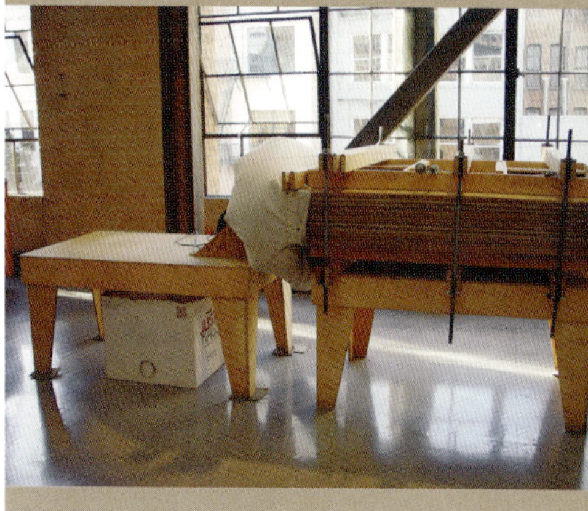

THE CROWN POINT DRYER.

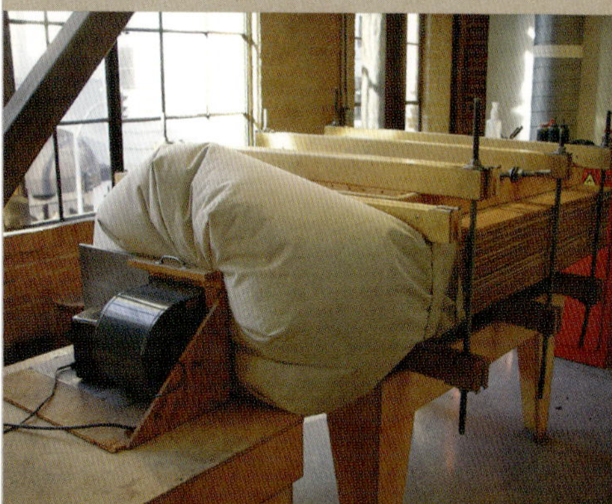

THE DRYER, SHOWING THE FUNNEL-SHAPED BAG AND BLOWER.

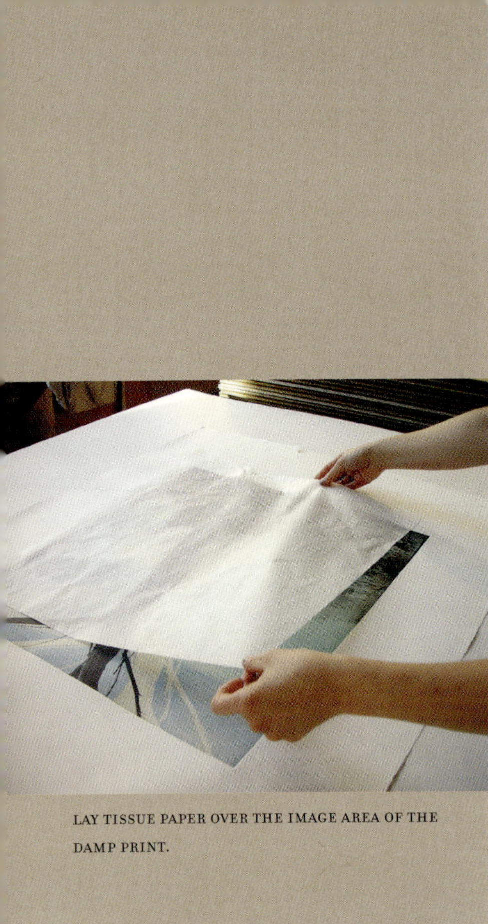



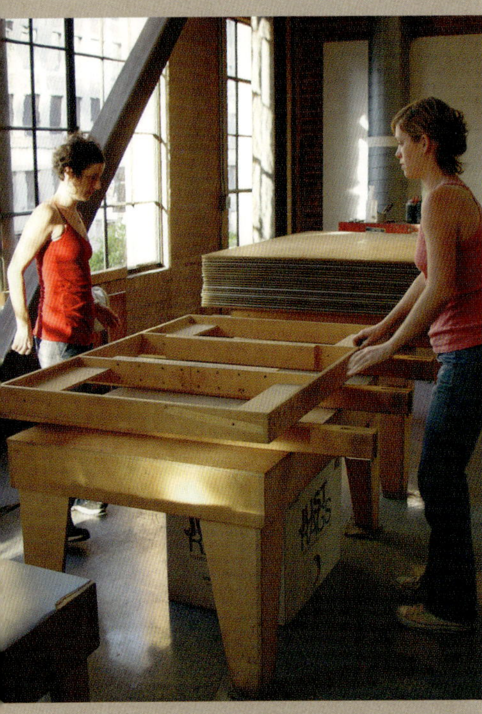



sign of discoloration from the drying process. The prints are in the dryer two days and nights, a short time, and a paper conservator has theorized that the movement of moisture from the paper into the Upson Board keeps any acid present in the board from migrating in the opposite direction. We are careful not to leave prints in the dryer for long periods after they have finished drying.

Your prints should be evenly damp, not wet, when they go in the dryer. At Crown Point, the prints usually have been kept in a damp pack after printing until the printers are ready to load the dryer. If a print has been air-dried, the printers mist it, wait for it to relax, and then blot it thoroughly before loading it.

Here are step-by-step instructions for loading a Crown Point forced-air dryer.

1. **PROTECT THE IMAGE AREA**

   If the ink is wet, lay a piece of tissue paper over the image area of each print. The tissue must be cut to fit inside the plate mark or be large enough to cover the entire sheet. If your image is larger than the tissue, butt sheets of tissue to cover it. Overlapping the pieces of tissue or leaving edges of the tissue on the margins of the prints during drying may cause embossed marks.

   TIP *The dryer maintains a clear plate mark, so normally nothing special needs to be done. However, if your prints are deeply embossed or an especially prominent plate mark is required, lay a piece of velveteen, large enough to cover the sheet entirely, under each print and another on top.*

2. **ARRANGE THE SLOTTED BRACES**

   The braces should be parallel and positioned so the slots hang over the edges of the table. On top of the braces, set the wooden frame on the braces that will hold the stack of cardboard and prints.

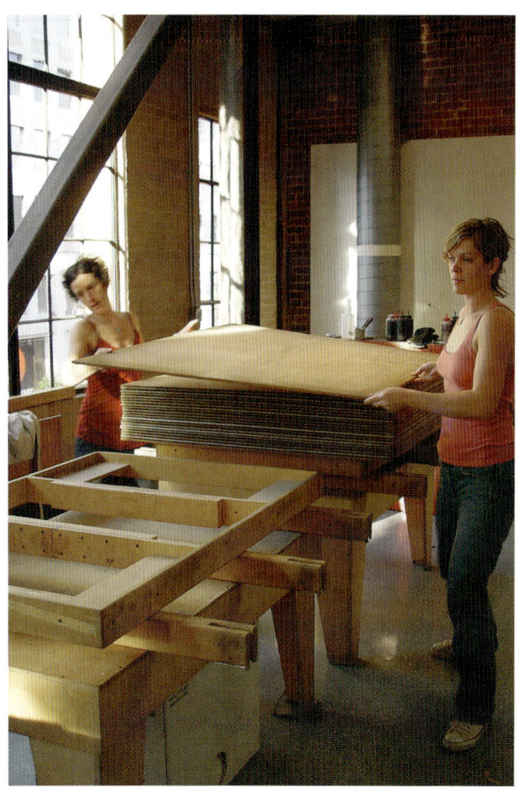

COVER THE FRAME WITH PLYWOOD.

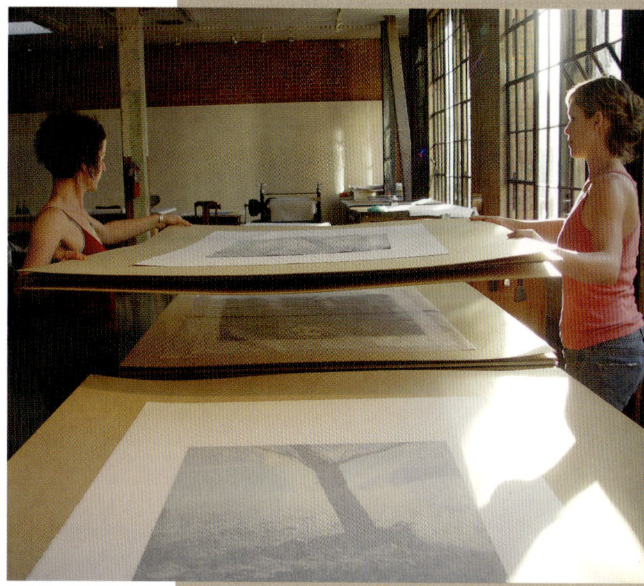

STACK THE PRINTS BETWEEN SHEETS OF SMOOTH BOARD WITH CORRUGATED SHEETS INTERLEAVED.

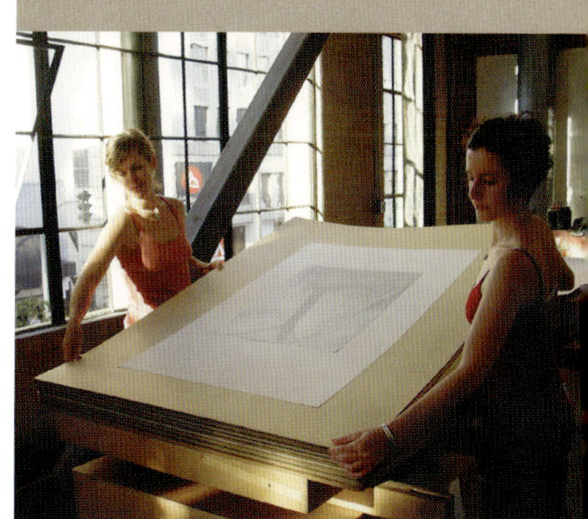

KEEP THE CORNERS ALIGNED.

3. **SET THE PLYWOOD IN PLACE**

Cover the frame with the sheet of plywood from the top of the dryer stack on the second table. Then add a sheet of corrugated cardboard and a sheet of smooth board (Upson Board, mat board, or similar). You will be transferring the sheets from the other stack and at the same time possibly removing dry prints.

4. **PLACE A PRINT BETWEEN SHEETS OF SMOOTH BOARD**

Remove a print from your damp pack, or from blotters, and set it on the smooth board. Cover the print with another sheet of smooth board, and then add a sheet of corrugated cardboard and a smooth sheet ready to receive the next print. The Crown Point printers pick up the three sheets together. As you build the stack, keep the corners aligned.

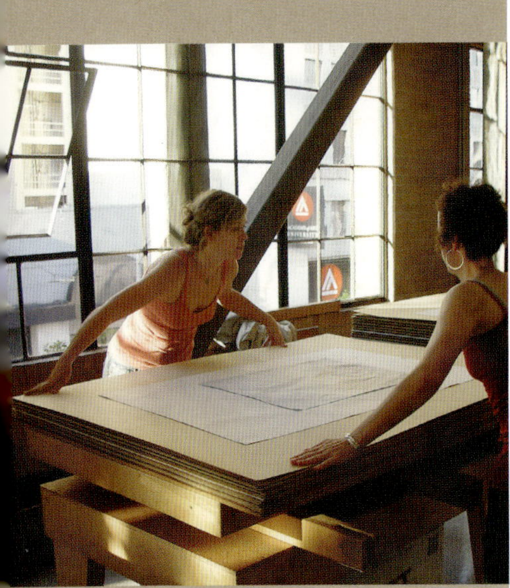



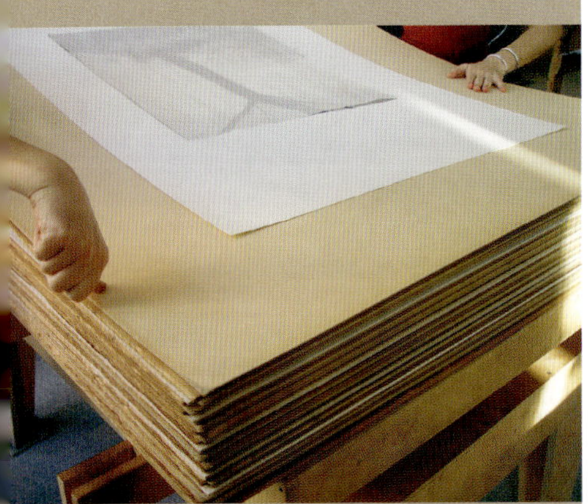



5. **KEEP BUILDING THE STACK**

Be sure to follow the same order: corrugated cardboard, followed by smooth board, a print, smooth board, corrugated cardboard, smooth board, a print, smooth board, and so on. After you have loaded all your prints, add any spare sheets of cardboard to the stack so that the air-funnel bag will fit.

TIP *If you find that the sheets of smooth board are warping, flip them so the opposite side is the one wicking the moisture.*

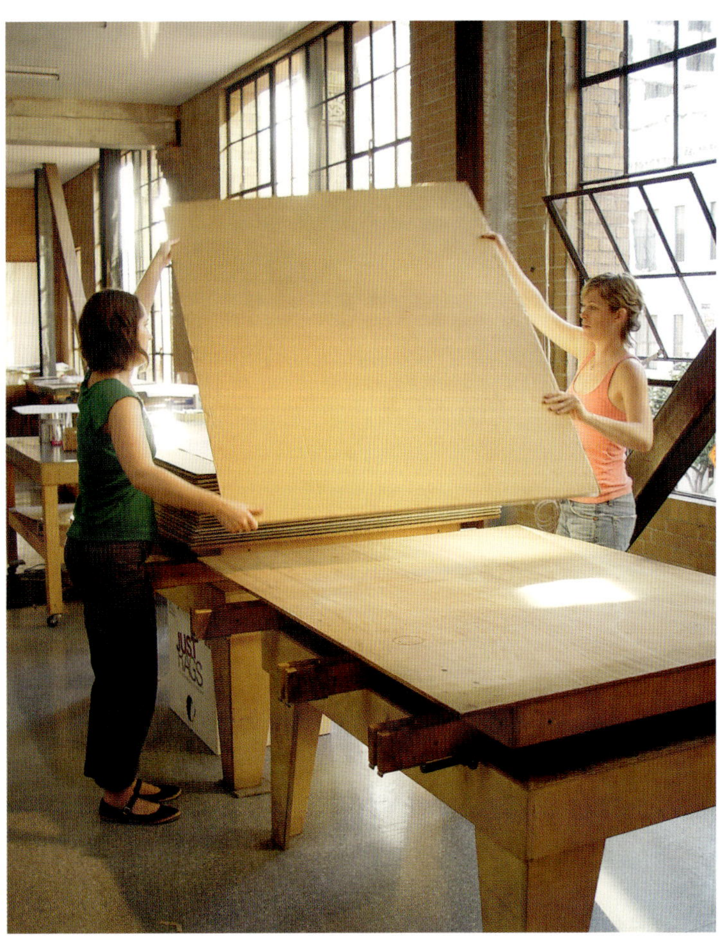

FLIP THE SHEETS OF SMOOTH BOARD OCCASIONALLY. EMILY YORK, CATHERINE BROOKS.

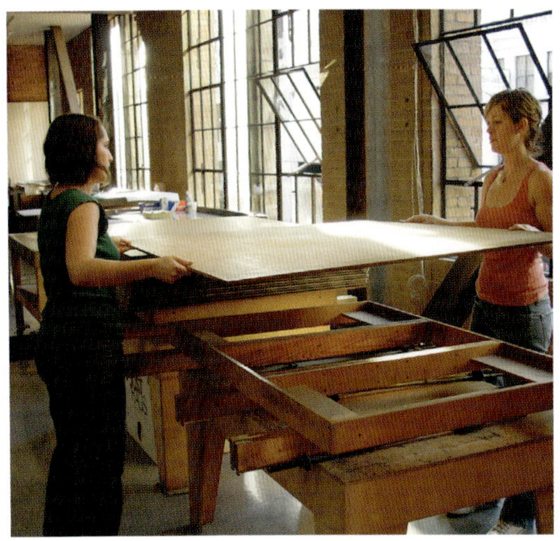

PUT PLYWOOD ON TOP OF THE STACK.

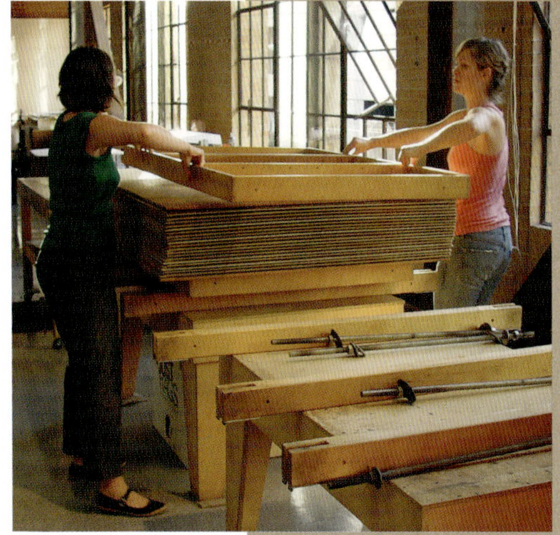

ADD THE FRAME.

6.  **COVER THE STACK**

    Top the stack with the plywood sheet from the bottom of
    the stack that you just dismantled.

7.  **SECURE THE STACK**

    Put the top frame in place and arrange the slotted braces
    parallel to one another and aligned with the braces on the
    bottom of the stack. Slide the universal thread stock into
    the slots and tighten the nuts with two wrenches. Hold the
    nut on the bottom with one wrench while you tighten the
    top nut with another.

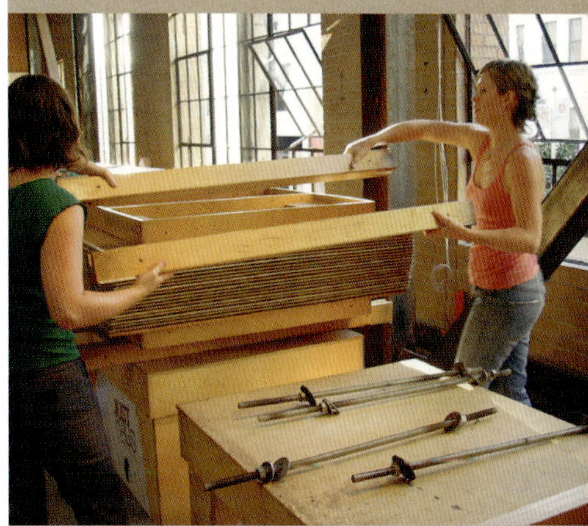

ADD THE SLOTTED BRACES AND ALIGN THEM.

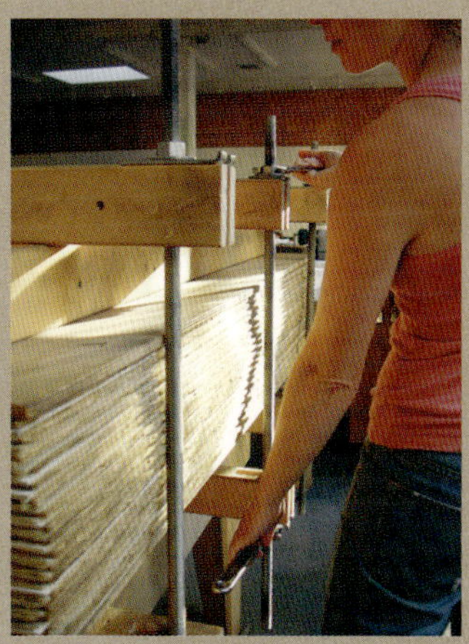

SLIDE THE THREAD STOCK INTO THE
SLOTS AND TIGHTEN.

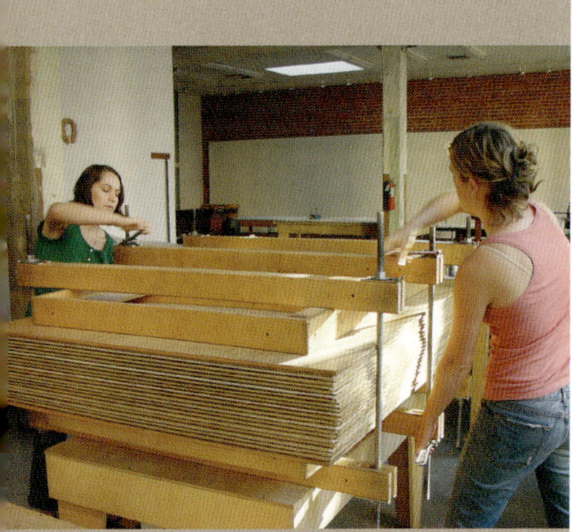

TIGHTEN BOTH SIDES EVENLY.

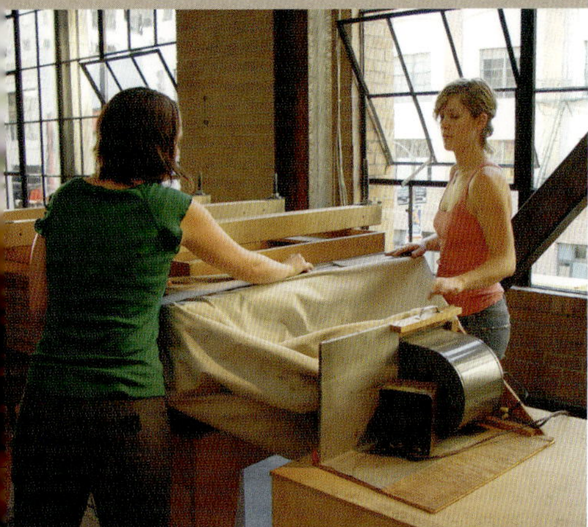

FASTEN THE LARGE END OF THE BAG OVER THE
STACK. SET THE HEATER NEXT TO THE BLOWER.

8. **TIGHTEN BOTH SIDES EVENLY**

Experience will teach you the proper amount of pressure.
Generally, the more damp prints you put in the dryer,
the more pressure you need because there will be more
shrinkage in the stack during drying.

9. **ATTACH THE BAG**

Fasten the large end of the bag over all the boards in the
stack using a tie or bungee cord if you don't have a special
clamp. The narrow end of the bag covers the mouth of the
squirrel cage blower. Set a small electric heater next to the
blower intake (but not touching it). Turn on the blower
and run the heater on medium. The dryer also works well
without a heater, but the drying time is longer.

10. **DRY THE PRINTS**

Warm air circulates through the corrugations, and the
smooth board wicks moisture from the prints. The Crown
Point printers recommend that prints stay two days and
two nights in the dryer. You will want to make adjustments
for type of paper, degree of moisture, and other factors.
Dry your prints at least overnight.

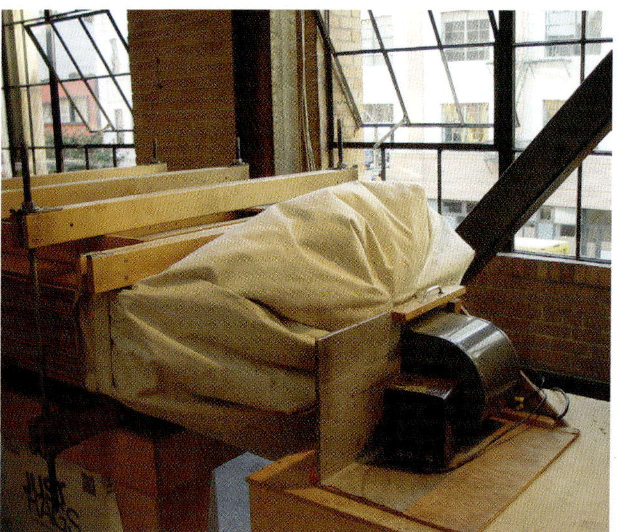

LEAVE THE PRINTS IN THE DRYER AT LEAST OVERNIGHT.

ROBERT BECHTLE   In 2005 the San Francisco Museum of Modern Art mounted a
retrospective (later traveling to the Modern Art Museum of Fort Worth, Texas, and
the Corcoran Gallery of Art, Washington, DC) of the paintings of Robert Bechtle
beginning with works done in 1964. Bechtle, who was born in San Francisco in
1932, has lived all his life in the San Francisco Bay Area, and his art is centered on
scenes from everyday life. In connection with the retrospective, Peter Schjeldahl
wrote in the *New Yorker* that in 1969, when he first noticed a Bechtle painting, he
was "rattled by the middle-class ordinariness of the scene." As he looked more
closely, he discovered "a feat of resourceful painterly artifice" that he gradually
realized was "beautiful." Schjeldahl concludes the article in this way: "Life is
incredibly complicated, and the proof is that when you confront any simple,
stopped part of it you are stupefied."

Bechtle began drawing and painting at a young age and won a scholarship
that paid for his first year of college by submitting a portfolio of artwork to a national
competition. After graduating from the California College of Arts and Crafts (now
the California College of the Arts) in Oakland, he was drafted into the U.S. Army
and sent to Berlin, where he painted murals in the mess hall and delighted in
visiting European museums. Back in California, he got an MA from CCAC and
began his teaching career there. Over the years he has taught in various Bay Area
institutions, especially San Francisco State University. Besides making paintings,
watercolors, and drawings, he is an accomplished printmaker: he worked in
lithography early in his career and mainly in etching after 1982 when Crown Point
Press began publishing his prints.

Bechtle was given his first solo museum exhibition in 1967 by the San
Francisco Museum of Art (now the San Francisco Museum of Modern Art), and
in 1970 the Whitney Museum of American Art in New York purchased a painting.
Since then, his work has been acquired by the Museum of Modern Art and the
Guggenheim Museum in New York, the Smithsonian Institution in Washington,
DC, and other museums in the United States, France, and Germany. Bechtle had
his first New York exhibition in 1971 at OK Harris Works of Art, where he continued
to show regularly until he joined the Barbara Gladstone Gallery in 2003. He is also
represented by Gallery Paule Anglim, San Francisco. —KB


BRAD BROWN   Brad Brown works predominantly on paper. About his working
process, he has said, "I have heaps of drawings and they are underfoot and in the
way, so they are being marked even when I'm not consciously working on them.
Sometimes I use a drawing as a drop cloth or a palette for another, and sometimes
my oil medium or something else drips or spills and stains a bunch of them. I want
all aspects of the process to be visible, and walking around the studio and stepping
on things is part of the process." Brown culls poetic fragments from his drawings
through folding, tearing, reassembling, and reworking them. Maria Porges wrote
in *Art in America* in 2001 that "Brown's drawings exude an air of poetic, random
inspiration, that of someone looking with intensity at anything and everything.
Brown draws primarily with charcoal, in a line simultaneously confident and
dreamy. Though other materials, oil paint and ink, are used to add splotches of

color, the compositions read as essentially black and white, dominated by the artist's virtuosic mark-making."

Brad Brown was born in 1964 in Raleigh, North Carolina. In 1987 he received his BFA in painting and printmaking from Virginia Commonwealth University and shortly thereafter moved to Brooklyn, New York. He moved to San Francisco in 1989 and lived there until 2003. He had his first solo exhibition in 1994 in San Francisco at the alternative art space Southern Exposure. Reviewing that exhibiton, Jamie Brunson, writing in *Art Issues*, spoke of "a visual experience that restores one's belief in the transcendental possibilities of art," and Kenneth Baker, writing in the *San Francisco Chronicle*, said the works "display a poise and freedom that comes to most artists, if ever, only after long experience."

Brown has done two projects in etching at Crown Point press, in 1999 and 2001. In the earlier project, he used dice to settle on whether to pour, paint, drip or blow the acid for each mark he made on a plate. Finally, he cut the plate into sixteen equal-sized pieces and asked the printers to assemble them randomly to produce a series of unique works rather than an edition. He has also worked extensively in lithography at Shark's Ink in Colorado.

Brad Brown has been a Richard C. Diebenkorn Teaching Fellow at the San Francisco Art Institute and was awarded a residency at Arcus Project in Moriya, Japan. He has had solo exhibitions at the Museum of Contemporary Art, Denver, and the Jundt Art Museum in Spokane, Washington. His work is in the collections of the Museum of Modern Art, New York; the San Francisco Museum of Modern Art; the Palace of the Legion of Honor, San Francisco; the Arkansas Art Center, Little Rock; and the Boise Art Museum, Idaho. Brad Brown lives and works in New York City. He is represented by the Larissa Goldston Gallery, New York. —DZ

ENRIQUE CHAGOYA "It is very important to understand the relationship between art and society," Enrique Chagoya has said. Chagoya combines imagery from art history and cartoons, appropriates images from various cultures, and juxtaposes disparate figures in satirical ways. In a 10-foot-long scroll, titled *An American Primitive in Paris*, for example, he mixed images of Superman, Jesus, and Aztec diagrams with portraits of Claude Monet and Che Guevara. In making his art, Chagoya has used painting, drawing, printmaking, video-animation, and installation. "My artwork is a conceptual fusion of opposite cultural realities that I have experienced in my lifetime," he says. Ken Johnson wrote in 2000 in the *New York Times*, "Enrique Chagoya is a gifted caricaturist and mimic. He grapples with the conflicts of his own hybrid inheritance, giving expression to an irreverent, wildly pluralistic imagination."

Chagoya was born in Mexico City in 1953. His father, a bank employee by day and painter by night, encouraged Chagoya's interest in art by teaching him to sketch at an early age. As a young adult, Chagoya enrolled in the Universidad Nacional Autónoma de México in 1975, where he studied political economy and drew political cartoons for labor union newsletters. In 1977 he immigrated to the United States and worked as a union organizer for farmers in Texas. Later he moved to Berkeley, California, where he embarked on a career in art. He began as a freelance illustrator and graphic

designer. In 1984 Chagoya earned a BFA in printmaking at the San Francisco Art
Institute and then pursued an MA and MFA at the University of California, Berkeley,
graduating in 1987. He is now an associate professor at Stanford University. He lives
in San Francisco.

Chagoya's early interest in political economy continues to inform his work.
"Humankind is at constant war with itself, and is perfectly capable of total
destruction," he has said. "This is the raw material of my work." He is a versatile
printmaker, working in his own studio and in the printmaking workshops Shark's
Ink in Colorado, Universal Limited Art Editions in New York, and Crown Point
Press for a 1997 project, *Why Draw a Live Model?*

Chagoya's work is represented in the collections of museums worldwide,
including the the Museum of Modern Art and the Metropolitan Museum of Art in New
York; the San Francisco Museum of Modern Art; and Centro/Arte Contemporaneo
in Mexico City. He has had many solo exhibitions, and in 2007 the Des Moines Art
Center in Iowa mounted a twenty five-year survey "Enrique Chagoya: Borderlandia."
Chagoya has received two National Endowment for the Arts fellowships, and in 1997
he won an Academy Award from the American Academy of Arts and Letters. Enrique
Chagoya is represented by Gallery Paule Anglim, San Francisco. —DZ

FRANCESCO CLEMENTE "Elegant and elusive, Francesco Clemente's paintings embrace
ambiguity in life, death, and art, often translating the chaste into the erotic with
unholy glee," wrote Lilly Wei in *Art + Auction* in 2006. Clemente is an extraordinary
iconographer. He draws from a cacophony of timeless symbols, themes, cultures,
periods, media, ways of thought, and of life. He has said that the tradition of art
"gives truthfulness to any image you come across." Clemente's signature concerns
revolve around the body, sexuality, and self-portraiture.

Clemente was born in Naples, Italy, in 1952. After early academic training in
classical languages and literature, he briefly, in 1970, studied architecture at the
University of Rome. Throughout the 1970s he made drawings based on childhood
memories and dreams. His first solo exhibition was at the Galleria Valle Giulia, Rome,
in 1971. The following year, Clemente met Alighiero e Boetti, whom he considered
a mentor. Clemente first visited India in 1973, a country to which he would return
for numerous sojourns. In 1974 he met Alba Primiceri, an actress in the Italian
theater, and later married her. She would become a frequent subject of his art. In 1981
Clemente moved to New York City, where he currently lives and works.

He has often engaged in collaborations. In Madras, India, he has worked
with sign painters, miniaturists, and local papermakers. In New York in 1984 he
collaborated on a number of works with Jean-Michel Basquiat and Andy Warhol. He
has published illustrated books in conjunction with poets Allen Ginsberg, Robert
Creeley, and René Ricard.

Clemente made his first prints at Crown Point Press in 1981 and over the
years has made many prints, drawings, and watercolors. His works on paper were
the focus of a retrospective organized by the Philadelphia Museum of Art in 1990,
which traveled within the United States and to the Royal Academy of Arts, London,
in 1991. Clemente's comprehensive body of work was the subject of a retrospective

at the Guggenheim Museum, New York, in 1999. It traveled to the Guggenheim Bilbao in Spain.

Clemente embarked on a series of midsized *alla prima* paintings in 2003 with tarotlike emblems, many of which were accomplished in a single day. This *Tandoori Satori* series was exhibited at the Museo Nazionale delle Arti del XXI Secolo, Rome, in 2006. Of these paintings Clemente has said, "They are a return to the source, to drawings I made in the '70s. I hold them fast, they are like a charm. They are amulets to protect myself with." In 2004 Clemente began a fresco project for the Museo d'Arte Contemporanea Donna Regina in his native city of Naples. In 2005 he exhibited self-portraits at the Gagosian Gallery in London. They reincarnated his perpetual themes of birth, death, and rebirth. Clemente has said, "A self-portrait is a way to register the constant appearing and disappearing of the self." Francesco Clemente's work is collected by many museums, among them the Museum of Modern Art and the Guggenheim Museum in New York, the Tate Collection in London, and the Kunstmuseum in Basel. He is represented by the Gagosian Gallery, New York. —DZ

CHUCK CLOSE In 1998 Chuck Close had a retrospective of his paintings at the Museum of Modern Art in New York. One of many laudatory reviews was in the *Wall Street Journal*, where Francine Prose wrote that "to spend time among these paintings is like acquiring a brand-new sense, or fine tuning an old one. What changes is our consciousness of how we see—and see the face, in particular. In their ability to make us mindful of the processes by which images come together in the brain, in life, and on canvas, Mr. Close's works offer revelatory, emotionally charged information about what's behind, and in front of, our eyes."

Close was born in Monroe, Washington, in 1940 and attended Everett Community College in 1958–60. In 1961 he won a coveted scholarship to the Yale Summer School of Music and Art, and the following year entered the degree program at the Yale School of Art. His fellow students included many artists who are influential today, among them Richard Serra, Nancy Graves, Brice Marden, Robert Mangold, and Sylvia Plimack Mangold. Close received both a BFA and an MFA from Yale. He lived in Vienna, Austria, on a Fulbright grant in 1964–65 and after that settled in New York City.

Close began exhibiting at New York's Bykert Gallery in 1970, the year it was founded, and showed there regularly until 1977, when he joined Pace Gallery. His first museum exhibition was at the Los Angeles County Museum of Art in 1971. In 1973 the Museum of Modern Art in New York presented a show focusing on one print, *Keith*, made at Crown Point Press a year earlier, along with working proofs. Close has been a printmaker throughout his career, with most of his prints published by Pace Editions, New York. Close's list of museum exhibitions is long and prestigious. His work is in the collections of most of the great international museums of contemporary art, including the Centre Georges Pompidou in Paris, the Tate Gallery in London, and the Walker Art Center in Minneapolis. An exhibition of his prints was organized in 2003 by the Art Museum of the University of Houston in Texas and traveled to the Metropolitan Museum of Art, New York, among other venues. The San Francisco Museum of Modern Art mounted a show in

2005 of Chuck Close's self portraits from 1967 to 2005. Close is represented by Pace Wildenstein in New York. —KB

MARY HEILMANN In 2007 a Mary Heilmann retrospective opened at the Orange County Museum, Newport Beach, California, before traveling to other venues, including the New Museum of Contemporary Art, New York, in 2009. In the catalog essay, Dave Hickey speaks of sharing with Heilmann "a tiny arc, a traverse through the historical world. We rode the same waves on adjacent beaches in Southern California. Alive with terror, we launched ourselves off the same diving platforms. . . . First and foremost (and as quaint as this may sound), we thought of ourselves as American. We are members, in fact, of the last generation for whom being an American seemed an intriguing and exciting proposition."

Hickey speaks of Heilmann's "resolutely high-style American painting," of her "cavalier informality," and of how "the canvas support on which she paints somehow manages to remain, in the minimalist tradition, a literal object—a literal object, however, that has been impudently decorated with painted marks." He says that "she has never trafficked in the 'new nostalgia' of current European painting," and at the end of his essay goes back to the metaphor of surfing. "Anything that goes well," he explains, "feels like dropping perfectly into the wave, like giving yourself up at the exact instant. . . For me, the confidence, anxiety, and relaxed intensity in Mary Heilmann's work speaks this physical/intellectual language." Dodie Kazanjian, writing in the August 2007 issue of *Vogue*, voices a similar feeling: "My eyes kept going back to the blue-and-white canvas. It was minimal but raw, an empty, sensuously brushed, somewhat sloppy blue square on an even emptier white ground, yet it contained a world of associations: water, sky, summer, youth, infinity. If I could look at this painting every day, I thought, I'd never need the simple beach house of my dreams."

Mary Heilmann was born in San Francisco in 1940 and grew up in Southern California. She has a BA in literature from the University of California, Santa Barbara, and an MA in ceramics and sculpture from the University of California, Berkeley. She moved to New York in 1968, where she was friendly with Bruce Nauman and Richard Serra, both of whom she had known in San Francisco. She was included in the Whitney Annual in 1972, and in 1975 joined the Holly Solomon Gallery, where she showed regularly through 1981.

Heilmann joined the Pat Hearn Gallery in New York in 1986 and until Hearn died in 2000 was part of an unusually close group of artists and friends associated with the gallery. In 1990 the Institute of Contemporary Art, Boston, presented a survey of Heilmann's painting. She produced print projects at Crown Point Press in 1998 and 2006 and has also worked in printmaking with Pace Editions in New York. In 1997 she had her first show at the Hauser & Wirth Gallery, Zurich and London, where she continues to exhibit regularly. Heilmann's paintings are in the collections of the Whitney Museum of American Art, New York; the Moderna Museet, Stockholm; and many other museums worldwide. She is represented by the 303 Gallery, New York. —KB

 Shoichi Ida, who died in 2006, was born in 1941 in Kyoto, Japan. He was trained in both Western and Eastern art traditions, but his work remained essentially Japanese. In 1997 Margaret Hawkins wrote in the *Chicago Sun-Times*, "In Ida's works there is a sense of purity and the feeling that he has uncluttered the vast abundance of nature so that we may see it more clearly." Since the mid-1960s, he often focused on a concept he called "The Surface Is the Between," which he first began to develop in printmaking and extended throughout his life to works in handmade paper, clay, bronze, steel, iron, and painting on paper and canvas. He explained his unifying concept in an interview published in the *Hara Museum Review* in 1987: "The surface can be the paper or canvas or whatever; it is the point of contact between me and the ideas I am working on. Through my work I try to make invisible phenomena visible by showing the point of contact."

Shoichi Ida earned a postgraduate degree from the Kyoto Municipal University of Art in 1964. He received a grant in 1968 from the French government to live and work in Paris and also lived briefly in New York and in San Francisco. He exhibited at the Holly Solomon Gallery in New York, the Perimeter Gallery in Chicago, and Don Soker Contemporary Art in San Francisco. In 1990 five of his prints were shown at the Cincinnati Art Museum.

Ida was perhaps best known as a paper artist and printmaker. He told Constance Lewallen in a 1989 interview that he was moved to begin making prints in the early 1960s when a stone left an impression on a piece of paper in his studio. In addition to a great deal of print work in Japan, he produced five etching projects with Crown Point Press between 1984 and 1992 and a woodcut in Crown Point's Japan program in 1986.

In 1986 Ida was presented with an Award for Excellence in International Cultural Exchange from the National Endowment for the Arts. In 1989 he was awarded the prestigious Suntory Prize in Japan. In 2003, in perhaps his final body of work, he collaborated with artist Robert Kushner on "East and West, Points of Contact," at the Sheehan Gallery in Walla Walla, Washington. He was given a retrospective at the Toyota City Museum in 2005.

Shoichi Ida's work is held in public collections around the world, including the Museum of Modern Art, New York; the Victoria and Albert Museum, London; and the National Museum of Modern Art, Tokyo. His estate is represented by the Perimeter Gallery in Chicago. —KLB

 "How to explain the living beauty, joyousness, and playful celebration in Robert Kushner's art?" Sara Lynn Henry asked in her catalog essay for Kushner's twenty-five-year retrospective at the New Jersey Center for Visual Arts in 1998. The explanation is personal, historical, and theoretical, the story of a career that is stubbornly original in its rejection of the idea that originality, or newness, is the main ingredient of good art. "I really believe the public deserves something beautiful," Kushner has said.

Robert Kushner was born in Pasadena, California, in 1949. He studied at the University of California at San Diego, where he developed a friendship with the art historian and critic Amy Goldin, who helped sharpen an interest in decorative art into a life project. On a trip to Turkey, Iran, and Afghanistan in 1974 with Goldin, Kushner recognized, he told Edward Gomez in *Art in America* in 2005, that in ancient Persia "the greatest minds had been making decoration." After that trip, Kushner moved to New York and became one of the founders of what was called the pattern and decoration movement. He was first known as a performance artist. His spontaneous, yet carefully researched paintings on pieced fabric would float and whirl on the back of a performer. The costumes were not accessories to the action. They were the action. As he moved into concentrating on painting and drawing, his allegiance to decoration stayed with him.

In 1980 Kushner was included in the Venice Biennale. In 1984 he had a solo show of paintings on paper at the Whitney Museum of American Art in New York. He is a dedicated printmaker, having worked in many media, especially etching, which he has done mainly at Crown Point Press. He participated in Crown Point's woodcut program in China in 1989 and went twice to Japan to work with Crown Point's master woodblock printer Tadashi Toda. Kushner has exhibited prints, paintings, and paper works widely in Japan.

Kushner's travels instilled in him the conviction, he says, that his work is "a slight update of a vast conservative tradition" that doesn't have borders. In 2005 he created a painting installation titled *Spring Scatter Summation*, filling the Great Room at the Wistariahurst Museum in Holyoke, Massachusetts. In the catalog essay, Peter Eleey wrote: "Maybe decorative painting can be an instrument through which we can harmonize the energies within and around us? Almost in spite of the horrors of the world, there remains a place to go, there is a refuge. There is, certainly, this room."

Robert Kushner's work is held in many museum collections around the world, including the Whitney Museum of American Art and the Metropolitan Museum of Art, New York; the National Gallery of Art, Washington, DC; the Tate Collection, London; the Uffizi Gallery, Florence; and the Kitakyushu Museum of Art, Japan. In 2006 the Mint Museum of Art in Charlotte, North Carolina, mounted an exhibition of his work. Kushner is represented by the DC Moore Gallery in New York. He lives and works in New York.—KLB


TOM MARIONI In a brochure for a 2005 exhibition titled "Sounds Like Drawing" at the Drawing Room in London, the show's curator, Anthony Huberman, describes Tom Marioni as "a seminal figure of the American conceptual art movement. He pioneered the use of social situations as art and explored performance as sculptural actions using sound, drawing, photography, and installation." Thomas McEvilley in the introduction to Marioni's 2003 memoir, *Beer, Art, and Philosophy*, says that "in terms of the history of art, the moment of Marioni's arrival was the beginning of a new era. All the rules were about to be rewritten and he would be a part of it."

Marioni was born in 1937 in Cincinnati, Ohio, attended the Cincinnati Art Academy, and in 1959 moved to San Francisco, where he still lives. His first sound work, *One Second Sculpture*, 1969, was celebrated in the 2005 Lyon Biennial as presaging the work of many artists today who use sound and duration as subjects. His first museum show was in 1970 at the Oakland Museum of California. Titled

"The Act of Drinking Beer with Friends Is the Highest Form of Art," it was an early example of social activity as art. Over the years, Marioni has been invited to repeat the work in various contexts around the world.

In 1970 Marioni founded the Museum of Conceptual Art (MOCA), which he described at the time as "a large-scale social work of art." Until the museum closed in 1984, he organized many groundbreaking shows, including "Sound Sculpture As" in 1970. MOCA has entered history as the first alternative art space in the United States. Marioni had one-person shows in several significant venues for early conceptual art, among them the Richard Demarco Gallery in Edinburgh in 1972 and Gallery Foksal in Warsaw in 1975. In 1977 he had a solo show, "The Sound of Flight," at the M. H. de Young Memorial Museum in San Francisco. He has done installation/performance works at the Whitechapel Gallery in London (1972), the Institute of Contemporary Art in London (1973), the Centre Georges Pompidou in Paris (1980), and the Folkwang Museum in Essen, Germany (1982), among other museums.

Marioni was included in important sound art shows: "For Eyes and Ears" (1980) at the Academy of Fine Arts in Berlin, "Live to Air" (1982) at the Tate Gallery in London, and "From Sound to Image" (1985) at the Stuttgart Staatsgalerie in Germany. His work was shown in "Out of Actions: Between Performance and the Object" in 1998, organized by the Museum of Contemporary Art in Los Angeles. Drawing is central to Marioni's art, and in 1999 he had a drawing retrospective at the Mills College Art Museum in Oakland. His prints have been published by Crown Point Press since 1974. In 2006 the Contemporary Arts Center in Cincinnati presented a survey exhibition of his work since 1968. Marioni was included in "The Art of Participation: 1950 to Now," in 2008 at the San Francisco Museum of Modern Art, and in 2009 in "The Third Mind: American Artists Contemplate Asia, 1860-1989" at the Guggenheim Museum, New York. His work is in the collections of the San Francisco Museum of Modern Art, the Museum of Modern Art in New York, the Stadtische Kunsthalle in Mannheim, Germany, and other museums. He is represented by Gallery Paule Anglim in San Francisco and the Margarete Roeder Gallery in New York. —KB

JULIE MEHRETU Julie Mehretu packs a great deal of information into her work: Chinese calligraphy, Japanese ink drawings, graffiti, video games, news imagery, weather systems, maps, blueprints, and city plans are all raw material for her paintings, drawings, and prints. Yet despite her dense collections of systems and shapes, her works remain light and full of great, sweeping space. Mehretu is interested in (as she has written) "the role of an individual within a larger context." Christopher Miles wrote in the September 2004 issue of *Artforum* that "Mehretu's paintings play disturbingly against a backdrop of recent disasters such as 9/11 and the disintegration of the space shuttle. Hers is a world in which things fall apart, but also fall together."

Julie Mehretu was born in Addis Ababa, Ethiopia, in 1970. She attended the Université Cheikh Anta Diop de Dakar in Senegal before moving to Kalamazoo, Michigan. She earned a BA from Kalamazoo College and an MFA from the Rhode

Island School of Design. A solo exhibition in 2003 at the Walker Art Center in Minneapolis was titled "Drawing into Painting," as her painting process is deeply rooted in drawing: she suggests movement, such as expanding spaces, through her dynamic use of line. Printmaking, like drawing, is of serious interest to her. For her complex prints made at Crown Point Press in 2006, she used multiple plates to layer many different processes over one another.

Mehretu was the recipient of the 2001 Penny McCall Award. In 2005 she received a MacArthur Fellowship and the American Art Award from the Whitney Museum of American Art. In 2007 she was awarded the Berlin Prize at the American Academy in Berlin. Her paintings are in the collections of the San Francisco Museum of Modern Art, the Walker Art Center, and the Museum of Modern Art in New York. In 2004 her work appeared at the Whitney Biennial and the São Paolo Biennial, and she has had solo shows at the Saint Louis Art Museum and the Walker Art Center. In 2007 exhibitions of her work were mounted at the Detroit Institute of Art; the Kunstverein, Hanover, Germany; and the Louisiana Museum of Contemporary Art, Denmark. In 2008 she had solo shows at Williams College, Massachusetts, and the Kresge Art Museum at Michigan State University. She is represented by The Project in New York and Los Angeles, the Barbara Davis Gallery in Houston, and Galerie Carlier in Berlin. She lives and works in New York and Berlin. —RL

SUSAN MIDDLETON Susan Middleton is a photographer specializing in portraits of animals and plants. She has been photographing rare and endangered species since 1986, and her work, with collaborator David Liittschwager, is collected in four books, two published by National Geographic Books and two by Chronicle Books. The working process developed by Middleton and Liittschwager is documented in an Emmy Award–winning National Geographic television special *America's Endangered Species: Don't Say Goodbye*, 1997. A book of Middleton's photographs with text by Mary Ellen Hannibal, *Evidence of Evolution: Darwin's Cabinet of Curiosities* was published by Abrams in 2009.

In pursuing her work, Middleton has traveled across the United States and has lived for extended periods in Africa and Hawaii. She is a certified diver and has accompanied scientific oceanographic expeditions. She generally isolates animals and plants in a studio-style setting with a plain backdrop, what she calls "mini-studios," even for live creatures photographed in the field. Biologist Edward O. Wilson has commented that "[her] remarkable portraits speak to the heart. In the end, their kind of testimony may count as much toward conserving life as all the data and generalizations of science."

Susan Middleton was born in 1948 and holds a BA in sociology, with a minor in art, from Santa Clara University, California. She apprenticed in photography by working as an assistant to Richard Avedon. Middleton chaired the department of photography of the California Academy of Sciences, San Francisco, from 1982 to 1995. In 2006 she produced a thirty-minute documentary film focusing on animals and plants of the northwestern Hawaiian Islands. In 2008 Crown Point Press in San Francisco published six photogravures of her images, four of them in color.

Middleton has said that she isolates her subjects from their environments so we can perceive them as individuals, "each in its own right." Many locations where she shoots are in remote and difficult terrain, and often she must wait long periods for an animal to become comfortable in the setup she creates for the photo. "When I photograph an animal, I always wonder how we, as humans, are known by that animal," she has said.

Her photographs have been exhibited in many museums, among them the American Museum of Natural History, New York; the National Academy of Sciences, Washington, DC; and the California Academy of Sciences, San Francisco. Her work is in the collections of those institutions and the Center for Creative Photography, Tucson; the Museum of Fine Arts, Houston; and the Honolulu Academy of Arts, among other public collections. She makes her home in San Francisco, California.–KB

CLAES OLDENBURG "Claes Oldenburg has always had a unique relationship with the commonplace. He has done more than extrapolate it from its habitual context; he has created it. He has exploited its dramatic and spectacular potential, finally giving it hypersignificance," wrote Germano Celant in *The Course of the Knife*, published in 1989. In his sculptures, Oldenburg takes an object from the everyday world such as a typewriter, lipstick, flashlight, hamburger, or tube of toothpaste, and lifts it out of its usual context by dramatically changing its scale or texture. He often uses soft, sensuous materials, making the familiar item strange and remarkable, yet uniquely humorous. Many pieces are metaphors for parts of the human body, often having sexual connotations. "I am for an art that is political, erotical, and mystical, that does something more than sit on its ass in a museum," Oldenburg famously wrote in 1961.

Oldenburg was born in 1929 in Stockholm, Sweden, and settled with his family in Chicago in 1936. He attended Yale University and received a BA degree in literature and art in 1950. Returning to Chicago, he worked as a reporter at the City News Bureau and took night courses at the Art Institute of Chicago.

In 1956 Oldenburg moved to New York City and became an active member of the thriving artistic community. Oldenburg's first New York exhibition, in 1958, was a selection of his drawings included in a group show at Red Grooms' City Gallery. In 1959 he had his first solo show in New York, an exhibit of drawings and sculpture at the Judson Gallery. *The New Realists* exhibition at the Sidney Janis Gallery in 1962, which defined Pop Art, included Oldenburg's work.

Oldenburg views his work as a "single-minded aim to give existence to fantasy" and always looks for "a passage from the impossible to the possible." The fantastic quality of his work can especially be seen in the large-scale, outdoor, public monuments he began executing in the mid-1960s. Among them are *Lipstick on Caterpillar Tracks* (1969), first erected at Yale University; *Giant Icebag* (1969–70), which is motorized and inflates and deflates; and *Flashlight* (1981), a 38-foot steel monument in Nevada. Many of his monumental outdoor installations have been executed in collaboration with his wife, sculptor Coosje van Bruggen. In 1975 and 1976 Oldenburg produced eleven etchings at Crown Point Press, which were published by Multiples, Inc.

In 1995 Claes Oldenburg had a solo exhibition at the Museum of Modern Art,

New York, and was given a retrospective organized by the National Gallery of Art, Washington, DC, and the Solomon R. Guggenheim Museum, New York. In 2002 Oldenburg and van Bruggen installed four large-scale sculptures in the roof garden of the Metropolitan Museum of Art. Oldenburg's work is represented in numerous public collections, including the Whitney Museum of American Art, New York; the Tate Gallery, London; and the San Francisco Museum of Modern Art. Oldenburg lives and works in New York and is represented by Pace Wildenstein, New York. —DZ

NATHAN OLIVEIRA "Nathan Oliveira's passion is for continuing an inner-directed artistic tradition attached to the human subject. . . . The evocation of mystery that the viewer experiences in Oliveira's work derives from a depth of feeling refracted through artistic tradition and transmitted to the spectator by the artist's hand," wrote Peter Selz in a catalog essay for Oliveira's 2002 retrospective at the San Jose Museum of Art, California.

Oliveira was born in 1928 in Oakland, California, to a family of Portugese immigrants. He studied painting and printmaking at the California College of Arts and Crafts (now the California College of the Arts) in Oakland, and in the summer of 1950 with Max Beckmann at Mills College in Oakland. After two years in the U.S. Army as a cartographic draftsman, he began teaching painting in 1955 at CCAC and drawing and printmaking at the California School of Fine Arts (now the San Francisco Art Institute). Since then he has had guest teaching appointments at many art schools and universities. He held a tenured teaching position at Stanford University from 1964 until he retired in 1995. He lives in Stanford, California.

In 1959 Oliveira was the youngest painter included in the important exhibition "New Images of Man" at the Museum of Modern Art in New York.     A survey of five years of his paintings and works on paper was shown at the Art Gallery of the University of California, Los Angeles, in 1963, and in 1973 the Oakand Museum of California showed a fifteen-year survey of his paintings. In 2002 a painting and printmaking retrospective with a major catalog initiated by the San Jose Museum of Art traveled to the Neuberger Museum of Art, Purchase, New York, and three other museums. Oliveira had a print retrospective in 1980 at California State University, Long Beach, and the California Palace of the Legion of Honor in San Francisco organized a survey of his work in monotype in 1997. In 2008 the Palo Alto Arts Center mounted an exhibition of his work titled "Nathan Oliveira: The Painter's Bronzes." Oliveira was elected to the American Academy of Arts and Letters in 1994 and has received many other awards, including a Guggenheim Fellowship, two honorary doctorates, and, in 2000, membership in a distinguished order conferred by the government of Portugal. His work is in the collections of many museums, among them the Art Institute of Chicago, the Carnegie Institute in Pittsburgh, the Metropolitan Museum of Art in New York, and the Museum of Modern Art in New York. He is represented by the DC Moore Gallery, New York; the Marsha Mateyka Gallery, Washington, DC; and the John Berggruen Gallery, San Francisco. —KB

JUDY PFAFF Judy Pfaff has been showing her work since the 1970s, but her spontaneous exploration of dimensions and materials continues to inspire younger artists to blur the distinctions between painting and sculpture. *New York Times* critic Roberta Smith has described her dense but uncluttered installations as "airy," "exhilarating," "elaborately impure, implicitly narrative environments." Another *Times* critic, Benjamin Genocchio, has observed that "it is remarkable how all the elements seem to hang together and develop on one another. She seems somehow to get order and disorder working for her at the same time . . . a very contemporary quality, given our lives today."

Pfaff studied at the Yale University School of Art with artist Al Held, who was a mentor to her personally and artistically. She has a strong, kinetic connection to her work. "Sometimes students ask me — they want to be told — 'How do you do this?' They do all the reading, but when they get their hands in it, they find out the stuff has a mind of its own. It's like having children, I would imagine," Pfaff has said. She seldom has an idea of what a completed artwork of hers will look like in the end. Pfaff gained international prominence in the 1980s, a decade when her work garnered an enthusiastic following among those interested in the connection between "high" and "low" art. Her forms seem both organic and highly engineered, but she invents them intuitively, so there is a freshness to her work that does not counteract its familiarity.

Pfaff was born in 1946 in London, England, and raised in Detroit. She received her BFA from Washington University in St. Louis and her MFA from Yale in 1973. Since then, she has mounted more than a hundred solo exhibitions and two hundred group exhibitions and has received numerous grants, including a 1983 Guggenheim Fellowship in sculpture and two grants from the National Endowment for the Arts. Her work is in collections in Germany and the United States nationwide, notably at the Museum of Modern Art in New York, the Whitney Museum of American Art in New York, and the Library of Congress in Washington, DC. Pfaff represented the United States in the Venice Biennale in 1982. In 2004 she was awarded a MacArthur Fellowship. She lives and works in New York City. —RL

TIM ROLLINS In the early 1980s Tim Rollins conducted art classes throughout the New York City school system under the auspices of a program called the Arts and Literacy Project. In 1982 he settled at a school in the South Bronx, where he taught art to junior high school students who had been classified as learning disabled, emotionally handicapped, truant, or otherwise at risk. Two years later, he launched the Art and Knowledge Workshop, working after school with a group of students aged sixteen to nineteen. He read aloud to the kids, and as he did, the kids drew. In time, he decided to attempt what he called "a strange and stumbling hybrid" and make his own art in collaboration with the kids, who chose to call themselves K.O.S., Kids of Survival. "What we're doing changes people's conception about who can make art, how art is made, who can learn and what's possible, because a lot of these kids had been written off by the school system," Rollins said.

In 1986, in the *New York Times*, Roberta Smith wrote: "Tim Rollins + K.O.S. are producing artwork of a remarkable sophistication, which refuses to conform to known categories but alternates between the literary and the visual, the modern and the naive."

Tim Rollins was born in Pittsfield, Maine, in 1955. He studied fine art at the
University of Maine and earned a BFA from the School of Visual Arts, New York, in
1978. Later, he pursued graduate studies in art education at New York University.
Rollins is a cofounder of Group Material (1979), a collective of socially committed
artists.

The imagery for paintings by Rollins + K.O.S. is drawn from American and
European literature—Melville's *Moby Dick*, Hawthorne's *The Scarlet Letter*, Kafka's
*Amerika*, and Schubert's song cycle *Winterreise*, for example. The kids paint highly
personalized forms and symbols over book pages pasted, usually, on mural-
sized canvas. "We vandalize the book, but we also honor it," Rollins says. In 1989
Rollins brought a group of K.O.S. members to the Crown Point Press studio in San
Francisco and they produced a portfolio of fourteen prints inspired by Gustave
Flaubert's prose-poem, "The Temptation of Saint Anthony." A second project in
1990 extended their work on the same text. Reviewing that work in 1990, for *SF
Weekly*, Glen Helfand wrote, "Collaborative, multicultural and visually striking,
the unlikely art-and-education work of Tim Rollins + K.O.S. is perhaps the
quintessential art of today."

Rollins continues to work with K.O.S. thirty years after the group's formation,
though the individual members have changed over time. The art of Rollins + K.O.S.
has been shown worldwide and is in the permanent collections of more than seventy
museums, including the Museum of Modern Art, New York; the Hirshhorn Museum
and Sculpture Garden, Washington, DC; the Tate Gallery, London; and the Museum
for Gegenwartskunst, Basel. Rollins lives and works in New York City, and Tim Rollins
+ K.O.S. is represented by Lehmann Maupin Gallery, New York. —DZ


WILSON SHIEH Chinese artist Wilson Shieh paints and draws in the *gongbi*, or fine-
line, style of Ming dynasty painters of the seventeenth century, but his subject
matter is humorously, stylishly, and politically contemporary. Ian Findlay wrote
in *Asian Art News* in 2001, "There is a timeless quality to Shieh's images that seems
to spring from another age and it is one that he suggests is intentional. Yet, at the
same time, he sees that he conforms to some extent with the tradition upon which
he draws."

Shieh was born in 1970 into a family of traders, the third generation of Hong
Kong residents in his family. His hometown, Kennedy Town, is a melting pot of
Chinese, Portugese, British, and South Asian cultures, and his work reflects that
diversity. Shieh's *Swimmer*, one of the prints he completed at Crown Point Press
in 2005, is derived from the *Four Swimmers* series he completed a year earlier
in watercolor and gouache on dyed silk. The titles of the individual paintings,
inscribed on the images themselves in English, Chinese, and Portugese, come from
famous Brazilian bossa nova songs Shieh heard during his childhood. The songs,
like his work, are characteristically both playful and unnerving. One finds oneself
questioning, for example, his swimmer's suggestive gesture—is it a wave of hello or
a drowning man's arm thrown up for help?

Shieh received his BFA in 1994 and his MFA in 2001, both from the Chinese
University of Hong Kong. His first solo exhibition was at the Hong Kong Arts Centre

in 1998; in 2002 he began showing at Grotto Fine Art, Hong Kong. Since then, he
has gained an international reputation. He won the Philippe Charriol Foundation
Art Competition in painting in 1997 and the Prize of Excellence at the Hong Kong
Art Biennial in 2003, the same year he was awarded an Asian Artists Fellowship
by the Freeman Foundation through the Vermont Studio Center. His work is in
the collections of many Hong Kong institutions, including the Museum of Art,
the Heritage Museum, the Philippe Charriol Foundation, and the British Council,
and in collections outside Hong Kong at the Queensland Art Gallery in Brisbane,
Australia, the Asian Art Museum in San Francisco, and the Ashmolean Museum of
Art and Archaeology at the University of Oxford. —RL

PAT STEIR "The career of the American artist Pat Steir has been one of pushing
against the current to reach a pinnacle of strength," wrote Herbert Muschamp in
a feature article in *Vogue* in 1990. "Steir has spent three decades navigating the
treacherous eddies of an increasingly competitive art world, finally reaching a
peak of achievement with the series of waterfall paintings that has preoccupied
her since 1987. Legendarily an artist's artist, Steir has managed to sidestep the
movements and factions that have snared so many of her contemporaries." Her
critical support has been enthusiastic as time has gone by. "Beauty and intellect join
forces in Pat Steir's impressive new paintings," reported Ken Johnson in the *New
York Times* in 1997. And in 2005 Susan Harris wrote in *Art in America* that "the joy
of Steir's work lies in its simultaneous occupation of real and metaphysical realms,
which is sourced as much in her surrender to the pulse of the universe as in the
process of making art."

Steir was born in 1938 in Newark, New Jersey, and lives in New York City. She
attended the Pratt Institute in New York in 1956–58 and Boston University College
of Fine Arts in 1958–60, then returned to Pratt to receive a BFA in 1962. Both
institutions have honored her: Boston University in 2001 with a Distinguished
Alumni Award and Pratt in 1991 with an honorary doctorate.

In 1962, the year she graduated from art school, Steir was included in a group
show at the High Museum of Art in Atlanta. In 1964 her work was in a show called
"Drawings" at the Museum of Modern Art in New York. Her first one-person
exhibition was at the Terry Dintenfass Gallery, New York, in 1964. During that time,
she worked in New York as an illustrator and a book designer. Around 1970 she
became friends with Sol LeWitt, Lawrence Weiner, and other conceptual artists,
and she made a trip to New Mexico to visit Agnes Martin.

Steir's first museum exhibition, in 1973 at the Corcoran Gallery of Art,
Washington, DC, marks the beginning of a career dense with painting exhibitions.
She has also made installation work (shown at Documenta IX, Kassel, Germany,
in 1992) and is an important printmaker. Crown Point Press began publishing her
prints in 1977, and in 1983 the Spencer Museum of Art, University of Kansas, gave
her a print and drawing exhibition. A print retrospective at the Cabinet des Estampes
in Geneva traveled to the Tate Gallery in London. Steir has had one-person painting
exhibitions at the Brooklyn Museum in 1984 and the New Museum of Contemporary
Art in New York in 1987, both of which traveled to other museums, many in Europe.

In 2007 her paintings were exhibited in the Reykjavik Art Museum in Iceland. Her work is in the collections of the Metropolitan Museum of Art, the Museum of Modern Art, the Guggenheim Museum, and the Whitney Museum of American Art in New York, and many other national and international museums, including the National Gallery of Art, Washington, DC, and the Tate Collection, London. She is represented by Cheim and Reid in New York. —KB  ·

WAYNE THIEBAUD "If the world were a perfect place," wrote Michael Kimmelman in the *New York Times* in 2001, "the Wayne Thiebaud retrospective that has just opened at the Whitney Museum would be nailed to the walls for good and we would be free to stop by whenever we needed to remind ourselves what happiness feels like." David Littlejohn reviewed the same show in the *Wall Street Journal* when it appeared in San Francisco at the California Palace of the Legion of Honor, which organized it in 2000. He praised "Mr. Thiebaud's way with light and shadow, his radiant rainbow outlines, his dance of brushstrokes, the rich white grounds on which he paints voluptuous colors and the rigidly controlled austerity of his compositions."

Thiebaud was born in 1920 in Mesa, Arizona, and resides in California, in Sacramento and San Francisco. As a child, he lived in Long Beach, California, and in Hurricane, Utah, where his family's farm failed during the Depression. The family moved back to Long Beach in 1933, and Thiebaud worked in his youth as a sign painter and as an "in-betweener" in the animation department of Walt Disney studios. He studied commercial art in a trade school, attended Long Beach Junior College, and worked as a shipfitter in the Long Beach harbor. In the U.S. Army from 1942 to 1945, stationed in California, he drew a cartoon strip for the base newspaper. After leaving the service, he worked as a designer and cartoonist at the Rexall Drug Company in Los Angeles, where a fellow employee was painter Robert Mallary, who encouraged him to begin painting. Studying under the GI Bill, Thiebaud received a BA and an MA from California State College (now California State University) in Sacramento. His first one-person exhibition was in 1951 at the E. B. Crocker Art Gallery (now the Crocker Art Museum) in Sacramento.

Thiebaud began teaching at Sacramento Junior College in 1951, and he has been a teacher ever since, working as a visiting professor in schools around the country from Colorado University to Harvard University and Yale University. At the same time he sustained a teaching commitment to the University of California at Davis begun in 1960. (He nominally retired in 1990.) He lived for a year in New York City in 1956–57, became friendly with Elaine and Willem de Kooning, and met other abstract expressionist artists.

His first exhibition in New York, at the Alan Stone Gallery in 1962, received tremendous critical attention, with reviews in *Newsweek*, *Art News*, the *New York Times*, and *Life* magazine. That same year he had a one-person exhibition at the de Young Museum in San Francisco. Thiebaud began making etchings at Crown Point Press in 1964. His first prints date from 1950, and he has been an active printmaker throughout his career. He has shown in numerous exhibitions and received many awards, including the National Medal of Arts presented by President Clinton in 1994. His paintings are in the collections of most major museums in the

United States including the Museum of Modern Art in New York, the San Francisco Museum of Modern Art, and the Art Institute of Chicago. He is represented by the Alan Stone Gallery, New York, and the Paul Thiebaud Gallery, San Francisco. —KB

RICHARD TUTTLE In 2005, in *Time* magazine, Richard Lacayo called Richard Tuttle "the man of small things." Lacayo was reviewing Tuttle's retrospective at the San Francisco Museum of Modern Art, which, he said, "sends you home with your senses briskly reconditioned." Tuttle, he added, "has been increasingly recognized as a genuine, if highly idiosyncratic, American master." The exhibition traveled to the Whitney Museum of American Art in New York, the Des Moines Art Center, the Dallas Museum of Art, the Museum of Contemporary Art in Chicago, and the Museum of Contemporary Art in Los Angeles.

Tuttle was born in 1941 in Rahway, New Jersey, and lives in New York City and New Mexico. He received a BA from Trinity College in Hartford, Connecticut, in 1963, and while in Hartford spent time in the Wadsworth Atheneum and became friendly with the curator of paintings there, Sam Wagstaff. Wagstaff, who organized what is considered the first exhibition of minimal art, introduced Tuttle to art ideas and also to many artists. In 1964 Tuttle moved to New York. He telephoned the painter Agnes Martin and asked if he could meet her. She not only introduced him to the director of the legendary Betty Parsons Gallery but also became an inspiration to him and a lifelong friend. Tuttle began working at the Betty Parsons Gallery as a gallery assistant in 1964. His first one-person exhibition was at the gallery in 1965. He showed there regularly until Parsons died in 1982.

In 1966 Tuttle spent a year in Paris through a grant that provided a studio and a stipend. In 1968 he had his first show in Europe, at the Galerie Schmela in Düsseldorf. That same year, at the Betty Parsons Gallery he showed shaped, dyed, unstretched canvases now considered key works of a movement variously called postminimal art, process art, or antiform. In 1969 his work was included in "When Attitudes Become Form" organized by the Kunsthalle in Bern. In 1972 Tuttle showed in the Projects Room at the Museum of Modern Art in New York, and in 1975 the Whitney Museum of American Art gave him a ten-year survey. In 1979 the Stedelijk Museum in Amsterdam mounted a survey of his small collage works. He has had many other one-person shows and has been in many important group shows, including "Drawing Now," organized by the Museum of Modern Art in New York in 1976. Tuttle has said that all his work is drawing centered.

He made his first prints, woodcuts, as part of an artist's book, in 1965. Tuttle has created prints and artist's books continuously during his career, many of them published by Brooke Alexander Editions, New York. Crown Point Press has published etching projects with him since 1998. His paintings are in many museum collections, including the Albright-Knox Art Gallery in Buffalo, the Fogg Art Museum at Harvard University, the Museum Ludwig in Cologne, the Metropolitan Museum of Art in New York, and the Wadsworth Atheneum in Hartford, Connecticut. He is represented by Sperone Westwater in New York. —KB

ROBERT BECHTLE

Plate 25, page 101. *Potrero Houses—Pennsylvania Avenue*, 1989. Color woodcut printed on silk by Sun Shumei, at Rongbaozhai Studio, Beijing and mounted on Rives Heavyweight Buff by Brian Shure at Crown Point Press. 11 × 16 inch image on 27 × 26 inch sheet. Edition 38. Published by Crown Point Press.

BRAD BROWN

Plate 19, page 63. *Textbook Comic Devices*, 2001. Color sugar lift and spit bite aquatints with drypoint printed on hosho paper chine collé on Somerset Textured White by Case Hudson. $23^{1}/_{2} \times 30^{3}/_{4}$ inch image on $30^{1}/_{2} \times 37^{1}/_{4}$ inch sheet. Edition 10. Published by Crown Point Press.

ENRIQUE CHAGOYA

Plate 21, page 67. *Abenteurer der Kannibalen Bioethicists*, 2001. Color lithograph, woodcut, and collage printed on natural Thai mulberry, white Thai mulberry, and Moriki papers chine collé on Amate by Bud Shark. $19 \times 61$ inch image on $24^{1}/_{2} \times 63$ inch sheet. Edition 30. Published by Shark's Ink, Lyons, Colorado.

FRANCESCO CLEMENTE

Plate 4, page 20. *Telemone #2*, 1981. Soft ground etching with aquatint and drypoint in black and silver on Farnsworth paper chine collé on Arches 88 with hard ground etching. Printed by Hidekatsu Takada. $61 \times 19$ inch image on $63 \times 24$ inch sheet. Edition 25. Published by Crown Point Press.

Plate 9, page 28. *Not St. Girolamo*, 1981. Color soft ground etching with aquatint and drypoint on Farnsworth paper chine collé on Arches 88 with hard ground etching. Printed by Hidekatsu Takada. $61 \times 19$ inch image on $63 \times 24$ inch sheet. Edition 25. Published by Crown Point Press.

Plate 24, page 99. *The Two Flames*, 1987. Woodcut on xuan zhi paper with silk brocade border printed at Rongbaozhai Studio, Beijing. $10^{1}/_{4} \times 6$ inch image on $7^{3}/_{4} \times 4$ inch sheet. Edition 100. Published by Crown Point Press.

CHUCK CLOSE

Plate 18, page 60. *Leslie/Fingerprint/Silk Collé*, 1986. Direct gravure printed on silk chine collé on d'Arches Aquarelle by Patrick Foy at Graphicstudio, University of South Florida, Tampa. $54^{1}/_{4} \times 40^{1}/_{4}$ inch sheet. Edition 10. Published by Graphicstudio and Pace Editions, New York. Photo courtesy of Pace Editions.

JUAN GARCIA

Plate 38, page 131. *Wall Street*, 2007. Mezzotint with gold leaf on Somerset Velvet. 11 × 11 inch image on 11 × 11 inch sheet. Edition 17. Published and printed by the artist.


MARY HEILMANN

Plate 10, page 39. *Clear Day*, 2006. Color spit bite and sugar lift aquatints printed on gampi paper chine collé on Somerset Satin White by Catherine Brooks. 15 × 11 inch image on 22½ × 17 inch sheet. Edition 10. Published by Crown Point Press.


SHOICHI IDA

Plate 5, page 24. *Between Vertical and Horizon—Descended Triangle (A)*, 1987. Color spit bite aquatint with drypoint printed on gampi paper chine collé on Somerset Satin White  by Nancy Anello. 7 × 14 inch image on 20 × 25 inch sheet. Edition 40. Published by Crown Point Press.

Plate 6, page 24. *Between Vertical and Horizon—Descended Triangle (B)*, 1987. Color spit bite aquatint with soft ground etching and drypoint printed on gampi paper chine collé on Somerset Satin White by Nancy Anello. 7 × 14 inch image on 20 × 25 inch sheet. Edition 40. Published by Crown Point Press.

Plate 7, page 25. *Between Vertical and Horizon—Descended Triangle (D)*, 1987. Color spit bite aquatint with drypoint printed on gampi paper chine collé on Somerset Satin White by Nancy Anello. 14 × 7 inch image on 26½ × 17 inch sheet. Edition 20. Published by Crown Point Press.


ROBERT KUSHNER

Plate 31, page 125. *Night Blooming Cereus XXIV*, 2006. Sugar lift aquatint printed on antique kimono silk and mounted on kozo paper by Paul Mullowney at HuiPress. Gold leafing added by the artist. 24 × 24 inches. From a series of 35 unique prints. Published by HuiPress, Makawao, Hawaii.

Plate 32, page 125. *Night Blooming Cereus IV*, 2006. Sugar lift aquatint printed on antique kimono silk and mounted on kozo paper by Paul Mullowney at HuiPress. Palladium leafing added by the artist. 24 × 24 inches. From a series of 35 unique prints. Published by HuiPress, Makawao, Hawaii.

Plate 33, page 126. *Red Hibiscus XXVII*, 2007. Screenprint on antique Japanese fabric and mounted on Somerset by Steven Sangenario at Brand X, New York. 28 × 28 inch image on 28 × 28 inch sheet. From a series of 52 unique prints. Published by the artist.

Plate 39, page 142. *Hand-Painted Daphne I, #46*, 1985–91. Color woodcut printed on Echizen kozo paper by Tadashi Toda with hand painting and silver leaf by the artist. 22½ × 19 inch image on 25 × 32½ inch sheet. From a series of 7 unique prints. Published by Crown Point Press.

Plate 40, page 146. *Tondo*, 1987. Color aquatint, drypoint, and sugar lift, spit bite and soap ground aquatints, with gold leafing printed on Somerset Textured White by Marcia Bartholme. 36 × 36 inch image on 41¼ × 40½ inch sheet. Edition 50. Published by Crown Point Press.

FRANCESCA LOHMANN
Plate 36, page 130. *Mitosis*, 2008. Installation work consisting of three-dimensional cells made from copper, beeswax, hand-blown glass, and print fragments, with spit bite aquatints from sixty various size plates printed on gampi paper and mounted on the wall, 96 × 36 inches.. Unique. Printed and published by the artist.

ROBERT MAPPLETHORPE
Plate 17, page 59. *Hyacinth*, 1986. Photogravure printed on silk chine collé on Saunders Waterford by Deli Sacilotto. 32¾ × 32½ inch image on 45 × 38 inch sheet. Edition 27. Published by Graphicstudio, University of South Florida, Tampa. Photo courtesy the Mapplethorpe Foundation, New York.

TOM MARIONI
Plate 1, page 7. *Finger Line*, 1991. Color soft ground and hard ground etching and spit bite aquatint with wood veneer and a drawing chine collé printed on Somerset Soft White Textured by Daria Sywulak. 27 × 17 inch image on 39½ × 27¼ inch sheet. Edition 10. Published by Crown Point Press.

Plate 3, page 12. *Pi*, 1988. Woodcut printed in red on silk by Xu Yinshe, Hanhzhou, China, and mounted on Arches Cover Buff by Brian Shure at Crown Point Press. 12½ × 14½ inch image on 22½ × 23¼ inch sheet. Edition 30. Published by Crown Point Press.

JULIE MEHRETU
Plate 30, page 122. *Entropia: Construction*, 2005. Lithograph printed on gampi paper chine collé on Somerset Satin by Cole Rogers at Highpoint Editions. 29½ × 39¾ inch image on 40 × 49¾ inch sheet. Edition 30. Published by Highpoint Editions, Minneapolis.

AGATA MICHALOWSKA

Plate 34, page 128. *in that one moment i can see the dust collect on my fingertips*, 2007. Installation work consisting of stones covered with silk and hand-dyed felt, with nine aquatints on abaca paper chine collé on mulberry paper mounted on a wall. 58½ × 37½ inch image. Edition 2. Printed and published by the artist.


SUSAN MIDDLETON

Plate 16, page 58. *Passenger Pigeon*, 2008. Photogravure printed on gampi paper chine collé on Somerset Satin White by Asa Muir-Harmony. 15 × 11½ inch image on 23 × 17½ inch sheet. Edition 10. Published by Crown Point Press.


ATSUKO MORITA

Page 78. *Self-Portrait as Female, Age 50*, 2008. Photogravure printed on gampi paper chine collé on Somerset Satin White by Ianne Kjorlie. Proof of impression. 12 × 10 inch image on 29¾ × 22¾ inch sheet. Created by the artist during the Crown Point Press Summer Workshop, 2008.


CLAES OLDENBURG

Plate 8, page 27. *Sailboat and Hat*, 1975. Hard ground etching with spit bite aquatint printed on Rives Lightweight Buff chine collé on Rives BFK by John Slivon at Crown Point Press. 6 × 4½ inch sheet on 24 × 17¼ inch sheet. Edition 35. Published by Multiples, New York.


NATHAN OLIVEIRA

Plate 11, page 42. *Copper Plate Nudes II (7)*, 2001. Color sugar lift and spit bite aquatints with texture from the back of a discarded plate printed on gampi paper chine collé on Somerset Satin White by Dena Schuckit. 17¾ × 13¾ inch image on 27¼ × 22½ inch sheet. Edition 20. Published by Crown Point Press.


JUDY PFAFF

Plate 28, page 119. *Six of One—Melone*, 1987. Color woodcut with collaged elements on hosho paper chine collé by Lawrence Hamlin. 55 × 63 inch image on 55 × 63 inch sheet. Edition 25. Published by Crown Point Press.


ODILON REDON

Page 10. *L'Oeil, Comme un Balloon se Dirige Verg L'Infiniti (The Eye Like a Strange Balloon Moves Toward Infinity)*, 1882. Lithograph printed chine collé. 10½ × 8 inch image on 11 × 7¾ inch sheet. Photograph courtesy the Museum of Art, Rhode Island School of Design. Gift of Murrary S. Danforth, Jr. Photography by Eric Gould.

SOLANGE ROBERDEAU

Plate 37, page 131. *Albion Faun* from the series *The Space Between: A Personal Bestiary*, 2005. Color hard ground etching with aquatint and spit bite aquatint on silk chine collé on Rives BFK Grey. 12 × 17 ½ inch sheet on 22 × 30 inch sheet. Edition 12. Printed and published by the artist.


TIM ROLLINS + K.O.S.

Plate 12, page 54. *Temptation of St. Antony I*, 1989. Spit bite aquatint with xerographic text printed on Rives Lightweight White chine collé on Lana Gravure White by Brian Shure. 8¼ × 5¼ inch sheet on 22½ × 15 inch sheet. Published by Crown Point Press.

Plate 13, page 54. *Temptation of St. Antony XI*, 1989. Aquatint with xerographic text printed on Rives Lightweight White chine collé on Lana Gravure White by Brian Shure. 8¼ × 5¼ inch sheet on 22½ × 15 inch sheet. Published by Crown Point Press.

Plate 14, page 54. *Temptation of St. Antony VII*, 1989. Aquatint with xerographic text printed on Rives Lightweight White chine collé on Lana Gravure White by Brian Shure. 8¼ × 5¼ inch sheet on 22½ × 15 inch sheet. Published by Crown Point Press.


WILSON SHIEH

Plate 15, page 57. *Three Angels*, 2005. Color direct gravure with aquatint and spit bite aquatint printed on gampi paper chine collé on Somerset Satin White by Catherine Brooks. 18 × 15 inch image on 27 × 23 inch sheet. Edition 30. Published by Crown Point Press.


BRIAN SHURE

Plate 20, page 65. *Museum Steps*, 2008. Lithograph on Indian khadi tea paper chine collé on Rives BFK. 14 × 21 inch image on 22½ × 30 inch sheet. Edition 12. Printed and published by the artist.

Plate 26, page 103. *Naiku*, 1989. Drypoint with spit bite aquatint printed in gold on aizomi gampi paper chine collé backed with udagami paper and mounted on a handscroll. Printed by Paul Mullowney. 18 × 68 inch image on 19¾ × 98 inch scroll. Edition 10. Published by Tokugenji Press.

Plate 27, page 103. *Geku*, 1989. Color drypoint with spit bite aquatint printed in silver on aizomi gampi paper chine collé with udagami paper and mounted on a handscroll. Printed by Paul Mullowney. 18 × 68 inch image on 19¾ × 98 inch scroll. Edition 10. Published by Tokugenji Press.

PAT STEIR

Plate 22, page 94. *Kweilin Dreaming, Part C, #60*, 1989. Color woodcut printed on silk at Rongbaozhai Studio, Beijing, with hand painting by the artist. Mounted on Somerset Textured White by Brian Shure at Crown Point Press. 26½ × 32¾ inch image on 37½ × 42¾ inch sheet. From a series of 16 unique prints. Published by Crown Point Press.

Plate 23, page 97. *Kweilin Dreaming, Part C, #58*, 1989. Color woodcut printed on silk at Rongbaozhai Studio, Beijing, with hand painting by the artist. Mounted on Somerset Textured White by Brian Shure at Crown Point Press. 26½ × 32¾ inch image on 37½ × 42¾ inch sheet. From a series of 16 unique prints. Published by Crown Point Press.


WAYNE THIEBAUD

Plate 2, page 8. *Marina Ridge*, 1997. Drypoint printed on gampi paper chine collé on Somerset Textured White by Daria Sywulak. 11 × 9 inch image on 21 × 17 inch sheet. Edition 35. Published by Crown Point Press.


MEG TURNER

Plate 35, page 129. *Bricks*, 2007. Installation consisting of twelve hard ground etchings with aquatint and drypoint on Rives Lightweight mounted on the wall. 98 × 76 inch image. Unique. Printed and published by the artist.


RICHARD TUTTLE

Plate 29, page 120, *Naked IX*, 2004. Color soft ground etching with hand staining printed on hosho paper with gampi chine collé by Rachel Fuller. 27 × 20 inch sheet. Edition 10. Published by Crown Point Press.

*Crown Point Press Master Printers 1962–2009*

Crown Point Press master printers are awarded that status by founder
Kathan Brown after having been trained in a three-year apprentice
program at the press and having demonstrated not only comprehensive
technical skills but also the ability to manage artist projects. Of the twenty-
nine master printers in the press's forty-seven year history to 2009,
thirteen founded their own successful presses, and an additional eight
accepted jobs as teachers and/or as professional printers in other shops.
One owns a gallery, and one has been a museum preparator, now retired.
Three "retired" to raise families. Three currently work at Crown Point.
Overlapping these careers, many also pursue their own work as artists.

<table>
<tr><td>Nancy Anello</td><td>Lothar Osterberg</td></tr>
<tr><td>Marcia Bartholme</td><td>Jeryl Parker</td></tr>
<tr><td>Renée Bott</td><td>Pamela Paulson</td></tr>
<tr><td>Patricia Branstead</td><td>Peter Pettengill</td></tr>
<tr><td>Catherine Brooks</td><td>Dena Schuckit</td></tr>
<tr><td>Kathan Brown</td><td>Brian Shure</td></tr>
<tr><td>Mark Callen</td><td>Doris Simmelink</td></tr>
<tr><td>Jeannie Fine</td><td>Paul Singdahlsen</td></tr>
<tr><td>Patrick Foy</td><td>John Slivon</td></tr>
<tr><td>Rachel Fuller</td><td>Daria Sywulak</td></tr>
<tr><td>Lawrence Hamlin</td><td>Hidekatsu Takada</td></tr>
<tr><td>Case Hudson</td><td>Stephen Thomas</td></tr>
<tr><td>David Kelso</td><td>Lilah Toland</td></tr>
<tr><td>Ianne Kjorlie</td><td>Emily York</td></tr>
<tr><td>Paul Mullowney</td><td></td></tr>
</table>

**Brian Shure** is a painter and printmaker living in Rhode Island. He received a BA from Antioch College, apprenticed with Ernest de Soto at Collectors Press Lithography Workshop in San Francisco, and worked as a professional lithographer for fifteen years. He and his wife, Evelyn Lincoln, published and printed intaglio editions for several years under their imprint, Smalltree Press, and he was a master printer and the coordinator of the China woodblock program at Crown Point Press from 1987 to 1994. In 2006 he completed three commissioned murals in the Pittsburgh Federal Courthouse. He has taught as a visiting artist at Brown and Cornell universities, has given workshops in the United States, Japan, and Mexico, and is on the advisory board of Highpoint Press in Minneapolis. Since 1996 he has taught at the Rhode Island School of Design, where he is assistant professor and coordinator of the graduate printmaking program. He is represented by the Katharina Rich Perlow Gallery in New York and the Lenore Gray Gallery in Providence, Rhode Island.

*Acknowledgments*

I extend my thanks to Kathan Brown, not only for her support for this book but for her dedication to the field of printmaking and her commitment to sharing its secrets and magic as widely as possible. She has done more than anyone to bring intaglio printmaking to the forefront of contemporary artistic exploration through her insistence on the continued relevance of its simple and elegant processes. Her high standards and boundless curiosity have inspired me as a teacher and an artist. Kathan and Sasha Baguskas have been endlessly patient with the processes of writing and designing that have taken much longer than the work on the original book. Javier Briones has miraculously edited the mass of video I gathered on my 2007 visit to China into coherent demonstrations that underlie the other material on the DVD. His well-organized filming and editing of the how-to demonstrations, along with Sasha's fine still photographs, make up a large and important part of the new material in this volume.

Painter and consummate printmaker Robert Kushner has been particularly helpful, opening his studio to us and generously sharing the metal leafing skills he has developed through trial and error over many years. Solange Roberdeau assisted him in the demonstration we filmed and photographed. Paul Mullowney made available the videotape of master Shosaku Yoshimura's scroll mounting workshop at the Hui Art Center in Hawaii. Paul's skill as a master printer is augmented by an encyclopedic knowledge of paper handling and pasting built on extensive experimentation and practice. His generosity is emblematic of the openness I have found among printers at the print shops I have worked with over the years. I want to acknowledge all professional printers who are extending the traditions and skills of printmaking in the crucible of the marketplace. That list begins with the current and past printers of Crown Point Press, especially Ianne Kjorlie and Asa Muir-Harmony, who appear in many of the step-by-step photos. I have had invaluable help from Cole Rogers and his staff at Highpoint Printmaking Workshop, Minneapolis; Bud Shark of Shark's Ink, Lyons, Colorado; Steven Sangenario and Bob Blanton of Brand-X, New York; and Bill Hall at Pace Prints, New York.

I thank the directors and staff members at Rongbaozhai in Beijing and Duoyunxuan in Shanghai for allowing me free access to their studios with my video camera. I am indebted to the Central Academy of Fine Art in Beijing for hosting me on my visit there, and to Xiu Ja, the assistant director of CAFA's international relations office for translating and making arrangements for me with Rongbaozhai and beyond. In Shanghai, I was hosted by the College of Fine Arts at Shanghai University. Helen Dong, assistant to the dean, took care of my arrangements with Duoyunxuan and lent me her excellent interpreting skills.

My visit to the woodblock workshops in China was supported by a faculty development fellowship from the Rhode Island School of Design. My colleagues at RISD have been supportive in many ways, providing me with encouragement, feedback, space, and assistance, and affording me the privilege of working with a continuous stream of disciplined students whose work shows that understanding traditional skills is crucial to the innovations in which they excel. Amy Diaz-Infante was my assistant for the collé lithography demonstration in this book.

Special thanks go to David Becker, the Claire W. and Richard P. Morse Curatorial Research Fellow in the Department of Prints, Drawings, and Photographs at the Museum of Fine Arts, Boston, for help in developing my understanding of the history of chine collé. He took the time to read the section on historical background in my earlier book and discuss it with me. Although that section is not part of this book, I learned a great deal from him. A history of the technical and cultural developments from which the chine collé process grew is a project I hope to take up in the future.

Finally I want to thank my most supportive teachers, Allan Jones and master lithographer Ernest de Soto. This book is dedicated to my mother, Ishbel, and as always, with everything, to Evie. —Brian Shure

Visit www.magical-secrets.com
for ongoing discussions about printmaking and for continually
updated information about printmaking supplies and equipment.
Crown Point Press publishes, exhibits, and sells etchings
produced by invited artists in its San Francisco studios.
The press offers workshops open to all.

The Crown Point Gallery and Bookstore are open to the public
Tuesday through Saturday, ten a.m. to six p.m.
20 Hawthorne St., San Francisco, CA 94105
Tel. 415.974.6273
www.crownpoint.com

*Magical Secrets about Chine Collé*
PASTING, PRINTING, MOUNTING, AND LEAFING STEP-BY-STEP

Copyright ©2009 Crown Point Press and Brian Shure
ISBN 978-1-891300-23-3
*Author:* Brian Shure
*Artists' biographies authors:* Kim L. Bennett, Kathan Brown, Rachel Lyon, Dana Zullo
*DVD editing and production:* Javier Briones

*Editors:* Kathan Brown, Judith Dunham
*Series concept:* Kathan Brown
*Cover image:* Tom Marioni

*Series book and cover design:* Catherine Mills
*Book and cover layout:* Sasha Baguskas
*Step-by-step design:* Sasha Baguskas

*Step-by-step photographs:* Sasha Baguskas, except pages 136–138 courtesy Cole Rogers
*Photos of artists:* Kathan Brown, except pages 15, 116, Brian Shure; pages 29, 53, Colin McRae;
page 26, unknown photographer
*Author photo:* Evelyn Lincoln

*Production:* Sasha Baguskas at Crown Point Press
*Printing:* in China through Colorcraft Ltd. Hong Kong
*Distributed by:* Small Press Distribution, SPD
        1341 7th Street, Berkeley, CA 94710
        (510) 524-1668